P M X

JANE AUSTEN AND HER TIMES

BY THE SAME AUTHOR

A BACHELOR GIRL IN LONDON
THE GIFTS OF ENEMIES
THE CHILDREN'S BOOK OF LONDON

MORNING EMPLOYMENTS

JANE AUSTEN
AND HER TIMES

BY

G. E. MITTON

WITH TWENTY-ONE ILLUSTRATIONS

NEW YORK: G. P. PUTNAM'S SONS
LONDON: METHUEN & CO.
1905

CONTENTS

CHAP.		PAGE
I.	PRELIMINARY AND DISCURSIVE	1
II.	CHILDHOOD	22
III.	THE POSITION OF THE CLERGY	34
IV.	HOME LIFE AT STEVENTON	49
V.	THE NOVELS	80
VI.	LETTERS AND POST	105
VII.	SOCIETY AND LOVE-MAKING	117
VIII.	VISITS AND TRAVELLING	148
IX.	CONTEMPORARY WRITERS	161
X.	A TRIO OF NOVELS	176
XI.	THE NAVY	196
XII.	BATH	212
XIII.	DRESS AND FASHIONS	229
XIV.	AT SOUTHAMPTON	249
XV.	CHAWTON	266
XVI.	IN LONDON	278
XVII.	FANNY AND ANNA	296
XVIII.	THE PRINCE REGENT AND *EMMA*	303
XIX.	LAST DAYS	313
	INDEX	327

LIST OF ILLUSTRATIONS

MORNING EMPLOYMENTS	*Frontispiece*	
From a Painting by BUNBURY.		
THE REV. GEORGE AUSTEN . . .	*Facing page*	16
From a Family Miniature.		
THE REV. JAMES AUSTEN	,, ,,	16
From a Family Miniature.		
JUVENILE RETIREMENT	,, ,,	26
From a Painting by JOHN HOPPNER.		
THE VICAR RECEIVING HIS TITHES . .	,, ,,	42
From a Drawing by H. SINGLETON.		
JANE AUSTEN	,, ,,	58
From a Portrait by her Sister CASSANDRA.		
THE HAPPY COTTAGERS	,, ,,	74
From a Painting by GEORGE MORLAND.		
MISS BURNEY (MADAME D'ARBLAY) . .	,, ,,	96
From a Portrait by EDWARD BURNEY.		
FROM A SUMMER'S EVENING . . .	,, ,,	156
From a Drawing by DE LOUTHERBOURG.		
TRAVELLERS ARRIVING AT EAGLE TAVERN, STRAND	,, ,,	159
From an Old Engraving.		
DOMESTIC HAPPINESS	,, ,,	170
From a Painting by GEORGE MORLAND.		
COWPER	,, ,,	192
From a Painting by GEORGE ROMNEY, in the possession of B. Vaughan Johnson, Esq.		

LIST OF ILLUSTRATIONS

VICTORY OF LORD DUNCAN (CAMPERDOWN), 1797 *Facing page*		208
From a Painting by J. S. COPLEY.		
FAÇADE OF THE PUMP ROOM, BATH, IN THE EIGHTEENTH CENTURY . . . ,, ,,		220
From a Contemporary Engraving.		
DRESSING TO GO OUT . . . . ,, ,,		230
From a Drawing by P. W. TOMKINS.		
INIGO JONES, HON. H. FANE, AND C. BLAIR . ,, ,,		246
From a Painting by Sir JOSHUA REYNOLDS.		
A PLATE FROM THE GALLERY OF FASHION . ,, ,,		260
CHARING CROSS, 1795 . . . . ,, ,,		285
From an Engraving in the Crace Collection.		
THE LITTLE THEATRE, HAYMARKET . . ,, ,,		291
From an Engraving by WILKINSON in *Londina Illustrata*.		
THE REV. GEORGE CRABBE . . . ,, ,,		293
From a Drawing by Sir F. CHANTREY, in the National Portrait Gallery.		
THE GARDEN OF CARLTON HOUSE . . ,, ,,		304
From a Painting by BUNBURY.		

JANE AUSTEN AND HER TIMES

CHAPTER I

PRELIMINARY AND DISCURSIVE

OF Jane Austen's life there is little to tell, and that little has been told more than once by writers whose relationship to her made them competent to do so. It is impossible to make even microscopic additions to the sum-total of the facts already known of that simple biography, and if by chance a few more original letters were discovered they could hardly alter the case, for in truth of her it may be said, "Story there is none to tell, sir." To the very pertinent question which naturally follows, reply may thus be given. Jane Austen stands absolutely alone, unapproached, in a quality in which women are usually supposed to be deficient, a humorous and brilliant insight into the foibles of human nature, and a strong sense of the ludicrous. As a writer in *The Times* (November 25, 1904) neatly puts it, "Of its kind the comedy of Jane Austen is incomparable. It is utterly merciless. Prancing victims of their illusions, her men and women are utterly bare to our understanding, and their gyrations are irresistibly comic." Therefore as a personality, as a central figure, too much cannot be written about her, and however much is said or written the mystery of her genius will still always baffle conjecture, always lure men on to fresh attempts to analyse and understand her.

The data of Jane Austen's life have been repeated several times, as has been said, but beyond a few trifling allusions to her times no writer has thought it necessary to show up the background against which her figure may be seen, or to sketch from contemporary records the environment amid which she developed. Yet surely she is even more wonderful as a product of her times than considered as an isolated figure; therefore the object of this book is to show her among the scenes wherein she moved, to sketch the men and women to whom she was accustomed, the habits and manners of her class, and the England with which she was familiar. Her life was not long, lasting only from 1775 to 1817, but it covered notable times, and with such an epoch for presentation, with such a central figure to link together the sequence of events, we have a theme as inspiring as could well be found.

In many ways the times of Jane Austen are more removed from our own than the mere lapse of years seems to warrant. The extraordinary outburst of invention and improvement which took place in the reign of Queen Victoria, lifted manners and customs in advance of what two centuries of ordinary routine would have done. Sir Walter Besant in his *London in the Eighteenth Century* says, "The passing of the Reform Bill in 1832, the introduction of steamers on the sea, the beginning of railways on land, make so vast a break between the first third and last two-thirds of the nineteenth century, that I feel justified in considering the eighteenth century as lasting down to the year 1837; in other words, there were so few changes, and these so slight, in manners, customs, or prevalent ideas, between 1700 and 1837, that we may consider the eighteenth century as continuing down to the beginning of the Victorian era, when change after change—change in the constitution, change in communications, change in the growth and extension of trade, change in religious thought, change in social standards— introduced that new time which we call the nineteenth century."

According to this reckoning, Jane Austen may be counted as wholly an eighteenth-century product, and such a view is fully justified, for the differences between her time and ours were enormous. It is impossible to summarise in a few sentences changes which are essentially a matter of detail, but in the gradual unfolding of her life I shall attempt to show how radically different were her surroundings from anything to which we are accustomed.

It is an endless puzzle why, when her books so faithfully represent the society and manners of a time so unlike our own, they seem so natural to us. If you tell any half-dozen people, who have not made a special study of the subject, at what date these novels were written, you will find that they are all surprised to hear how many generations ago Jane Austen lived, and that they have always vaguely imagined her to be very little earlier than, if not contemporary with, Charlotte Brontë or George Eliot. So far as I am aware, no writer on Jane Austen has ever touched on this problem before. Her stories are as fresh and real as the day they were written, her characters might be introduced to us in the flesh any time, and, with the exception of a certain quaintness of eighteenth-century flavouring, there is nothing to bring before us the striking difference between their environment and our own. It is true that the long coach journeys stand out as an exception to this, but they are the only marked exception. If we had never had an illustrated edition of Jane Austen, nine people out of ten at least would have formed mental pictures of the characters dressed in early Victorian, or perhaps even in present-day, costume. It is only since Hugh Thompson and C. E. Brock have put before us the costumes of the age, that our ideas have accommodated themselves, and we realise how Catherine Morland and Isabella Thorpe looked in their high-waisted plain gowns, when they had arrived at that stage of intimacy which enabled them to pin "up each other's trains for the dance." Or how attractive Fanny Price was in her odd high-crowned hat, with its nodding plume, and the open-necked short-sleeved dress, as she surveyed herself in the glass while Miss Crawford snapped the chain round her neck. The knee-breeches of the men, their slippers and cravats, the neat, close-fitting clerical garb, these things we owe to the artists,—they are taken for granted in the text. It would have seemed as ridiculous to Jane Austen to describe them, as for a present-day novelist to mention that a London man made a call in a frock-coat and top-hat.

Yet her word-pictures are living and detailed, filled in with innumerable little touches. How can we reconcile the seeming inconsistency? The explanation probably is, that without acting consciously, she, with the unerring touch of real genius, chose that which was lasting, and of interest for all time, from that which was ephemeral. In her sketches of human nature, in the strokes with which she describes character, no line is too fine or too delicate for her attention; but in the case of manners and customs she gives just the broad outlines that serve as a setting. Her novels are novels of character.

But the problem is not confined to the books; in her

letters to her sister, though there is abundant comment on dress, food, and minor details which should mark the epoch, yet the letters might have been written yesterday. Austin Dobson in one of his admirable prefaces to the novels says: "Going over her pages, pencil in hand, the antiquarian annotator is struck by their excessive modernity, and after a prolonged examination discovers, in this century-old record, nothing more fitted for the exercise of his ingenuity that such an obsolete game at cards as 'Casino' or 'quadrille.'"

And this is true also of her letters. More remarkable still is the entire absence of comment on the great events which thrilled the world; with the exception of an allusion to the death of Sir John Moore, we hear no whisper of the wars and upheavals which happened during her life. It is true that the Revolution in France, which shook monarchs on their thrones, occurred before the first date of the published letters, yet her correspondence covers a time when battles at sea were chronicled almost continuously, when an invasion by France was an ever-present terror; Trafalgar and Waterloo were not history, but contemporary events; but though Jane must have heard and discussed these matters, no echo finds its way into her lively and amusing budgets of chit-chat to her sister. Of course women were not supposed to read the papers in those days, but with two sailor brothers the news must have often been personal and intimate, and she was, according to the notions of her time, well educated; yet we search in vain for any allusion to such contemporary matters. It may be objected that the letters of a modern girl to a sister would hardly touch on questions which agitate the public, but there are several replies to this: in the first place, few such exciting events have occurred in recent times as happened during Jane Austen's life; our war in Africa was a mere trifle in comparison with the bloody field of Waterloo, where Blucher and Wellington lost 30,000 men, or the thrilling naval victory of Trafalgar; and stupendous as have been the recent battles between Russia and Japan, they affect us only indirectly—England is not herself involved in them, nor are her sons being slain daily. In the second place, surely even the South African War would probably produce some comment in letters, especially if the writer had brothers in the army as Jane had brothers in the navy. Thirdly, letters in Jane Austen's time were one great means of news, for newspapers were not so easy to get, and were much more costly than now, so that we expect to find more of contemporary events in letters than at a time like the present, when telegrams and columns of print save us the trouble of recording such matters in private.

In the forty-two years between 1775 and 1817, vast discoveries of world-wide importance were made. When Jane Austen was born, Captain Cook was still in the midst of his exploration, and the map of the world was being unrolled day by day. Though New Zealand and Australia had been discovered by the Dutch in the previous century, they were all but unknown to England. Six years only before her birth had the great navigator charted and mapped New Zealand for the first time, also the east coast of Australia, and had christened New South Wales. When she was four years old, Cook was murdered by the natives at Hawaii.

The atlas from which she learnt her earliest geography lessons was therefore very different from those now in use. The well-known cartographer, S. Dunn, published an atlas in 1774, where Australia is marked certainly, but as though one saw it through distorted glasses; the east coast, Cook's discovery, is clearly defined, the rest is very vague; and the fact that Tasmania was an island had not then been discovered, for it appears as a projecting headland. In the same general way is New Zealand treated, and neither has a separate sheet to itself; beyond their appearance on the map of the world, they are ignored. Japan also looks queer to modern eyes, it almost touches China at both ends, enclosing a land-locked sea.

The epoch was one of change and enlargement in other than geographical directions. In the thirty years before Jane Austen's birth an immense improvement had taken place in the position of women. Mrs. Montagu, in 1750, had made bold strokes for the freedom and recognition of her sex. The epithet "blue-stocking," which has survived with such extraordinary tenacity, was at first given, not to the clever women who attended Mrs. Montagu's informal receptions, but to her men friends, who were allowed to come in the grey or blue worsted stockings of daily life, instead of the black silk considered *de rigueur* for parties. Up to this time, personal appearance and cards had been the sole resources for a leisured dame of the upper classes, and the language of gallantry was the only one considered fitting for her to hear. By Mrs. Montagu's efforts it was gradually recognised that a woman might not only have sense herself, but might prefer it should be spoken to her; and that because the minds of women had long been left uncultivated they were not on that account unworthy of cultivation. Hannah More describes Mrs. Montagu as "not only the finest genius, but the finest lady I ever saw . . . her form (for she has no body) is delicate even to fragility; her countenance the most animated in the world; the sprightly vivacity of fifteen, with the judgment and experience of a Nestor."

In art there had never before been seen in England such a trio of masters as Reynolds, Gainsborough, and Romney. Isolated portrait painters of brilliant genius, though not always native born, there had been in England,—Holbein, Vandyke, Lely, Kneller, and Hogarth are all in the first rank,—but that three such men as the trio above should flourish contemporaneously was little short of miraculous.

In 1775, Sir Joshua had passed the zenith of his fame, though he lived until 1792. Gainsborough, who was established in a studio in Schomberg House, Pall Mall, was in 1775 at the beginning of his most successful years; his rooms were crowded with sitters of both sexes, and no one considered they had proved their position in society until they had received the hall-mark of being painted by him. He was only sixty-one at his death in 1788. Romney, who lived to 1802, never took quite the same rank as the other two, yet he was popular enough at the same time as Gainsborough; Lady Newdigate (*The Cheverels of Cheverel Manor*) mentions going to have her portrait painted by him, and says that "he insists upon my having a rich white satin with a long train made by Tuesday, and to have it left with him all the summer. It is the oddest thing I ever knew." Sir Thomas Lawrence and Hoppner carried on the traditions of the portrait painters, the former living to 1830; with names such as these it is easy to judge art was in a flourishing condition.

Among contemporary landscape painters, Richard Wilson, who has been called "the founder of English Landscape," lived until 1782. But his views, though vastly more natural than the stilted conventional style that preceded them, seem to our modern eyes, trained to what is "natural," still to be too much conventionalised. Among others the names of Gillray, Morland, Rowlandson stand out, all well on the way to fame while Jane was still a child.

These preliminary remarks have been made with a view to giving some general idea of that England into which she was born, and they refer to those subjects which only affected her indirectly. All those things which entered directly into her life, such as her country surroundings, contemporary books, prices of food, fashions, and a host of minor details, are dealt with more particularly in the course of the narrative.

As we have said, matters of history are not mentioned or noticed in Jane Austen's correspondence, which is taken up with her own environment, her neighbours, their habits and manners, and illumined throughout by a bright insight at times rather too biting to be altogether pleasant. Of her immediate surroundings we have a very clear idea.

Of all the writers of fiction, Jane Austen is most thoroughly English. She never went abroad, and though her native good sense and shrewd gift of observation saved her from becoming insular, yet she cannot be conceived as writing of any but the sweet villages and the provincial towns of her native country. Even the Brontës, deeply secluded as their lives were, crossed the German Ocean, and saw something of Continental life from their school at Brussels. Nothing of this kind fell to Jane Austen's share. Yet people did travel in those days, travelled amazingly considering the difficulties they had to encounter, among which were the horrors of a sailing-boat with its uncertain hours. Fielding, in going to Lisbon, was kept waiting a month for favourable winds! There was also the terrible embarking and landing from a small boat before such conveniences as landing-stages were built.

In one of Lord Langdale's letters, dated 1803, we have a vivid description of these horrors: "We left that place [Dover] about six o'clock last Saturday morning, and arrived at Calais at four in the afternoon. Our passage was rather disagreeable, the wind being chiefly against us, and rain sometimes falling in torrents. I never witnessed a more curious scene than our landing. When the packet-boat had come to within two miles of the coast of France, we were met by some French rowing boats in which we were to be conveyed on shore. The French sailors surrounded us in the most clamorous and noisy manner, leaping into the packet and bawling and shouting so loud as to alarm the ladies on board very much. To these men, however, we were to consign ourselves, and we entered their boats, eight passengers going in each. When we got near the shore, we were told it was impossible for the boat to get close to land, on account of the tide being so low, and that we must be carried on the men's shoulders. We had no time to reflect on this plan before we saw twelve or fourteen men running into the water,—they surrounded our boat and laid hold of it with such violence, that one might have thought they meant to sink it, and fairly pulled us into their arms. . . . For my part I laughed heartily all the time, but a lady who was with us was so much frighted, that I was obliged to support her in my arms a considerable time before she was able to stand."

It was not only in the arms of men that passengers were thus carried ashore, in *Napoleon's British Visitors and Captives*, by J. G. Alger, there is a still more extraordinary account quoted from a contemporary letter. "In an instant the boathead was surrounded by a throng of women up to their middles and over, who were there to carry us on shore. Not being aware of this manœuvre, we did not throw ourselves into the arms of these sea-nymphs so instantly as we ought, whereby those who sat at the stern of the boat were deluged with sea spray. For myself, I was in front, and very quickly understood the clamour of the mermaids. I flung myself upon the backs of two of them without reserve, and was safely and dryly borne on shore, but one poor gentleman slipped through their fingers, and fell over head and ears into the sea."

From the same entertaining book we learn that, "For £4, 13s. you could get a through ticket by Dover and Calais, starting either from the City at 4.30 a.m. by the old and now revived line of coaches connected with the rue Notre Dame des Victoires establishment in Paris, or morning and night by a new line from Charing Cross. Probably a still cheaper route, though there were no through tickets, was by Brighton and Dieppe, the crossing taking ten or fifteen hours. By Calais it seldom took more than eight hours, but passengers were advised to carry light refreshments with them. The diligence from Calais to Paris, going only four miles an hour, took fifty-four hours for the journey, but a handsome carriage drawn by three horses, in a style somewhat similar to the English post-chaise, could be hired by four or five fellow-travellers, and this made six miles an hour."

During a great part of Jane Austen's life, much of the Continent was closed to English people because of the perpetual state of war between us and either Spain or France, but in any case such an expedition would seem to have lain quite outside her limited daily round, and was never even mooted.

Steventon Rectory, where she was born on December 16, 1775, has long ago vanished, and a new rectory, more in accordance with modern luxurious notions, has been built. Of the old house, Lord Brabourne, great-nephew to Jane Austen, writes: "The house standing in the valley was somewhat better than the ordinary parsonage houses of the day; the old-fashioned hedgerows were beautiful, and the country around sufficiently picturesque for those who have the good taste to admire country scenery."

Steventon is a very small place, lying in a network of lanes about seven miles from Basingstoke. The nearest points on the high-roads are Deane, on the Andover Road, and Popham Lane on the Winchester Road. There is an inn at the corner of Popham Lane to this day, and that there was an inn there in Jane Austen's time we know, for Mrs. Lybbe Powys, writing in 1792, says: "We stopped at Winchester and lay that night at a most excellent inn at Popham Lane." At this time, curiously enough, her fellow-travellers were Dr. Cooper, Jane Austen's uncle, and his son and daughter, though whether the party made a détour to visit the rectory we do not know. Of course at that time Jane was of no greater importance than any seventeen-year-old daughter of a country clergyman, and there would be no reason to mention her.

It is difficult to find Steventon, so little is there of it, and that so much scattered; a few cottages, a farm, and beyond, half a mile away, the church, with a pump in a field near to mark the site of the old rectory house where Jane Austen was born. This is all that remains of her time. The new rectory stands on the other side of the narrow road, raised above it, and sheltered by a warm backing of trees in which evergreens are conspicuous. A very substantial-looking building it is, much superior to what was considered good enough for a clergyman in the eighteenth century. The country is well wooded, and the roads undulating, so that there are no distant views. Probably a good deal of the planting has been done since Jane Austen's time, but that there were trees then we know from her own account, and some of the fine oaks that still stand can have altered but little since then. Mr. Austen-Leigh's account of the house in which she was born is worth quoting—

"North of the house, the road from Deane to Popham Lane ran at a sufficient distance from the front to allow a carriage drive through turf and trees. On the south side, the ground rose gently, and was occupied by one of those old-fashioned gardens in which vegetables and flowers are combined, flanked and protected on the east by one of the thatched mud walls common in that country, and overshadowed by fine elms. Along the upper or southern side of this garden ran a terrace of the finest turf, which must have been in the writer's thoughts when she described Catherine Morland's childish delight in 'rolling down the green slope at the back of the house.'"

Though there is so little left to see, and the church has been "restored," yet it is worth while to pass through this country to realise the environment in which the authoress spent her childhood. There are still left in the neighbourhood, notably at North Waltham, some of the old diamond-paned, heavily-timbered brick houses with thatched roofs, to which she must have been accustomed. The gentle curves of the roads, the oak and beech and fir overshadowing the sweet lanes, the wild clematis, which grows so abundantly that in autumn it looks like hoar-frost covering all the hedgerows, these things were prominent objects in the scenery amid which she lived. It is not likely she looked on her surroundings in the same way as any ordinarily educated person would now look on them. Love of scenery had not then been developed. The artificial and formal landscape gardening, with "made" waterfalls, was the correct thing to admire. Genuine nature, much less homely nature, was only then beginning to be observed. This is strange to us, for, as Professor Geikie says, "At no time in our history as a nation has the scenery of the land we live in been so intelligently appreciated as it is to-day."

But Jane was not in advance of her times, and though she loved her trees and flowers, we find in her writings no reflections of the scenes amid which she daily walked; in her books scenery is simply ignored. We know if it rained, because that material fact had an influence on the actions of her heroines, but beyond that there is little or nothing; yet she greatly admired Cowper, one of the earliest of the "natural" poets.

Mr. Austen-Leigh, her own nephew, speaks of the scenery around her first home as "tame," and says that it has no "grand or extensive views," though he admits it has its beauties, and says that Steventon "from the fall of the ground, and the abundance of its timber, is certainly one of the prettiest spots." But this quiet prettiness, without the excessive richness to be found in other south-country villages, is perhaps more thoroughly characteristic of England than any other.

The impressions of childhood are invariably deep, and are cut with a clearness and minuteness to which none others of later times attain. Just as a child examines a picture in a story-book with anxious and searching care, while an adult gains only a general impression of the whole, so a child knows the place where it has played in such detail that every bough of the trees, every root of the lilacs, every tiny depression or ditch is familiar. And thus Jane must have known the home at Steventon.

Writing about a storm in 1800, she says: "I was

just in time to see the last of our two highly valued elms descend into the Sweep!!! The other, which had fallen, I suppose, in the first crash, and which was the nearest to the pond, taking a more easterly direction, sunk amid our screen of chestnuts and firs, knocking down one spruce fir, beating off the head of another, and stripping the two corner chestnuts of several branches in its fall. This is not all. One large elm out of the two on the left-hand side as you enter, what I call, the elm walk, was likewise blown down; the maple bearing the weathercock was broke in two, and what I regret more than all the rest is that all the three elms which grew in Hall's meadow, and gave such ornament to it, are gone."

This bespeaks her intimate acquaintance with the trees, of which each one was a friend.

The country and the writer suited each other so wonderfully, that one pauses for a moment wondering whether, after all, environment may not have that magic influence claimed for it by some who hold it to be more powerful than inherited qualities. Influence of course it has, and one wonders what could possibly have been the result if two such natures as those of Jane Austen and Charlotte Brontë had changed places; if Jane had been brought up amid the wild, bleak Yorkshire moors, and Charlotte amid the pleasant fields of Hampshire. As it is, the surroundings of each intensified and developed their own peculiar genius.

Jane was born of the middle class, her father, George Austen, being a clergyman in a day when clergymen were none too well thought of, yet taking a better position than most by reason of his own family and good connections. George Austen had early been left an orphan, and had been adopted by an uncle. He showed the possession of brains by obtaining first a scholarship at St.

John's College, Oxford, and subsequently a fellowship.

He took Orders which, in the days when rectories were looked upon simply as "livings," was a recognised mode of providing for a young man, whether he had any vocation for the ministry or not. But he seems to have fulfilled his duties, or what were then considered sufficient duties, creditably enough. Of George Austen one of his sons wrote—

"He resided in the conscientious and unassisted discharge of his ministerial duties until he was turned of seventy years." He was a "profound scholar" and had "exquisite taste in every species of literature."

The subject of the clergy at that date, and the examples of them which Jane has herself given us in her books, is an interesting one, and we shall return to it. The rectory of Steventon was presented to George Austen by Mr. Knight, the same cousin who afterwards adopted his son Edward; and the rectory of Deane, a small place about a mile distant, was bought by an uncle who had educated him, and given to him. The villages were very small, only containing about three hundred persons altogether. In those days parish visiting or parochial clubs and entertainments were unthought of, Sunday schools in their earliest infancy, and we hear nothing whatever throughout the whole of Jane Austen's correspondence which leads us to think that she, in any way, carried out the duties which in these days fall to the lot of every clergyman's daughter. This is not to cast blame upon her, it only means that she was the child of her times; these things had not then been organised.

George Austen married Cassandra, youngest daughter of the Rev. Thomas Leigh, who was of good family, her uncle was Dr. Theophilus Leigh, Master of Balliol

THE REV. JAMES AUSTEN

THE REV. GEORGE AUSTEN

College, a witty and well-known man. These things are not of importance in themselves, but they serve to show that the family from which Jane sprang was on both sides of some consideration. The Austens lived first at Deane, but moved to Steventon in 1771. They had undertaken the charge of a son of Warren Hastings, who died young, and they had a large family of their own, as was consistent in days when families of ten, eleven, and even fifteen were no uncommon thing.

There were five sons and two daughters in all, and Jane was the youngest but one. (See Table, p. 326.) James, the eldest, was probably too far removed in age from his younger sister ever to have been very intimate with her. It is said that he had some share in her reading and in forming her taste, but though she was very fond of him she never seems, as was very natural, to have had quite the same degree of intimate affection for him as she felt for those of her brothers nearer to her own age. James was twice married, and his only daughter by his first wife was Anna, of whom Jane makes frequent mention in her letters, and to whom some of the published correspondence was addressed. His second wife was Mary Lloyd, whose sister Martha was the very devoted friend, and frequent guest, of the girl Austens, and who late in life married Francis, one of Jane's younger brothers. The son of James and Mary was James Edward, who took the additional name of Leigh, and was the writer of the *Memoir* which supplies one of the only two sources of authoritative information about Jane Austen. He died in 1874.

The next brother, Edward, as already stated, was adopted by his cousin Mr. Knight, whose name he took. He came into the fine properties of Chawton House in Hampshire and Godmersham in Kent, even during the lifetime of Mr. Knight's widow, who looked on him as a son and retired in his favour. Edward married Elizabeth Bridges, and had a family of eleven children, of whom the eldest, Fanny Catherine, married Sir Edward Knatchbull, and their eldest son was created Lord Brabourne; to him we owe the *Letters* which are the second of the authoritative books on Jane Austen.

Jane Austen was attached to her niece Fanny Knight in a degree only second to that of her attachment to her own sister Cassandra. Fanny's mother, Mrs. Edward Austen or Knight (for the change of name seems not to have taken place until her death), died comparatively young, and the great responsibility thrown upon Fanny doubtless made her seem older, and more companionable, than her years; of her, her famous aunt writes—

"I found her in the summer just what you describe, almost another sister, and could not have supposed that a niece would ever have been so much to me. She is quite after one's own heart. Give her my best love and tell her that I always think of her with pleasure."

The third Austen brother, Henry, interested himself much in his sister's writing, and saw about the business arrangements for her, when, after many years, she decided to publish one of her own books at her own risk. He was something of a rolling stone, filling various positions in turn, and at length taking Orders and succeeding his brother James in the Steventon living. During part of his life he lived in London, where Jane often stayed with him. He married first his cousin Eliza, the daughter of George Austen's sister; she was the widow of a Frenchman, the Count de Feuillade, who had suffered death by the guillotine. Eliza was very popular with her girl cousins, as we can see from Jane's remarks; she died in 1813, and in 1820 Henry married Eleanor, daughter of Henry Jackson. The two youngest brothers, Francis and Charles, came above and below Jane, with about three years' interval on either side. They both entered the navy, and both became admirals.

Frank rose to be Senior Admiral of the Fleet, and was created G.C.B.; he lived to be ninety-two. He, like another of his brothers, was twice married,—a habit that ran abnormally in the family,—and his second wife was Martha, the sister of his brother James's wife, mentioned above. Charles married first Fanny Palmer, and was left a widower in 1815 with three small daughters. He married secondly her sister Harriet. The two Fannies, Mrs. Charles Austen and the eldest daughter of Edward Knight, sometimes cause a little confusion. Jane Austen mentions calling with the younger Fanny on the motherless children of her brother, one of whom was also Fanny, soon after their loss. "We got to Keppel Street, however, which was all I cared for, and though we could only stay a quarter of an hour, Fanny's calling gave great pleasure, and her sensibility still greater; for she was very much affected at the sight of the children. Little Fanny looked heavy. We saw the whole party."

It has been necessary to give a few details respecting the brothers who played so large a part in Jane's life, because her visits away from home were nearly all to their houses, her letters are full of allusions to them, and the great family affection which subsisted between them all made the griefs and joys of the others the greatest events in a very uneventful life. The dearest, however, of the whole family was the one sister Cassandra, who, like Jane herself, never married, which seems the stranger when we consider how many of the brothers married twice. There was a sad little love-story in Cassandra's life. She was engaged to a young clergyman who had promise of promotion from a nobleman related to him. He accompanied this patron to the West Indies as chaplain to the regiment, and there died of yellow fever. There is perhaps something more pathetic in such a tale than in any other, the glowing ideal has not been smirched by any touch of the actual sordid daily life, it is snatched away and remains an ideal always, and the happiness that might have been is enhanced by romance so as to be a greater deprivation than any loss of the actual.

The two sisters were sisters in reality, sharing the same views, the same friendships, the same interests. When away, Jane's letters to Cassandra are full and lively, telling of all the numberless little events that only a sister can enjoy. And if Jane's own estimate is to be believed, Cassandra's are to the full as vivacious.

"The letter which I have this moment received from you has diverted me beyond moderation. I could die of laughter at it, as they used to say at school. You are indeed the finest comic writer of the present age."

Cassandra lived to 1845, long enough to see that her beloved sister's letters would in all probability be published; she was of a reticent nature, with a strong dislike to revealing anything personal or intimate to the public, she therefore went through all these neatly written letters from Jane, which she had so carefully preserved, and destroyed anything of a personal nature. One cannot altogether condemn the action, greatly as we have been the losers; the letters that remain, many in number, deal almost entirely with outside matters, trivialities of everyday life, and they are written so brightly that we can judge how interesting the bits of self-revelation by so expressive a pen would have been.

In 1869, when Mr. Austen-Leigh published his

Memoir, only one or two of Jane Austen's letters were available; but in 1802, on the death of Lady Knatchbull (*née* Fanny Knight), the letters above referred to, which Cassandra Austen had retained, were found among her belongings, having come to her on her aunt's death. Her son, created Lord Brabourne, therefore published these in two volumes in 1884, and when quotations and extracts are given in this book without further explanation, it must be inferred that these are taken from letters of Jane to Cassandra, as given by Lord Brabourne.

CHAPTER II

CHILDHOOD

OF Jane Austen's childhood in the quiet country rectory we know little, probably because there is not a great deal to know. It was the custom in those days to put babies out to nurse in the village, sometimes until they were as much as two years old, a point often overlooked when the mothers of what is now extolled as a domestic period are held up as patterns to a more intellectual and roving generation. Certainly it was an easy and cheap method of getting rid of the care and trouble involved by a baby in the house, and it probably answered well, as the child would learn to do without too much attention, and at an early age, faddists notwithstanding, could hardly suffer from any influence of its surroundings, other than physically, and it may be taken for granted that the material necessities were well provided and kept under supervision. Nevertheless, a mother who adopted this course at the present day could hardly escape the epithet of "heartless," which would assuredly be levelled at her.

In the time of Jane's childhood the old days of rigid severity toward children were past, no longer were mere babies taken to see executions and whipped on their return to enforce the example they had beheld. In fact a period of undue indulgence had set in as a reaction, but this does not seem to have affected the Austen family, who were brought up very wisely, and perhaps even a little more repressively than would be the case in a similar household to-day. Jane herself was evidently a diffident child.

She says of a little visitor many years afterwards: "Our little visitor has just left us, and left us highly pleased with her; she is a nice natural open-hearted, affectionate girl, with all the ready civility one sees in the best children in the present day; so unlike anything that I was myself at her age, that I am often all astonishment and shame.

"What is become of all the shyness in the world? Moral as well as natural diseases disappear in the progress of time and new ones take their place. Shyness and the sweating sickness have given way to confidence and paralytic complaints."

Her own attitude toward children is peculiar. Though on indisputable testimony she was the most popular and best loved of aunts, the fact remains that she had no great insight into child nature, nor does she seem to have had any general love of children beyond those who were specially connected with her by close ties. She loved her nieces, but much more as they grew older than as children.

Mr. Austen-Leigh says: "Aunt Jane was the delight of all her nephews and nieces. We did not think of her as being clever, still less as being famous; but we valued her as one always kind, sympathising, and amusing," and he quotes "the testimony of another niece—'Aunt Jane was the general favourite with children, her ways with them being so playful, and her long circumstantial stories so delightful.'" And again, "Her first charm to children was great sweetness of manner ... she could make everything amusing to a child."

The truth probably is that her innate kindness of

heart and unselfishness compelled her to be as amusing as possible when thrown with little people, but perhaps because she took so much trouble to entertain them she found children more tiresome than other people who accept their company more placidly. However this may be, it is undeniable that the attitude she takes toward children in her books is almost always that of their being tiresome, there never appears any genuine love for them or realisation of pleasure in their society; and she continually satirises the foolish weakness of their doting parents. It is recorded as a great feature in the character of Mrs. John Knightley "that in spite of her maternal solicitude for the immediate enjoyment of her little ones, and for their having instantly all the liberty and attendance, all the eating and drinking, and sleeping and playing, which they could possibly wish for, without the smallest delay, the children were never allowed to be long a disturbance to him [their grandfather] either in themselves or in any restless attendance on them."

Poor Anne in *Persuasion* is tormented by "the younger boy, a remarkably stout forward child of two years old, . . . as his aunt would not let him tease his sick brother, [he] began to fasten himself upon her, in such a way, that busy as she was about Charles, she could not shake him off. She spoke to him, ordered, entreated, insisted in vain. Once she did contrive to push him away, but the boy had the greater pleasure in getting upon her back again directly."

Perhaps to Anne this annoyance was a blessing in disguise, as it brought forward the whilom lover to her assistance, but that is beside the point!

The children of Lady Middleton in *Sense and Sensibility* are particularly badly behaved and odious.

"Fortunately for those who pay their court through such foibles, a fond mother, though in pursuit of praise for her children the most rapacious of human beings, is likewise the most credulous; her demands are exorbitant, but she will swallow anything, and the excessive affection and endurance of the Miss Steeles towards her offspring were reviewed therefore by Lady Middleton without the smallest surprise or distrust. She saw with maternal complacency all the impertinent encroachments and mischievous tricks to which her cousins submitted. She saw their sashes untied, their hair pulled about their ears, their workbags searched and their knives and scissors stolen away, and felt no doubt of its being a reciprocal enjoyment.

"'John is in such spirits to-day!' said she, on his taking Miss Steele's pocket-handkerchief and throwing it out of the window, 'he is full of monkey-tricks.'

"And soon afterwards on the second boy's violently pinching one of the same lady's fingers, she fondly observed, 'How playful William is!'

"'And here is my sweet little Anna-Maria,' she added, tenderly caressing a little girl of three years old, who had not made a noise for the last two minutes; 'and she is always so gentle and quiet, never was there such a quiet little thing!'

"But unfortunately in bestowing these embraces a pin in her ladyship's head-dress slightly scratching the child's neck produced from this pattern of gentleness such violent screams as could hardly be outdone by any creature professedly noisy . . . her mouth stuffed with sugar-plums . . . she still screamed and sobbed lustily, and kicked her two brothers for offering to touch her.

. . . .

"'I have a notion,' said Lucy [to Elinor] 'you think the little Middletons are too much indulged. Perhaps they may be the outside of enough, but it is so natural in Lady Middleton, and for my part I love to see children full of life and spirits; I cannot bear them if they are tame and quiet.'

"'I confess,' replied Elinor, 'that while I am at Barton Park I never think of tame and quiet children with any abhorrence!'"

Those children in the novels who are not detestable are usually lay-figures, such as Henry and John Knightley, rosy-faced little boys not distinguished by any individuality. Others are merely pegs on which to hang their parents' follies, such as little Harry Dashwood, who serves his parents as an excuse for their unutterable meanness. The fact remains there are only two passable children in the whole gallery, and one is the slightest of slight sketches in that little-known and half-finished story *The Watsons*. Here the little boy, Charles, spoken of as "Mrs. Blake's little boy," is a real flesh-and-blood child, who at his first ball when thrown over remorselessly by his grown-up partner, though "the picture of disappointment, with crimsoned cheeks, quivering lips, and eyes bent on the floor," yet contrives to utter bravely, "'Oh, I do not mind it!'" and whose naïve enjoyment at dancing with Emma Watson, who offers herself as a substitute, is well done. His conversation with her is also very natural, and his cry, "'Oh, uncle, do look at my partner; she is so pretty!'" is a human touch.

The other instance is a sample of a very nervous, shy child, perhaps drawn from the recollections of Jane Austen's own feelings in childhood, this is Fanny Price, whose loneliness on her first coming to Mansfield Park is carefully depicted, but Fanny herself is unchildlike and exceptional. Her younger brothers rank among the gallery of bad children, for by "the superior noise of Sam, Tom, and Charles chasing each other up and down stairs, and tumbling about and hallooing, Fanny was almost stunned. Sam, loud and overbearing as he

JUVENILE RETIREMENT

was, . . . was clever and intelligent. . . . Tom and Charles being at least as many years as they were his juniors distant from that age of feeling and reason which might suggest the expediency of making friends, and of endeavouring to be less disagreeable. Their sister soon despaired of making any impression on them; they were quite untamable by any means of address which she had spirits or time to attempt. . . . Betsy, too, a spoilt child, trained up to think the alphabet her greatest enemy, left to be with servants at her pleasure, and then encouraged to report any evil of them."

But Jane Austen's abundant pictures of over-indulged, badly-behaved children are not the only ones to be found in contemporary fiction; in Hannah More's *Cœlebs in Search of a Wife* the children come in for dessert, "a dozen children, lovely, fresh, gay, and noisy . . . the grand dispute, who should have oranges, and who should have almonds and raisins, soon raised such a clamour that it was impossible to hear my Egyptian friend . . . the son and heir reaching out his arm to dart an apple across the table at his sister, roguishly intending to overset her glass, unluckily overthrew his own brimful of port wine." And of another and better behaved family it is observed as a splendid innovation that the children are not allowed to come into dessert, to clamour and make themselves nuisances, but are limited to appearing in the drawing-room later.

One of the characters in *Cœlebs* is made to observe, "This is the age of excess in everything; nothing is a gratification of which the want has not been previously felt. The wishes of children are all so anticipated, that they never experience the pleasure excited by wanting and waiting." He speaks also of the "too great profusion and plethora of children's books," which is certainly not a thing we are used to attribute to that age.

Several of the children's books of that date are kept alive to the present day by a salt of insight into child nature, and are published and re-published perennially. Many a child still knows and loves *The Story of the Robins*, by Mrs. Trimmer, first brought out in 1786; and as for *Sandford and Merton*, by Thomas Day, which was at first in three volumes, published respectively in 1783, 1787, and 1789, many a boy has revelled in it, not perhaps entirely from the point of view in which it was written, but with a keen sense of the ridiculous in the behaviour of the little prig Harry. Mrs Barbauld's (and her brother's) *Evenings at Home* still delights many children; and Miss Edgeworth's *Parent's Assistant*, of which the first volume appeared in 1796, is a perennial source of amusement in nurseries and schoolrooms. *The Fairchild Family* suffers from an excess of religiosity, and a terrible belief in the innate wickedness of a little child's heart, which is not now tolerated. When Emily and Lucy indulge in a childish quarrel, they are taken to see what remains of a murderer who has hung on a gibbet until his clothes are rotting from him, and the warning is enforced by a long sermon; but in spite of much that would not be suitable according to present ideas for a child to hear, *The Fairchild Family*, the first part of which came out a year subsequently to the death of Jane Austen, contains much that is very human in behaviour and action. Though later in date than the others mentioned as surviving, it really is quite as early in treatment, as it is a record of what Mrs. Sherwood, born in the same year as Jane Austen, remembered of her own childhood.

The book contains many examples of the spoilt-child phase, in contrast with which the strict upbringing of the young Fairchilds is shown as the better way. What Mrs. Sherwood puts into the mouth of Mrs. Fairchild about her childhood is probably autobiographical, and may be quoted as an instance of the sterner modes which were then rapidly passing out of vogue.

"I was but a very little girl when I came to live with my aunts, and they kept me under their care until I was married. As far as they knew what was right, they took great pains with me. Mrs. Grace taught me to sew, and Mrs. Penelope taught me to read; I had a writing and music master, who came from Reading to teach me twice a week; and I was taught all kinds of household work by my aunts' maid. We spent one day exactly like another. I was made to rise early, and to dress myself very neatly, to breakfast with my aunts. After breakfast I worked two hours with my aunt Grace, and read an hour with my aunt Penelope; we then, if it was fine weather, took a walk; or, if not, an airing in the coach, I and my aunts, and little Shock, the lap-dog, together. At dinner I was not allowed to speak; and after dinner I attended my masters or learned my tasks. The only time I had to play was while my aunts were dressing to go out, for they went out every evening to play at cards. When they went out my supper was given to me, and I was put to bed in a closet in my aunts' room."

A modern child under such treatment would probably develop an acute form of melancholia.

The home education of the time, for girls at least, was very superficial. We gather something of what was supposed to be taught from the remarks of the Bertram girls in *Mansfield Park* when they plume themselves on their superiority to Fanny—

"'Dear mamma, only think, my cousin cannot put the map of Europe together—or my cousin cannot tell the principal rivers in Russia, or she never heard of Asia Minor, or she does not know the differences between water colours and crayons! How strange! Did you ever hear anything so stupid?'

"'My dear,' their considerate aunt would reply, 'it is very bad, but you must not expect everybody to be as forward and quick at learning as yourself.'

"'But, aunt, she is really so very ignorant. Do you know we asked her last night which way she would go to get to Ireland, and she said she should cross to the Isle of Wight. I cannot remember the time when I did not know a great deal that she has not the least notion of yet. How long ago is it, aunt, since we used to repeat the chronological order of the kings of England, with the dates of their accession, and most of the principal events of their reigns?'

"'Yes,' added the other, 'and of the Roman Emperors as low as Severus, besides a great deal of the heathen mythology, and all the metals, semi-metals, planets, and distinguished philosophers.'"

The rattle-pate, Miss Amelia, in *Cœlebs* thus gives an account of her education: "I have gone on with my French and Italian of course, and I am beginning German. Then comes my drawing-master; he teaches me to paint flowers and shells, and to draw ruins and buildings, and to take views. . . . I learn varnishing, gilding, and Japanning. And next winter, I shall learn modelling and etching and engraving in mezzotint and aquatinta. Then I have a dancing-master who teaches me the Scotch and Irish steps, and another who teaches me attitudes, and I shall soon learn to waltz. Then I have a singing-master, and another who teaches me the harp, and another for the pianoforte. And what little time I can spare from these principal things, I give by odd minutes to ancient and modern history, and geography and astronomy, and grammar and botany, and I attend lectures on chemistry, and experimental chemistry."

Jane's early childhood was probably a very happy one; what with the companionship of Cassandra, with the liveliness and constant comings and goings of the brothers who were educated at home by Mr. Austen himself, with all the romps of a large family having unlimited country as a playground, it can hardly have failed to be so. While she was still too young to profit much by school teaching on her own account, she was sent to a school at Reading kept by a Mrs. Latournelle, because Cassandra was going, and the two sisters could not bear to be parted. How long she was at this school I do not know, but the subjects taught were probably those scheduled in the comprehensive summary of smatterings given by the two Miss Bertrams. This school was a notable one, and among the later pupils was Mrs. Sherwood, who followed Jane after an interval of nine years. She probably went to school as late as Jane went early, which would account for the gap in time between two who should have been contemporary.

Miss Mitford was also a pupil; she went in 1798 when the school had been removed to Hans Place, London. She gives a lively account of it. It was kept by M. St. Quintin, "a well-born, well-educated, and well-looking French emigrant," who "was assisted, or rather chaperoned, in his undertaking by his wife, a good-natured, red-faced Frenchwoman, much muffled up in shawls and laces; and by Miss Rowden, an accomplished young lady, the daughter and sister of clergymen, who had been for some years governess in the family of Lord Bessborough. M. St. Quintin himself taught the pupils French, history, geography, and as much science as he was master of, or as he thought it requisite for a young lady to know; Miss Rowden, with the assistance of finishing masters for Italian, music, dancing, and drawing, superintended the general course of study; while

Madame St. Quintin sat dozing, either in the drawing-room, with a piece of work, or in the library with a book in her hand, to receive the friends of the young ladies or any other visitors who might chance to call."

Miss Mitford says further that the school was "excellent," that the pupils were "healthy, happy, well-fed, and kindly treated," and that "the intelligent manner in which instruction was given had the effect of producing in the majority of the pupils a love of reading and a taste for literature."

Of course Jane, being such a child when she went, can hardly have taken full use of the opportunities which were afforded her, but perhaps she laid at school the foundations of that cleverness in neat sewing and embroidery which is manifested in the specimens still in the possession of her relatives.

There is a portrait of Jane painted when she was about fifteen. It shows a bright child with shining eyes and one loose lock of hair falling over her forehead; not particularly pretty, but intelligent and with character. She is standing, and is dressed in the simple white gown, high waist, short sleeves, and low neck which little girls wore as well as their elders, and round her neck is a large locket slung on a slender chain. Her portrait was painted by Zoffany when she was about fifteen, on her first visit to Bath, but whether this reproduction, which appears in the beginning of Lord Brabourne's *Letters of Jane Austen*, is from that picture I have not been able to ascertain.

Mr. Austen-Leigh says of her—

"In childhood every available opportunity of instruction was made use of. According to the ideas of the time she was well-educated, though not highly accomplished, and she certainly enjoyed that important element of mental training, associating at home with persons of

CHILDHOOD

cultivated intellect." He says in another place, "Jane herself was fond of music, and had a sweet voice, both in singing and conversation; in her youth she had received some instruction on the pianoforte . . . she read French with facility, and knew something of Italian."

In French she had at one time a great advantage in the continual association with Madame de Feuillade, her cousin, and afterwards her sister-in-law, who, as already mentioned, had been married to a Frenchman.

The illustration on p. 26 is a portrait group of the children of the Hon. John Douglas of the Morton family. It was painted by Hoppner, who lived 1758–1810; and, in the costumes of the little boy and elder girl especially, gives a good notion of the dress of the better-class children of the period.

CHAPTER III

THE POSITION OF THE CLERGY

JANE AUSTEN was a clergyman's daughter. At the present time there are undoubtedly wide differences in the social standing of the clergy according to their own birth and breeding, but yet it may be taken for granted that a clergyman is considered a fit guest for any man's table. It was not always so. There was a time when a clergyman was a kind of servant, ranking with the butler, whose hospitality he enjoyed; we have plenty of pictures of this state of affairs in *The Vicar of Wakefield*, to go no further. But before Jane was born, matters had changed. The pendulum had not yet swung to the opposite extreme of our own day, when the fact of a man's being ordained is supposed to give him new birth in a social sense, and a tailor's son passes through the meagrest of the Universities in order that he may thus be transformed into a gentleman without ever considering whether he has the smallest vocation for the ministry. In the Austens' time the status of a clergyman depended a very great deal on himself, and as the patronage of the Church was chiefly in the hands of the well-to-do lay-patrons, who bestowed the livings on their younger sons or brothers, there was very frequently a tie of relationship between the vicarage and the great house, which was sufficient to ensure the vicar's position. In the case of relationship the system was probably at its best, obviating any inducement to servility; but there was a very evil side to what may be called local patronage, which was much more in evidence than it is in our time. Archbishop Secker, in his charges to the clergy of the diocese of Oxford, when he was their Bishop in 1737, throws a very clear light on this side of the question. He expressly enjoins incumbents to make no promise to their patrons to quit the benefice when desired before entering into office. " The true meaning therefore is to commonly enslave the incumbent to the will and pleasure of the patron." The motive for demanding such a promise was generally that the living might be held until such time as some raw young lad, a nephew or younger son of the lord of the manor, was ready to take it. The evils of such a system are but too apparent. We can imagine a nervous clergyman who would never dare to express an opinion contrary to the will of the benefactor who had the power to turn him out into the world penniless; we can imagine the timeserver courting his patron with honied words. This debased type is inimitably sketched in the character of Mr. Collins in *Pride and Prejudice*. "'It shall be my earnest endeavour to demean myself with grateful respect towards her ladyship, and be very ready to perform those rites and ceremonies which are instituted by the Church of England.' Lady Catherine [he said] had been graciously pleased to approve of both the discourses which he had already had the honour of preaching. She had also asked him twice to dine at Rosings, and had sent for him only the Saturday before, to make up her pool of quadrille in the evening. Lady Catherine was reckoned proud, he knew, by many people, but he had never seen anything but affability in her. She had always spoken to him as she would to any other gentleman; she made not the smallest objection to his joining in the society of the neighbourhood."

In his delightful exordium to Elizabeth as to his reasons for proposing to her, he says—

"'My reasons for marrying are, first, that I think it a right thing for every clergyman in easy circumstances (like myself) to set the example of matrimony in his parish; secondly, that I am convinced it will add very greatly to my happiness; and, thirdly, which perhaps I ought to have mentioned earlier, that it is the particular advice and recommendation of the very noble lady whom I have the honour of calling patroness. Twice has she condescended to give me her opinion (unasked too!) on this subject; and it was but the very Saturday night before I left Hunsford—between our pools at quadrille while Mrs. Jenkinson was arranging Miss de Bourgh's footstool—that she said, 'Mr. Collins, you must marry. A clergyman like you must marry. Choose properly, choose a gentlewoman for my sake, and for your own; let her be an active useful sort of person, not brought up high, but able to make a small income go a good way.'"

And when, after his marriage with her friend, Elizabeth goes to stay with them, and is invited to dine with them at the Rosings, Lady Catherine's place, he thus encourages her—

"'Do not make yourself uneasy, my dear cousin, about your apparel. Lady Catherine is far from requiring that elegance of dress in us which becomes herself and daughter. I would advise you merely to put on whatever of your clothes is superior to the rest, there is no occasion for anything more. Lady Catherine will not think the worse of you for being simply dressed. She likes to have the distinction of rank preserved.'"

In the case of Mr. Collins, the patron happened to be a lady, but the instances were numberless in which clergymen spent all their time toadying and drinking with a fox-hunting squire.

Arthur Young says of the French clergy—

"One did not find among them poachers or fox-hunters, who, having spent the morning scampering after hounds, dedicate the evening to the bottle, and reel from inebriety to the pulpit," from which we may infer that many English clergymen did.

Cowper's satire on the way in which preferment is secured is worth quoting in full—

> "Church-ladders are not always mounted best
> By learned clerks and Latinists professed.
> The exalted prize demands an upward look,
> Not to be found by poring on a book.
> Small skill in Latin, and still less in Greek,
> Is more than adequate to all I seek.
> Let erudition grace him or not grace,
> I give the bauble but the second place;
> His wealth, fame, honours, all that I intend
> Subsist and centre in one point—a friend.
> A friend whate'er he studies or neglects,
> Shall give him consequence, heal all defects.
> His intercourse with peers and sons of peers—
> There dawns the splendour of his future years;
> In that bright quarter his propitious skies
> Shall blush betimes, and there his glory rise.
> 'Your lordship' and 'Your Grace,' what school can teach
> A rhetoric equal to those parts of speech?
> What need of Homer's verse or Tully's prose,
> Sweet interjections! if he learn but those?
> Let reverend churls his ignorance rebuke,
> Who starve upon a dog-eared pentateuch,
> The parson knows enough who knows a duke."

At the end of the eighteenth century the Church was at its deadest, enthusiasm there was none. Torpid is the only word that fitly describes the spiritual condition of the majority of the clergy. Secker says, "An open and professed disregard of religion is become, through a variety of unhappy causes, the distinguishing character of the present age"; and the clergy, as the salt of the earth, had certainly lost their savour, and did little or nothing to resist an apathy which, too commonly, extended to themselves.

The duties of clergymen were therefore almost as light as they chose to make them. One service on Sunday, and the Holy Communion three times yearly, at Christmas, Easter, and Whitsuntide, was considered enough.

"A sacrament might easily be interposed in the long interval between Christmas and Whitsuntide, and the usual season for it, the Feast of St. Michael, is a very proper time, and if afterwards you can advance from a quarterly communion to a monthly one, I make no doubt you will." (Secker.)

Baptisms, marriages, and funerals were looked on as nuisances; the clergyman ran them together as much as possible, and often arrived at the last minute, flinging himself off his smoking horse to gabble through the service with the greatest possible speed; children were frequently buried without any service at all.

The churches were for the most part damp and mouldy; there were, of course, none of the present conveniences for heating and lighting. Heavy galleries cut off the little light that struggled through the cobwebby windows. There were mouse-eaten hassocks, curtains on rods thick with dust, a general smell of mouldiness and disuse, and a cold, but ill-ventilated, atmosphere.

In some old country churches there still survive the family pews, which were like small rooms, and in which the occupants could read or sleep without being seen by anyone; in one or two cases there are fire-grates in these; and in one strange example at Langley, in Bucks, the pew is not only roofed in, but it has a lattice in front, with painted panels which can be opened and shut at the occupants' pleasure, and there is a room in connection with it in which is a library of books, so that it would be quite possible for anyone to retire for a little interlude without the rest of the congregation's being aware of it!

The church, only opened as a rule once a week, was left for the rest of the time to the bats and birds. Compare this with one of the neat, warm, clean churches to be found almost everywhere at present; churches with polished wood pews, shining brass fittings, tessellated floor in place of uneven bricks, a communion table covered by a cloth worked by the vicar's wife, and bearing white flowers placed by loving hands. A pulpit of carved oak, alabaster, or marble, instead of a dilapidated old three-decker in which the parish clerk sat below and gave out the tunes in a droning voice.

Organs were of course very uncommon at the end of the eighteenth century in country parishes, and though there might be at times a little local music, as an accompaniment, the hymns were generally drawled out without music at all. This is Horace Walpole's idea of church in 1791: "I have always gone now and then, though of late years rarely, as it was most unpleasant to crawl through a churchyard full of staring footmen and apprentices, clamber a ladder to a hard pew, to hear the dullest of all things, a sermon, and croaking and squalling of psalms to a hand organ by journey-men brewers and charity children."

The sermons were peculiarly dry and dull, and it would have taken a clever man to suck any spiritual nourishment therefrom. They were generally on points of doctrine, read without modulation; and if, as was frequently the case, the clergyman had not the energy to prepare his own, a sermon from any dreary collection sufficed. The black gown was used in the pulpit.

Cowper gives a picture of how the service was often taken—

> "I venerate the man whose heart is warm;
> Whose hands are pure, whose doctrine and whose life
> Coincident, exhibit lucid proof
> That he is honest in the sacred cause.
> A messenger of grace to guilty men.
> Behold the picture! Is it like? Like whom?
> The things that mount the rostrum with a skip,
> And then skip down again; pronounce a text,
> Cry, ahem! and reading what they never wrote,
> Just fifteen minutes, huddle up their work,
> And with a well-bred whisper, close the scene."

In this dismal account the average only is taken, and there were many exceptions; we have no reason to suppose, for instance, that the Rev. George Austen marred his services by slovenliness or indifference, though no doubt the most earnest man would find it hard to struggle against the disadvantages of his time, and the damp mouldy church must have been a sore drawback to church-going.

Twining's *Country Clergyman* gives us a picture of an amiable sort of man of a much pleasanter type than those of Cowper or Crabbe.

We gain an idea of a man of a genial, pleasant disposition, cultured enough, and fond of the classics; who kept his house and garden well ordered, who enjoyed a tour throughout England in company with his wife, who thoroughly appreciated the lines in which his lot was cast, but who looked upon the living as made for him, and not he for the parishioners. A writer in the *Cornhill* some years ago gives a series of pleasant little pen-pictures of typical clergymen of this date. "Who cannot see it all—the curate-in-charge himself sauntering up and down the grass on a fine summer morning, his hands in the pockets of his black or drab 'small clothes,' his feet encased in broad-toed shoes, his white neckcloth voluminous and starchless, his low-crowned hat a little on one side of his powdered head, his eye wandering about from tree to flower, and from bird to bush, as he chews the cud of some puzzling construction in Pindar, or casts and recasts some favourite passage in his translation of Aristotle."

There was the fox-hunter who in the time not devoted to sport was always "welcome to the cottager's wife at that hour in the afternoon when she had made herself tidy, swept up the hearth, and was sitting down before the fire with the stockings of the family before her. He would chat with her about the news of the village, give her a friendly hint about her husband's absence from church, and perhaps, before going, would be taken out to look at the pig."

Or "the pleasant genial old gentleman in knee-breeches and sometimes top-boots, who fed his poultry, and went into the stable to scratch the ears of his favourite cob, and round by the pig-stye to the kitchen garden, where he took a turn for an hour or two with his spade or his pruning knife, or sauntered with his hands in his pockets in the direction of the cucumbers . . . coming in to an early dinner."

Mr. Austen seems to have been a mixture of the first and third of these types, for he was certainly a good scholar, and yet some of his chief interests in life were connected with his pigs and his sheep.

But though these are charming sketches, and their counterparts were doubtless to be found, we fear they are too much idealised to be a true representation of the generality of the clergy of that time; and, charming as they are, there is an easy freedom from the responsibility of office which is strange to modern ideas.

Livings, many of which are bad enough now, were

then even worse paid; £25 a year was the ordinary stipend for a curate who did most of the work. Massey (*History of England in the Reign of George II.*) estimates that there were then five thousand livings under £80 a year in England; consequently pluralism was oftentimes almost a necessity. Gilbert White, the naturalist, was a shining light among clergymen; he was vicar of Selborne, in Hampshire, until his death in 1793; but while he was curate of Durley, near Bishop's Waltham, the actual expenses of the duty exceeded the receipts by nearly twenty pounds in the one year he was there. To reside at all was a great thing for a clergyman to do, and we may be sure, from what we gather, that the Rev. George Austen had this virtue, for he resided all the time at Steventon.

But though the clergy frequently left all the work to their curates, they always took care to receive the tithes themselves. In the picture engraved by T. Burke after Singleton, in the period under discussion, we see the fat and somewhat cross-looking vicar receiving these tithes in kind from the little boy, who brings his basket containing a couple of ducks and a sucking pig into the vicarage study.

Hannah More gives us an account of the usual state of things in regard to non-residence—

" The vicarage of Cheddar is in the gift of the Dean of Wells; the value nearly fifty pounds per annum. The incumbent is a Mr. R., who has something to do, but I cannot find out what, in the University of Oxford, where he resides. The curate lives at Wells, twelve miles distant. They have only service once a week, and there is scarcely an instance of a poor person being visited or prayed with. The living of Axbridge . . . annual value is about fifty pounds. The incumbent about sixty years of age. Mr. G. is intoxicated about

THE VICAR RECEIVING HIS TITHES

six times a week, and very frequently is prevented from preaching by two black eyes, honestly earned by fighting."

"We have in this neighbourhood thirteen adjoining parishes without so much as even a resident curate."

"No clergyman had resided in the parish for forty years. One rode over three miles from Wells to preach once on a Sunday, but no weekly duty was done or sick persons visited; and children were often buried without any funeral service. Eight people in the morning, and twenty in the afternoon, was a good congregation."

She evidently means that the service was sometimes held in the morning, and sometimes in the afternoon, as she says there were not two services.

She also speaks of it as an exceptionally disinterested action of Dr. Kennicott that he had resigned a valuable living because his learned work would not allow him to reside in the parish.

By far the best account of what was expected from a contemporary clergyman is to be gathered from Jane Austen's own books. It is one of her strong points that she wrote only of what she knew, and as her own father and two of her brothers were clergymen, we cannot suppose that she was otherwise than favourably inclined to the class. Her sketch of Mr. Collins is no doubt something of a caricature, but it serves to illustrate very forcibly one great error in the system then in vogue—that of local patronage.

The other clergymen in her books are numerous: we have Mr. Elton in *Emma*, Edmund Bertram and Dr. Grant in *Mansfield Park*, Henry Tilney in *Northanger Abbey*, and Edward Ferrars in *Sense and Sensibility*.

It is impossible to deny that Edmund Bertram is a prig, or perhaps, to put it more mildly, is inclined to be sententious, so sometimes one almost sympathises with the gay Miss Crawford, whose ideas so shocked him and Fanny; yet though those ideas only reflected the current opinion of the times, they were reprehensible enough. When Miss Crawford discovers, to her chagrin, that Edmund, whom she is inclined to like more than a little, is going to be a clergyman, she asks—

"'But why are you to be a clergyman? I thought that was always the lot of the youngest, where there were many to choose before him!'

"'Do you think the Church itself never chosen, then?'

"'Never is a black word. But yes, in the never of conversation which means not very often, I do think it. For what is to be done in the Church? Men love to distinguish themselves, and in either of the other lines distinction may be gained, but not in the Church. A clergyman is nothing.'"

And in reply to Edmund's defence, she continues—

"'You assign greater consequence to a clergyman than one has been used to hear given, or than I can quite comprehend. One does not see much of this influence and importance in society, and how can it be acquired where they are so seldom seen themselves? How can two sermons a week, even supposing them worth hearing, supposing the preacher to have the sense to prefer Blair's to his own, do all that you speak of, govern the conduct and fashion and manners of a large congregation for the rest of the week? One scarcely sees a clergyman out of his pulpit!'

"'You are speaking of London, I am speaking of the nation at large.'"

But it is noteworthy that even Edmund, who is upheld as a bright example, does not in his defence assert anything relative to the careful looking after the lives of his flock which nowadays is a chief part of a parish clergyman's duty. He speaks of conduct, and declares that "as the clergy are or are not what they ought to be, so are the rest of the nation," but all the retort he wins from the girl he so much admires is that she is just as much surprised at his choice as ever, and that he really is fit for something better!

In another place, where the same discussion is reopened, she says: "'It is indolence, Mr. Bertram, indeed—indolence and love of ease—a want of all laudable ambition, of taste for good company, or of inclination to take the trouble of being agreeable, which make men clergymen. A clergyman has nothing to do but to be slovenly and selfish, read the newspaper, watch the weather, and quarrel with his wife. His curate does all the work, and the business of his own life is to dine.'"

This type is exemplified in the same book by Dr. Grant, who is not drawn vindictively, but is described by his own sister-in-law, Miss Crawford, as "'an indolent, selfish *bon vivant*, who must have his palate consulted in everything; who will not stir a finger for the convenience of anyone; and who, moreover, if the cook makes a blunder, is out of humour with his excellent wife. To own the truth, Henry and I were driven out this very evening by a disappointment about a green goose, which he could not get the better of. My poor sister was forced to stay and bear it.'"

And when Edmund is about to enter on the living, Henry Crawford gaily observes, "'I apprehend he will not have less than seven hundred a year. Seven hundred a year is a fine thing for a younger brother; and as, of course, he will still live at home, it will be all for his *menus plaisirs;* and a sermon at Christmas and Easter, I suppose, will be the sum total of sacrifice.'"

After all this, it is pleasant to know that some upright and serious men, even in those days, thought differently of the life and duties of a clergyman, for Jane makes Sir Thomas Bertram reply—

"'A parish has wants and claims which can be known only by a clergyman constantly resident, and which no proxy can be capable of satisfying to the same extent. Edmund might, in the common phrase, do the duty of Thornton, that is, he might read prayers and preach without giving up Mansfield Park; he might ride over every Sunday to a house nominally inhabited, and go through divine service; he might be the clergyman of Thornton Lacey every seventh day, for three or four hours, if that would content him. But it will not. He knows that human nature needs more lessons than a weekly sermon can convey; and that if he does not live among his parishioners, and prove himself by constant attention to be their well-wisher and friend, he does very little either for their good or his own.'"

It is also striking to see how very much the taking of Orders depended upon some living to be obtained; there seems to have been no special idea of suitability, and still less of preparation, only the merest and most perfunctory examination was demanded of the candidate for Orders. There is a story of this date of one examination for ordination where only two questions were asked, one of which was, "What is the Hebrew for a skull?"

In an entertaining book on Jane Austen by Miss Constance Hill, published in 1902, there is a quotation from a letter anent the ordination examination of Mr. Lefroy, who married Anna, Jane's niece. "The Bishop only asked him two questions, first if he was the son of Mrs. Lefroy of Ashe, and secondly if he had married a Miss Austen."

It is said also that Brownlow North, Bishop of Winchester, examined his candidates for ordination in a cricket-field during a match. One candidate is described by Boswell as having read no books of divinity, not even the Greek Testament. There were, of course, serious and learned bishops enough; Burnet, Bishop of Salisbury, who lived from 1643 to 1715, was horrified at the ignorance of candidates, who apparently had never read the Old Testament and hardly knew what was in the New. "They cry, and think it a sad disgrace to be denied Orders, though the ignorance of some is such that in a well-regulated state of things they would appear not to know enough to be admitted to the Holy Sacrament."

It is probable that the Bishops judged a great deal more, on the whole, by the appearance and manners of the man before them, and the prospects he had of holding a living, than by his own knowledge, and in the case of a well-born, serious-minded man like Edmund Bertram there would be no difficulty whatever about his lack of divinity.

Of Henry Tilney's duties in *Northanger Abbey*, very little can be said or gathered, he never appears like a clergyman at all. We are told that the parsonage was a "new built, substantial stone house." We know that he had to go there, much to Catherine Morland's distress, when she was a guest at his father's house, Northanger Abbey, because the engagements of his curate at Woodston obliged him to leave on Saturday for a couple of nights. But at all events he does seem to have spent most of his time at the parsonage, though he still kept on his room at home.

Of Edward Ferrars' clerical avocations we also hear so very little that he might almost as well have been of any other profession.

The only other clergyman in the novels is Mr. Elton, a specimen not quite so egregious as Mr. Collins, but sufficiently so to be very amusing. On him the waves of Emma's match-making break with force—

"'Poor Mr. Elton! You like Mr. Elton, papa! I must look about for a wife for him. There is nobody in Highbury who deserves him, and he has been here a whole year, and has fitted up his house so comfortably that it would be a shame to have him single any longer; and I thought when he was joining their hands to-day, he looked so very much as if he would like to have the same kind office done for him!'"

Emma thinks he will do admirably for her somewhat ambiguously placed friend Harriet Smith, while Mr. Elton himself fixes his eyes on the heiress Emma. A nice little illustration of the social status of the cleric, who would not have been thought entirely out of the question for the heiress, though doubtless a little beneath her. Mr. Elton is represented as a handsome, ingratiating, debonair young man, who spends his time playing the gallant, reading aloud, making charades with the young ladies, and preaching sermons that please everybody. However, he meets his match in the dashing and vulgar Mrs. Elton, whom he picks up, soon after his rejection by Emma, at a watering place, and thereafter they spend their time in a blissful state of mutual admiration.

CHAPTER IV

HOME LIFE AT STEVENTON

FOR the first five-and-twenty years of her life, from her birth in December 1775 to the spring of 1801, Jane lived at Steventon, in her father's rectory, as peaceful and quiet a home as even she could have wished. But though her own circumstances were peaceful and happy, the great world without was full of flux and reflux.

Wars and rumours of wars, revolutions and upheavals, which changed the whole face of Europe, were going on year by year, but of these things, as I have said, hardly an echo reaches us in her writing; not even in the correspondence with her sister, which begins in 1796 when the turmoil was at its height, which is the more surprising when we consider that her own sailor brothers were taking an active part in affairs; and her cousin, the Countess de Feuillade, had fled to the Austens for shelter when her husband suffered death by the guillotine. What depths these things stirred in Jane, or whether she lacked the imagination to bring home to her their enormous importance relative to the small details of immediate surroundings, we shall never know. Her minute observation, her unrivalled faculty for using that which lay under her hand, the stores of little human characteristics which, by her transmuting touch, she invested with such intense interest, lead one to suppose that such a clear, near-sighted mental vision carried with it defective mental long sight. There are a number of persons who, deeply and warmly interested in that which immediately appeals to them, cannot throw their sympathy far out over unseen events and persons. We are all prone to this, there is not one of us who is not more affected by a single tragic death in the neighbourhood than by the loss of a hundred lives in America; life in this world would be intolerable were it not so, this is one of the provisions of a merciful providence for making it endurable. But there are some more near-sighted in this respect than others, and from internal evidence in the letters we may judge that Jane belonged to them; it is only conjecture, but it is often the case in life, that virtues carry corresponding faults, that extreme cleverness in one direction induces a little want of perception in another. The law of balance and compensation is so omnipresent, that Jane's intensely clear vision in regard to near objects may have been paid for by absorption in them, somewhat to the exclusion of larger interests.

In 1789, while she was yet but fourteen years old, there began that Revolution which, taking it altogether, is the most tremendous fact in the history of Europe France was seething, but as yet the ferment had not affected other nations. In the July of that year the tricolour was adopted as the national flag, excess reigned supreme, and the nobles began to emigrate. It was not until 1792 that France began to grasp the lands of others, and reached forth the first of those tentacles, which, like those of an octopus, were to spread all over Europe. In the beginning Austria and Prussia opposed her, but after the murder of the French King, in January 1793, England was forced to join in to protect Holland, and to uphold the general status of nations. Treaties were signed between almost all the civilised nations of Europe, for the crushing of a common enemy; Switzerland alone, of those affected by France's movements, remaining perfectly neutral.

The echoes of the Reign of Terror that followed must have reached even to the remotest recesses of England, and it is impossible to believe that the Austens were not deeply affected.

Walpole's forcible language on the Revolution shows its effect on contemporary opinion: "I have wanted to vent myself, Madam [the Countess of Ossory], but the French have destroyed the power of words. There is neither substantive nor epithet that can express the horror they have excited! Brutal insolence, bloody ferocity, savage barbarity, malicious injustice, can no longer be used but of some civilised country, where there is still some appearance of government. Atrocious frenzy would, till these days, have sounded too outrageous to be pronounced of a whole city—now it is too temperate a phrase for Paris, and would seem to palliate the enormity of their guilt by supposing madness the spring of it—but though one pities a herd of swine that are actuated by demons to rush into the sea, even those diabolical vagaries are momentary, not stationary, they do not last for three years together nor infect a whole nation—thank God it is but one nation that has ever produced *two massacres* of Paris."

"But of all their barbarities the most inhuman has been their *not* putting the poor wretched King and Queen to death three years ago. If thousands have been murdered, tortured, broiled, it has been extempore; but Louis and his Queen have suffered daily deaths in apprehension for themselves and their children."

The newspapers gave long extracts from the doings of the National Assembly, but of course these always appeared some days subsequently to the events. The news of the death of the French King was known, by rumour at least, with extraordinary quickness, about two days after it happened, and was received with execration. Detailed accounts did not come in until some days after. The first notice is thus announced in the *St. James's Chronicle:* "The murder took place at four in the morning on Monday, and was conducted in the most private manner. The guillotine was erected in a court of the Temple. A hole dug under it into which the King's head fell, and his body was precipitated after." This was incorrect in some particulars, as the murder did not take place until after ten in the morning. In all the newspapers of the time, there are little sentences that strike us sadly even now, and when freshly recorded, as having just happened, they must have moved many persons to deep sorrow. July 1, 1793, "A greater regard is shown for the august prisoners. A small waggon has been sent in loaded with playthings for the son of the unfortunate Louis XVI." "After many entreaties the widow of Capet finally resolved to deliver up to us her son, who has been conducted to the apartments designed for him under the care of citizen Simon." Charlotte Corday's bold speech, when she was brought up to answer for her murder of the tyrant, is quoted: "I did not expect to appear before you; I always thought that I should be delivered up to the rage of the people, torn in pieces, and that my head, stuck upon the top of a pike, would have preceded Marat on his state bed to serve as a rallying point to Frenchmen, if there still are any worthy of that name."

In August of the same year, the death of Marie Antoinette was daily expected. "The queen was dressed in white lawn and wore a black girdle . . . her cell is only eight feet long, and eight feet wide. Her couch consists of a hard straw bed and very thin coverings; her diet, soup and boiled meat."

But in an anguish of mind which must have made her indifferent to the horrors of material surroundings, the poor Queen was kept alive until October, when finally news came of her execution. "As soon as the ci-devant queen left the Conciergerie to ascend the scaffold, the multitude cried out *brava* in the midst of plaudits. Marie Antoinette had on a white loose dress, her hands were tied behind her back. She looked firmly round her on all sides, and on the scaffold preserved her natural dignity of mind."

This is the kind of reading of contemporary events that would greet Jane when the household received its bi-weekly or tri-weekly paper.

All through 1794 war continued, while the French slowly bored their way into the Continent. Of the splendid naval victories of these years we speak in the chapter on the Navy; these surely must have affected Jane, and made her heart beat high at the thought of what her brothers might be called upon to undergo any day. Toward the end of 1795, Austria and Britain alone were left to uphold the right of nations against the all-devouring French. In England food was at famine prices, and there was actually a party who wished the enemy to win in order that the war might end. London was in a state of great agitation, so that public meetings were suppressed in the interests of public safety. In 1796, Spain declared war against Great Britain, having previously patched up peace with her dangerous neighbour. In this year Napoleon Buonaparte first began to be heard of outside his own country, by his successes in his Italian campaign.

England, in sore straits, attempted to make peace, but the arrogance of France left her no other course compatible with honour than to continue the war, and the opening of 1797 found her in great difficulties. On all sides invasion by France was dreaded; in fact, in the previous December an attempt at such an invasion by landing on the coast of Ireland, which was in a state of bitter rebellion, was made. In February the victory of St. Vincent put a little heart into the English people, and did away for a time with the possibility of another attempt at invasion by Hoche, whose fleet was scattered by a storm. In May of 1797 a dangerous mutiny broke out among the sailors, followed by another at the Nore, but these were firmly quelled.

In 1798, Napoleon's Egyptian campaign must have been followed with tense interest, though news would be slow in coming, and it would probably be many days before the news of Lord Nelson's glorious victory at the Battle of the Nile, which had smashed up the French fleet and left Napoleon stranded, was received in England. This victory gave renewed spirit to the Allies in Europe. A whole string of affiliated Republics had now been established by France, made out of her conquests—including Switzerland, whose strict neutrality had not preserved her from invasion. Yet Austria carried on her share of the war bravely, and in the autumn of 1799 the English made a desperate attempt to retrieve the integrity of Holland, but after a short campaign were compelled to evacuate the country. In October 1799, Napoleon, finding his dreams of establishing a great Eastern kingdom impracticable, returned to France, and in the December of the same year was acclaimed First Consul.

Thus, from her early girlhood, Jane would hear of events which greatly affected her own country, she would be accustomed to a perpetual state of war, she would share in the apprehensions of invasions, and the name of Napoleon, ever swelling into greater and greater menace, would continually strike upon her ear.

In November 1800, Jane makes one of her few allusions to historical events, and then only because it concerned her brother. "The *Petterel* with the rest of the Egyptian squadron was off the Isle of Cyprus, whither they went from Jaffa for provisions, and whence they were to sail in a day or two for Alexandria, there to await the result of the English proposals for the evacuation of Egypt."

In 1800, with Buonaparte at the head of a military despotism, a new era began in the war. The two terrific battles of Marengo and Hohenlinden, hotly contested, left the French victors; and at the latter seven thousand of the Allies were taken prisoners, and seven thousand killed and wounded.

In this year, at home the most important event was the Union of Ireland with Great Britain.

When the Continental war was going on, the news from the field of battle was generally eight or nine days old. But this, of course, was nothing to the time which elapsed in the case of India, for events which had happened there in February were given to the public as news in August! Then, indeed, to send a boy to the East was to part with him in reality. There was a long voyage round the Cape, prolonged indefinitely by wind and weather, to encounter. It would be a year from his setting out before the news of his arrival could reach his relations in England. It is the enormous difference made by the telegraph that strikes us most in the contemplation of this era. Of course the officials in India could not get instructions from home, they were responsible for the conduct of affairs, and the sense of responsibility and the impossibility of being checked in anything they wished to do, no doubt gave them that splendid decision which won for us our Indian Empire.

It was in 1784 that the India Act, introduced by Pitt, had given England power over Indian affairs. In the following year, Hastings had returned home, and his celebrated trial, ending in his complete acquittal in 1795, must have taught the English more about Indian matters than they had ever known before. To attend the trial in Westminster Hall was one of the society diversions of the day.

In 1791, in one day, the Duchess of Gordon "went to Handel's music in the Abbey; she then clambered over the benches and went to Hastings' trial in the Hall; after dinner to the play; then to Lady Lucan's assembly; after that to Ranelagh, and returned to Mrs. Hobart's faro table; gave a ball herself in the evening of that morning, into which she must have got a good way, and set out for Scotland the next day."

Long before Jane's death, the mighty Empire of India had passed almost completely under British control. But if her lifetime saw the foundation of one Empire it witnessed also the loss of another country. The United States were declared independent in the first year of her life, and before she was of an age to take any practical note of politics they had been recognised by France as an independent nation. She lived, indeed, in an epoch when history was made, and she lived on into a new era of things, when Buonaparte was finally subdued, France settled, the Continent at peace. At present we have only briefly outlined the extraordinary series of events which filled the five-and-twenty years during which she, living in her sheltered nook at Steventon, heard only echoes. There is something peculiarly suitable in picturing her in this tranquil backwater.

As far as Jane's personal appearance is concerned, we

can gather some notion of her, though the materials are slight. The only portrait preserved of her when grown up is from a water-colour drawing by her sister, and represents a bright, intelligent, but not very prepossessing face, with large eyes and a straight nose. There is humour and decision in the expression, and in spite of the quaint cap and the simple dress with elbow-sleeves and tucked chemisette, which make it look a little odd to modern eyes, there is distinct personality. It may be a good likeness of her as she was then, but, on the other hand, one must allow something for the treatment of an amateur, and we can afford to think of her as being more attractive than she is here represented. A contemporary verbal description left of her is that given by Sir Egerton Brydges, who knew her personally. He says: "She was fair and handsome, slight and elegant, but with cheeks a little too full." We may well believe that, as to looks, she was in that middle state of neither exceptional beauty nor exceptional plainness, which is certainly the happiest. Emma Woodhouse is supposed to have resembled her more than any of her other heroines, and she herself describes Emma by the mouth of one of the other characters in the book: "'Such an eye! the true hazel eye, and so brilliant! Regular features, open countenance, with a complexion—oh, what a bloom of full health; and such a pretty height and size, such a firm and upright figure. There is health, not merely in her bloom, but in her air, her head, her glance. One sometimes hears of a child being "the picture of health," now Emma always gives me the idea of being the complete picture of grown-up health.'"

The most exact personal description we have of Jane is to be found in the preface to the first edition of *Northanger Abbey*, written by her brother Henry. Allowing for the fact that this was penned at a time when the hearts of all who knew her were bleeding for the early death by which she had been taken from them, and that her gentle and gradual decline had previously softened and toned down the whole of that bright lively nature, so that any small imperfections had been entirely smoothed away, we may gather a good picture of her from his words—

"Her stature was that of true elegance, it could not have been increased without exceeding the middle height. Her carriage and deportment were quiet yet graceful. Her features were separately good. Their assemblage produced an unrivalled expression of that cheerfulness, sensibility, and benevolence, which were her real characteristics. Her complexion was of the finest texture. Her voice was extremely sweet." He says also that "she excelled in conversation as much as in composition; she was faultless, and never commented with unkindness even on the vices of others; she always sought in the faults of others something to excuse, forgive, or forget. She never uttered a hasty, a silly, or a severe expression." He speaks further of her good memory, of her fondness for landscape, and her musical skill, and says that Johnson was her favourite author in prose, Cowper in verse.

Yet though bright and clever, and animated by indisputable genius, she was not intellectual; the world of ideas held no place in her mind. We can see very well from her books that the great fundamental laws so important to a wide, deep mind were entirely ignored by her. She was of the mental calibre of her own Elizabeth Bennet, a bright intelligent companion, without depth or brain force. We cannot imagine her grasping abstractions or wrestling with theories; her mind was formed for practicalities and facts.

Jane, we know, was very healthy and full of spirits,

JANE AUSTEN

we hear of no ailments beyond a weakness of the eyes from which she certainly suffered; she says, " My eyes have been very indifferent since it [the last letter] was written, but are now getting better once more; keeping them so many hours open on Thursday night, as well as the dust of the ballroom, injured them a good deal. I use them as little as I can, but you know, and everybody who has ever had weak eyes knows, how delightful it is to hurt them by employment, against the advice and entreaty of all one's friends."

The Austens had special advantages in their position in the fact that they were relatives of Mr. Knight, to whom the whole parish belonged. Mr. Austen seems to have been referred to, in the absence of Mr. Knight, as a kind of squire. He lived simply, but had apparently enough money to allow his daughters the privileges of gentlewomen, and they went to all the dances and balls in the neighbourhood, and paid frequent visits to their brothers' houses for weeks at a time. Mr. Austen kept a carriage and pair, though that meant less than it would do now, as private means of conveyance was much more necessary and there was no carriage tax to add to the expense.

Mrs. Austen seems to have been constantly ailing, which threw the housekeeping a good deal into the hands of her daughters. It is possible that her ailments were more imaginary than real, as she lived to a great age, and in her old age employed herself about the garden and poultry, and is spoken of as being brisk and bright. Perhaps she grew more energetic as she grew older, a not uncommon process. Jane's allusions to her mother's health are frequent, and sometimes seem to point to the fact that she did not altogether believe in them—

" Now indeed we are likely to have a wet day, and though Sunday, my mother begins it without any ailment."

"It began to occur to me before you mentioned it, that I had been somewhat silent as to my mother's health for some time, but I thought you could have no difficulty in divining its exact state—you, who have guessed so much stranger things. She is tolerably well, better upon the whole than she was some weeks ago. She would tell you herself that she has a very dreadful cold in her head at present, but I have not much compassion for colds in the head without fever or sore throat."

"My mother continues hearty; her appetite and nights are very good, but she sometimes complains of an asthma, a dropsy, water in her chest, and a liver disorder."

"For a day or two last week my mother was very poorly with a return of one of her old complaints, but it did not last long, and seems to have left nothing bad behind it. She began to talk of a serious illness, her two last having been preceded by the same symptoms, but thank heaven she is now quite as well as one can expect her to be in the weather which deprives her of exercise."

In the family memoirs, Mrs. George Austen is always spoken of as a person of wit and imagination, in whom might be found the germs of her daughter's genius; such opinion based on recollections must be deferred to, but such is not the picture we gather from the letters. There, Mrs. Austen seems to have exercised none but the slightest influence on her daughters' lives, and when they do mention her, it is only to remark on her health, or the care of her in a journey, or that she will not have anything to do with choosing the furniture for the new home in Bath.

It is a curious circumstance, taken in conjunction with this, that all the mothers of Jane's heroines, when living, are described as fools or worse. It is not intended to hint that she drew such characters from the home circle or from her mother's friends, but it is plainly

HOME LIFE AT STEVENTON

to be seen that she did not look for, or expect from women of this standing, the wit and sense she found elsewhere. Indeed, when one thinks of the bringing up of women in those days, their narrowness of education and extraordinary ignorance of the world, it is wonderful how many did possess keen sense and mother wit. The most notable of the examples in point in the books is Mrs. Bennet in *Pride and Prejudice*, who, with her foolish indulgence of her younger children, her mad desire to get her daughters married to anyone who could furnish a home of whatever sort, is the worst specimen of her kind. "'Oh, Mr. Bennet, you are wanted immediately; we are all in an uproar. You must come and make Lizzie marry Mr. Collins, for she vows she will not have him; and if you do not make haste he will change his mind and not have her.'" Mr. Bennet's subsequent calm rebuke in his admonition to his daughter, "'An unhappy alternative is before you, Elizabeth. From this day you must be a stranger to one of your parents. Your mother will never see you again if you do not marry Mr. Collins, and I will never see you again if you do,'" heightens the effect of his wife's folly.

Mrs. Bennet's fatuous self-complacency, selfishness, and want of sense might have been almost too painful to cause amusement even in a book, had they not been set off by her husband's sardonic humour, just the touch that Jane Austen knew so well how to give.

But Mrs. Bennet is not the only one. Mrs. Jennings, in *Sense and Sensibility*, is "a good-humoured, merry, fat, elderly woman, who talked a great deal, seemed very happy and rather vulgar." She is perpetually making the Dashwood girls wince with her outspoken allusions, and seems altogether deficient in taste and sense, though extremely kind-hearted.

As for Mrs. Dashwood senior, in the same book, in her belief in the charming but double-faced Willoughby, she is, if possible, one degree more credulous than her most foolish daughter. Lady Bertram of *Mansfield Park* is kind enough to her niece in her own way, but "she did not go into public with her daughters. She was too indolent even to accept a mother's gratification in witnessing their success and enjoyment at the expense of any personal trouble." "Lady Bertram did not at all like to have her husband leave her; but she was not disturbed by any alarm for his safety or solicitude for his comfort, being one of those persons who think nothing can be dangerous or difficult or fatiguing to anyone but themselves."

Mrs. Musgrove senior, in *Persuasion*, is nothing but a soft-hearted fool, and "Captain Wentworth should be allowed some credit for the self-command with which he attended to her large fat sighings over the destiny of a son whom, alive, nobody had cared for."

The middle-aged women without daughters, such as Lady Russell and Mrs. Croft, in the same book, are allowed to be sensible, but a mother with grown-up daughters seems always to be mercilessly delineated by Jane.

Of Mr. Austen not much is known; he was a quiet, reserved man, noted for his good looks, and clever enough to educate his sons for the University himself. In his younger days he took pupils, and it was one of these pupils who in after years became so much attached to Cassandra that he entered into the engagement with her which terminated so sadly. Mr. Austen probably kept a restraining hand over his large household, and was responsible for the sensible and kindly upbringing which his daughters received; he seems to have placed no restraint whatever on their pleasures as they grew up.

It may be noted that the husbands of all the foolish women in Jane's books noted above are sensible, self-restrained, capable men.

As for the surroundings and small details of the home where Jane remained with her sister and parents when the brothers went out into the world, it is very difficult to give an adequate picture. There was a great simplicity, and an absence of many things which are now turned out in profusion by machinery but were then not known. We have all of us been in old houses of the simpler kind, and noted the severity of uncorniced walls, the smallness of the inconvenient sash-windows, the plainness of the whole aspect. To the furniture, also, the same remarks would apply, there would be fewer things and of a more solid kind. "Perhaps we should be most struck with the total absence of those elegant little articles which now embellish and encumber our drawing-room tables. We should miss the sliding bookcases, and picture stands, the letter weighing machines and envelope cases, the periodicals and illustrated newspapers—above all, the countless swarm of photograph books which now threaten to swallow up all space." (Mr. Austen-Leigh in the *Memoir*.)

By the following quotation from Jane herself before the removal to Bath, what a vision is instantly conjured up of the yellow speckled prints in cheap, varnished frames, the crude colours and stereotyped subjects of those old pictures which still occasionally remain in the spare rooms of country houses—

"As to our pictures, the battle piece, Mr. Nibbs, Sir William East, and all the old heterogeneous miscellany, manuscript, scriptural pieces dispersed over the house are to be given to James. Your own drawings will not cease to be your own, and the two paintings on tin will be at your disposal. My mother says that the French agricultural prints in the best bedroom were given by Edward to his two sisters."

In regard to minor matters of domestic comfort, lucifer matches were not in general use until 1834, though the fact that they were anticipated by some genius in advance of his time is evidenced by this advertisement in the *Morning Post* of 1788—

"For Travellers, Mariners, etc., Promethean Fire and Phosphorus.

"G. Watts respectfully acquaints the public that he has prepared a large variety of machines of a portable and durable kind, with Promethean fire, paper and match enclosed, most admirably calculated to prevent those disagreeable sensations which most frequently arise in the dreary hour of midnight, from sudden alarm, thieves, fire, or sickness."

Considering this, it is probable that some sort of sulphur match was in use before 1834, though the general method would be the tedious flint and steel.

For firing, wood was, of course, largely used, the cottagers depended totally on "pilfering, breaking hedges, and cutting trees." Coal was very expensive, being of course mined with difficulty in the pre-machinery days; here is a contemporary account of a visit to a coal-mine in Yorkshire. "We had the curiosity to walk and take a near outside view of one seventy yards deep. The manner they work them is strange and not a little dangerous, as they are obliged to have candles, and sometimes with a roof so low that men dig on their knees. . . . They have two boxes which are alternately pulled up and down by pullies worked by a horse, which goes round and round in a sort of well."

Added to the expense of mining was the expense of carriage, which, in the days before railways, had to be done by canal or sea, and the term sea-coal so frequently used in the literature of the day refers to this sea-borne coal. Sometimes after a storm the vessels were delayed, so that the scarcity of coal ran up the price enormously.

This is a brief sketch of the details at the rectory. In such a home there was plenty of occupation for a bright spirit like Jane's, and we can hardly imagine her ever to have been idle. When her sister was away, she undertook the housekeeping, and writes playfully—

"My mother desires me to tell you that I am a good housekeeper, which I have no reluctance in doing, because I really think it my peculiar excellence, and for this reason—I always take care to provide such things as please my own appetite, which I consider as the chief merit in housekeeping. I have had some ragout veal, and I mean to have some haricot mutton to-morrow. We are to kill a pig soon."

"I am very fond of experimental housekeeping, such as having an ox-cheek now and then; I shall have one next week, and I mean to have some little dumplings put into it."

At another time, speaking of the family doctor, she says—

"I was not ashamed of asking him to sit down to table, for we had some pease-soup, a sparerib, and a pudding."

Dinner at that date (1799) was, for the unfashionable, at the hour of three, and for the fashionable not earlier than five, and sometimes much later. Lady Newdigate (*The Cheverels of Cheverel Manor*) says, "The hours of the family are what the polite world would not conform to, viz., breakfast at half past eight, dine at half past three, supper at nine, and go to bed at ten."

Jane Austen in her home life was not in a fashionable set, and her people did not ape the manners of society; she writes at another time, "We dine now at half past three, and have done dinner I suppose before you begin; we drink tea at half past six."

When she went to stay at Godmersham, which she frequently did, she mingled with county people and noted their manners and ways; but she was entirely free from snobbishness, and her quiet satire of those who imitated all the superficial details in the life of a higher class than their own is seen in her account of Tom Musgrave in *The Watsons*, who condescends to stay and play cards with the Watsons until nine, when "the carriage was ordered to the door, and no entreaties for his staying longer could now avail; for he well knew that if he stayed he would have to sit down to supper in less than ten minutes, which, to a man whose heart had long been fixed on calling his next meal a dinner, was quite insupportable."

It is not difficult to trace the evolution of the dinner-hour; in the time of Pepys, busy men rose early and took hardly any breakfast, perhaps a glass of wine or a draught of ale with a bit of bread.

M. Grosley, a Frenchman who visited England about the middle of the eighteenth century, says that "the butter and tea, which the Londoners live upon from the morning till three or four o'clock in the afternoon, occasion the chief consumption of bread, which is cut in slices, and so thin that it does as much honour to the address of the person who cuts it as to the sharpness of the knife. Two or three of these slices furnish out a breakfast."

After this slight repast, corresponding to the Continental coffee and roll, men worked hard until dinner-time, a meal that occupied several hours, and at which they consumed an enormous amount; and they did little or no work afterwards. It is easy to imagine how, on account of work, the early dinner-hour of the poorer classes at noon began to be postponed among men who were more or less their own masters until they could feel, in a common phrase, they had "broken the back of the day's work"; hence the curious hour of three. In out-of-the-way places to this day the Sunday dinner-hour is at four o'clock. When breakfast became more usual, it was not necessary to have dinner so early as three; and with our present fashion of breakfast and lunch, to say nothing of afternoon tea, which we have transferred from after to before dinner, the dinner may be postponed to as late an hour as is desired without inconvenience.

Mrs. Lybbe Powys (then Caroline Girle) mentions in her lively Journal: "We had a breakfast at Holkham in the genteelest taste, with all kinds of cakes and fruit, placed undesired in an apartment we were to go through, which, as the family were from home, I thought was very clever in the housekeeper, for one is often asked by people whether one chooses chocolate, which forbidding word puts (as intended) a negative on the question."

Table decorations were unknown even at large banquets, people sat on benches and were served in the simplest manner. Lady Newdigate gives an account of suppers and prices when she was staying at Buxton—

"Being examined by the Bart in regard to our suppers and what we paid, he [her cousin] owned that we were charged but one shilling and it seems they pay two. Upon this poor Mrs. Fox [the landlady] was attacked and abused in very gross terms. So she came to us with streaming eyes to beg we would explain to the Edmonstones that our suppers were never anything more than a tart and cold chicken which we eat when the company went to supper above, whereas the E.'s order a hot supper of five or six dishes to be got at nine o'clock."

She also gives many details as to the items constituting her meals: " We are going to sup upon crawfish and roasted potatoes. Our feast [dinner] will consist of neck of mutton, lamb steaks, cold beef, lobsters, prawns, and tart."

This is the menu of a dinner given to Prince William of Gloucester in 1798—

Salmon Trout.
Soles.
Fricando of Veal.   Raised Giblet Pie.
Vegetable Pudding.
Chickens.   Ham.
Muffin Pudding.
Curry of Rabbits.   Preserve of Olives.
Soup.   Haunch of Venison.
Open Tart Syllabub.   Raised Jelly.
Three Sweetbreads Larded.
Maccaroni.   Buttered Lobster.
Peas.
Potatoes.
Baskets of Pastry.   Custards.
Goose.

Forks were two-pronged and not in universal use; knives were broad-bladed at the ends, and it was the fashion to eat peas with them.

" The taste for cleanliness has preserved the use of steel forks with two prongs. . . . With regard to little bits of meat, which cannot so well be taken hold of with the two pronged forks, recourse is had to the knife, which is broad and round at the extremity."

It is to be wished that two-pronged forks still survived in the public restaurants of to-day, as the use of the present forks in such places is one of the minor trials of daily life.

Mrs. Papendick's account of the plate and services

acquired at her marriage gives us an idea of what was then thought necessary in this respect. She says, " Two of our rooms were furnished by her Majesty, and a case of plate was also sent by her, which contained cruets, saltcellars, candle-sticks, and spoons of different sizes, silver forks not being then used. From the Queen came also six large and six small knives and forks, to which mamma added six more of each, and a carving knife and fork. Our tea and coffee set were of common Indian china, our dinner service of earthenware, to which, for our rank, there was nothing superior, Chelsea porcelain and fine India china being only for the wealthy. Pewter and Delft ware could also be had, but were inferior." Though Mr. Papendick was attached to the Court, he was anything but wealthy.

Turning to the novels, we find food frequently mentioned in *Emma*, when the little suppers of minced chicken and scalloped oysters, so necessary after an early dinner, were always provided at the Woodhouses. Poor Mr. Woodhouse's feelings on these occasions are mixed. " He loved to have the cloth laid because it had been the fashion of his youth; but his conviction of suppers being very unwholesome, made him rather sorry to see anything put upon it; and while his hospitality would have welcomed his visitors to everything, his care for their health made him grieve that they would eat. Such another small basin of thin gruel as his own was all that he could, with thorough self-approbation, recommend; though he might constrain himself, while the ladies were comfortably clearing the nicer things, to say—

"' Mrs. Bates, let me propose your venturing on one of these eggs. An egg boiled very soft is not unwholesome. Serle understands boiling an egg better than anybody. I would not recommend an egg boiled by anyone else, but you need not be afraid, they are very small you see—one of our small eggs will not hurt you. Miss Bates, let Emma help you to a little bit of tart—a very little bit. Ours are all apple tarts. You need not be afraid of unwholesome preserves here. I do not advise the custard. Mrs. Goddard, what say you to half a glass of wine? A small half glass put into a tumbler of water? I do not think it could disagree with you.'"

Arthur Young, who made a tour through the southern counties of England in 1771, gives us carefully tabulated facts, from which we learn that the average price for meat of all kinds, beef, mutton, veal, and pork, was no more than $3\frac{1}{2}$d. per pound. Butter was $6\frac{1}{2}$d. per pound, and bread a $1\frac{1}{4}$d. By 1786 we find that "meat, taking one kind with another, was fivepence a pound; a fowl ninepence to a shilling; a quartern loaf fourpence; sugar fourpence a pound; tea six shillings a pound and upwards."

With these prices it must be remembered that wages ruled much lower than at present. By 1801, when Jane was in Bath, the incessant state of war had raised everything. She writes: "I am not without hopes of tempting Mrs. Lloyd to settle in Bath; meat is only 8d. per pound, butter 12d., and cheese $9\frac{1}{2}$d. You must carefully conceal from her, however, the exorbitant price for fish; a salmon has been sold at 2s. 9d. per pound the whole fish."

In 1800 the price of the quartern loaf was 1s. $10\frac{1}{2}$d., and then peace was declared. In the preceding ten years the scarcity of flour had been so great that all sorts of changes were suggested in the making of bread. The members of the Privy Council set the example in their own households of not eating puddings, or anything that required flour, excepting the necessary bread, which was to be half made of rye. Flour as powder for wigs was no more used, being needed for consumption, and rice was recommended to the poor.

In 1800, also, was passed the Brown Bread Act, forbidding the sale of pure white wheaten bread, or the consumption of any sort of bread new, as if it were stale it was thought it would go farther. In the seven years before 1800 the prices of not only bread, but meat, butter, and sugar, had risen to double what they had been previously.

With a small household of only three persons, in the absence of Cassandra, the ordering at Steventon Rectory cannot have occupied much time or thought.

Though there would possibly be rather more active superintendence of the domestics than at present, ladies of comfortable means did not then, any more than now, spend all their mornings in the kitchen, as is sometimes erroneously supposed. Jane would doubtless fill up her time with a little practising, a little singing, the re-trimming of a hat, correspondence, and the other small items that go to make up a country girl's life. In the usual avocations of a genteel young lady, "the pianoforte, when they were weary of the harp, copying some indifferent drawings, gilding a set of flower pots, and netting white gloves and veils," we see a tedious inanition quite foreign to our conception of Jane.

Though gardening was not then a hobby, as it is now, there would be general superintendence of the gardener, and many a lingering walk by the borders and flower-beds on sunny mornings. Jane evidently loved flowers, as she often refers to them in her letters.

"Hacker has been here to-day, putting in the fruit trees. A new plan has been suggested concerning the plantation of the new enclosures on the right-hand side of the elm walk; the doubt is whether it would be better to make a little orchard of it by planting apples, pears, and cherries, or whether larch, mountain ash, and acacia."

There was at this time a reaction against the stiff and formal gardening which had been in fashion since introduced by William III. "It is from wild and uncultivated woods, that is from pure nature, that the present (1772) English have borrowed their models in gardening ... daisies and violets irregularly scattered form the borders of them. These flowers are succeeded by dwarf trees, such as rose buds, myrtle, Spanish broom, etc." (Grosley.)

M. Grosley also speaks of wages for gardeners being very high: "I have myself seen a spot of ground, not exceeding an acre, occupied partly by a small house, partly by gravel walks, with two beds of flowers, where the gardener, who was lodging in the house, had a salary of twelve guineas a year."

Wages for all classes were, as has been said, much lower than now; in regard to this question the cry of a "Constant Reader" to *The Times* in 1795 is amusing—

"Tell a servant now, in the mildest manner, they have not done their work to please you, and you are told to provide for yourself, and, should you offer to speak again, they are gone. . . . I look upon their exorbitant increase of wages as chiefly conducive to their impertinence; for when they had five or six pounds a year, a month being out of place was severely felt; but now their wages are doubled, they have in great measure lost their dependence. And what is this increase of wages for? Not in order to lay by a little in case of sickness, but to squander in dress. No young woman now can bear a strong pair of leather shoes, but they must wear Spanish leather, and so on in every article of dress."

By Arthur Young's account wages were less even than above, he says that dairymaids received an average of £3, 12s. yearly, and other maids £3, 6s. Prices possibly varied in different places, being higher in London where labour was scarcer. " Wages are very considerable . . . a fat Welsh girl who has just come out of the country, scarce understood a word of English, capable of nothing but washing, scouring, and sweeping the rooms . . . [received] six guineas a year, besides a guinea a year for her tea, which all servant maids either take in money, or have it found for them twice a day. The wages of a cook maid who knows how to roast and boil amount to twenty guineas a year." (Grosley.)

When the household details had been attended to, the members of the Austen family must sometimes have walked in the rough lanes. In order to avoid the mud in winter or wet weather, ladies wore pattens, which had an iron ring underneath and raised the foot, these pattens clinked as they walked, and must have been very bad in causing an awkward drag in the gait. But country lane walking was not greatly in favour then, women's gowns, with long clinging skirts, were not adapted for such promenades, and it is amusing to think how surprised either Jane or Cassandra would have been could they have met a modern tailor-made girl, with gaiters, and comfortable, trim short skirt well clearing the ground.

Though visiting the poor was not a regular duty, it is evident from many indications that the girls took pleasure in knowing the parishioners, and they must have been to see them occasionally.

The life of labourers was at that time extremely dull, and it is little to be wondered at that they were rough boors when they were left entirely without reasonable means of recreation, and without any mental nourishment. The public-house was often the working-man's sole chance of relaxation. Very few could read or write; in the long winter evenings there was nothing for them to do but to sit in a draughty cottage over a small wood-fire, without any of the luxuries that are now considered necessaries in every labourer's cottage. The interiors resembled a Highland crofter's hut, with beaten earth flooring, often damp; rough uncovered walls, no gay prints, or polished furniture. The introduction of machinery has in this case, as in so many others, altered the entire aspect of life. When sofa legs can be turned out by the hundred by a machine for little cost, everyone can afford sofas; when the process of reproduction of pictures is reduced to a minimum, every wall is adorned. Even the woven quilts and patterned chair-covers, now so little thought of as to be hardly noticed, were then unknown; plain dyes for materials were all that could be had.

Though probably Cowper's dismal picture is an extreme case, it has the merit of being contemporary—

> "The frugal housewife trembles when she lights
> Her scanty stock of brushwood, blazing clear,
> But dying soon like all terrestrial joys.
>
> . . . The brown loaf
> Lodged on the shelf, half eaten without sauce
> Of savoury cheese, or butter costlier still.
>
> . . . All the care
> Ingenious parsimony takes but just
> Saves the small inventory, bed and stool,
> Skillet and old carved chest, from public sale."

But to set against this we have the idyllic pictures of cottage life to be found amid the works of Morland and his *confrères*. One of these, engraved by Grozer, is

THE HAPPY COTTAGERS

given as an illustration. Here, though the cottage is low and dark, with thatched roof and small windows, the healthy, smiling faces of the cottagers themselves are very attractive. The truth probably lay in the mean between Cowper's realism and the artist's idealism, health and good temper may have been found even amid dirt and squalor.

At that time the state of the roads cut off the dweller in a small village from any neighbouring town. At present the three or four miles of good solid road in and out of a provincial town are nothing to a young man who starts off after his work on Saturday evenings, and in many cases he has a bicycle with which to run over them more easily still. At that time the roads, even main roads, were in a filthy state; the Act of 1775, by making turnpike roads compulsory, did much to improve them, but previously they were often mere quagmires with deep ruts, similar to the roads running by the side of a field where carting has been going on. Many and many a record is there of the coaches being stuck or overturned in the heavy mud.

The days of village merry-making and sociability seemed to have passed away in Puritan times never to revive, and had not been replaced by the personal pleasures of the present time. A labourer of Jane Austen's days had the bad luck to live in a sort of intermediate time. Not for him the reading-room with its bright light and warm fire, the concert, the club, and the penny readings, the smooth-running bicycle or the piano. Here is Horace Walpole's picture of suburban felicity: " The road was one string of stage coaches loaded within and without with noisy jolly folks, and chaises and gigs that had been pleasuring in clouds of dust; every door and every window of every house was open, lights in every shop, every door with women sitting in the street, every inn crowded with drunken topers; for you know the English always announce their sense of heat or cold by drinking. Well! It was impossible not to enjoy such a scene of happiness and affluence in every village, and amongst the lowest of the people; who are told by villainous scribblers that they are oppressed and miserable."

Wages for labourers, as in the case of servants, were very low. Arthur Young gives an interesting digest of the wages then in vogue in the southern counties. He divides the year into three parts: harvest, five weeks; hay-time, six weeks; and winter, forty-one weeks; the average of weekly wages for these three respective periods was 13s. 1d., 9s. 11d., and 7s. 11d., making a weekly medium of about 8s. 8d. all the year round. The writer is very severe on the labourers for what he considers their gross extravagance in the matter of tea and sugar, indeed his remarks sound so queer to our ears now that they are worth quoting at some length—

"All united in the assertion that the practice [of having tea and sugar] twice a day was constant, and that it was inconceivable how much it impoverished the poor. This is no matter of trivial consequence; no transitory or local evil; it is universal and unceasing; the amount of it is great . . . this single article cost numerous families more than sufficient to remove their real distresses, which they will submit to rather than lay aside their tea. And an object, seemingly, of little account, but in reality of infinite importance, is the custom, coming in, of men making tea an article of their food, almost as much as women; labourers losing their time to come and go to the tea table; nay, farmers' servants even demanding tea for their breakfast, with the maids! Which has actually been the case in East Kent. If the men come to lose as much of their time at tea as the women, and injure their health by so bad a beverage, the poor, in general, will find themselves far more distressed than ever. Wants, I allow, are numerous, but what name are we to give to those that are voluntarily embraced in order for indulgence in tea and sugar? ... There is no clearer fact than that two persons, the wife and one daughter for instance, drinking tea once a day amounts, in a year, to a fourth of the price of all the wheat consumed by a family of five persons; twice a day are half; so that those who leave off two tea drinkings can afford to eat wheat at double the price (calculated at six shillings a bushel)."

Tea was, of course, then very expensive. Lady Newdigate writes to her husband in 1781, "I enclose Mr. Barton's account for tea, the sum frights one, but if the common tea runs—as Mr. B. says it does—near eighty pounds the chest, it will answer well. The best is full 16s. a pound, but Mundays and Newdigates who have also a lot and have also had from the shops since the new tax was laid, say it is better than what you can buy for 18s." (*The Cheverels of Cheverel Manor.*)

Besides other occupations, such as have been slightly indicated, there was one in Jane's life about which she seldom spoke to anyone; from her earliest childhood the instinct to write had been in her, and she had scribbled probably in secret. Such a thing would not be encouraged in a child of her time. Nowadays, when every little Rosina and Clarence has a page to themselves in the weekly papers, and can see her or his own childish effusions in print, winning thereby the proud and admiring commendations of mother and father, the case is different; Jane wrote because she had to write, it was there and it must come out, but she probably looked on her writing as something to be ashamed of, a waste of time, and only read her compositions to her brothers and sisters under compulsion when no adults were present. Mr. Austen-Leigh says, "It is impossible to say at how early an age she began to write. There are copy books extant containing tales, some of which must have been composed while she was a young girl, as they had amounted to a considerable number by the time she was sixteen. Her earliest stories are of a slight and flimsy texture, and are generally intended to be nonsensical, but the nonsense has much spirit in it."

He gives as an instance "The Mystery, a short unfinished Comedy." He says later, "But between these childish effusions and the composition of her living works, there intervened another stage of her progress, during which she produced some stories, not without merit, but which she never deemed worthy of publication."

It was one of these, at first called *Elinor and Marianne*, which became the germ of *Sense and Sensibility*, and perhaps from these early stories she might, had she lived, have developed and produced other books.

The beautiful old town of Winchester, once the capital of the kingdom, lies only twelve miles from Steventon, and though there was no smooth, hard highroad as we know it, the Austens' carriage horses were probably stoutly-built animals who pulled their load through the mire with right goodwill. Many an expedition to the town must Jane have made, and well would she know the ancient part by the Cathedral and College, so little altered now that we may look upon it with her eyes. The red walls, with their garnishing of lichen and ferns, the beautiful nooks and sunny corners, would all be very familiar to her; and in these happy days, when she was still a light-hearted girl without a thought of fame, how little would she think that one day she should pass away close to the old grey Cathedral, which itself should form her burial-place, and which would be visited on that account by hundreds yet unborn, who knew her only in her books.

CHAPTER V

THE NOVELS

THE life of a genius is, after all, secondary to the works by which he lives; no one would want to know anything about him had not the works aroused their interest. The personality when revealed is ofttimes disappointing, sometimes repulsive, but that cannot alter the value of the work. There is certainly no fear that we shall find anything repulsive in the simple life of Jane Austen, or that we shall be disappointed in knowing her as she was, but for all that the works are the thing.

One writer on Jane Austen, in what purports to be a book, has devoted three hundred and thirty-two pages out of three hundred and eighty-six to a synopsis of the plots of the novels, told in bald and commonplace language, without any of the sparkle of the original, so that even the extracts embedded in such a context seem flat and uninteresting. This sort of book-making is worse than useless, it is positively harmful. Anyone who read the volume before reading the original novels would assuredly never go to them after having seen them flattened out in this style. There is no place for such a book; anyone who is interested in Jane Austen at all should read her works as they are. There can be no excuse on the ground of length, the longest, *Emma*, runs to four hundred and thirty-six pages of clear type in duodecimo form. For the publication of an abridged form of Richardson's works, there might be excuse; anyone who read such an abridgement might be forgiven, for Richardson's masterpiece filled seven volumes! But with Jane Austen there is nothing to abridge, every sentence tells, there is no prolixity, every word has its intrinsic value, and to retell her sparkling little stories in commonplace language is indeed to attempt the painting of the rose.

This book, at all events, is intended only for those who know the novels at first hand, and there shall be no explaining, no pandering to that laziness that prefers hash to joints. Taking it for granted that everyone knows the six complete novels, we enter here on a discussion of the excellencies common to all, leaving them to be discussed singly as they occur chronologically in the life of their author. The first question that occurs to anyone in this connection is, how is it that these books, without plot, without adventures, without *double entendre*, have managed to entrance generations of readers, and to be as much alive to-day as when they were written? The answer is simple and comprehensive,—they are of human nature all compact. This is the first and greatest quality. We have in them no heroes and heroines, no villains, but only men and women; and while the world lasts stories of real live flesh-and-blood characters will hold their own. The second characteristic, which is the salt of fiction, is the keen sense of humour that runs throughout. Jane Austen's observation of the foibles of her fellow-creatures was unusually sharp, her remarks in her letters are not always kind, but in the novels this sharp and keen relish of what is absurd is softened down so as to be nowhere offensive. Like her own Elizabeth, she might say, " I hope I never ridicule what is wise or good.

Follies and nonsense, whims and inconsistencies, do divert me, I own, and I laugh at them whenever I can."

A third characteristic, which is the result of genius alone, is her dainty sense of selection. She never gives anything redundant either in the actions or words of her characters, just enough is said or done to reveal the people themselves to us. One has only to think of writers deficient in this quality to realise how essential it is to enjoyment. In Miss Ferrier's *Marriage*, for instance, there are good and striking scenes, but in her conversations she never knows when to stop, the tedious long-winded sentences have to be skipped in order to get on with the story. The art of selection is that which distinguishes real dramatic talent from photographic realism. To be able to put down on paper exactly what average people say is certainly a gift, for few can do it, but a far higher gift is to select and combine just those speeches and actions which give the desired effect without leaving any sense of omission or incompleteness. Jane Austen had the power also of giving a flash of insight into a state of mind or a personal feeling in a few words more than any writer before or since. It is one of her strongest points. Take for example that scene when Henry Tilney instructing Catherine "talked of foregrounds, distances, and second distances; side screens and perspectives; lights and shades; and Catherine was so hopeful a scholar, that when they gained the top of Beechen Cliff, she voluntarily rejected the whole city of Bath as unworthy to make part of the landscape"; or the opening sentences of *Mansfield Park*. "Miss Maria Ward of Huntingdon, with only seven thousand pounds, had the good luck to captivate Sir Thomas Bertram of Mansfield Park, in the county of Northampton, and to be thereby raised to the rank of a baronet's lady, with all the comforts and consequences of a handsome house and large income. All Huntingdon exclaimed on the greatness of the match; and her uncle, the lawyer, himself, allowed her to be at least three thousand pounds short of any equitable claim to it."

It is by touches such as these that the characters are made to live before us, Jane never condescends to the device of tricks which Dickens allowed himself to use with such wearisome iteration; we have none of "the moustache went up and the nose came down" style. It is by a perfect perspective, by light touches given with admirable effect, that we know the difference between Fanny Price and Anne Elliot, both good, sweet, retiring girls; or between Elinor Dashwood and Emma Woodhouse, who both had the generosity of character to sympathise with another's love affairs while hiding their own. Henry Tilney and Edmund Crawford were both young clergymen of a priggish type, but Henry's didactic reflections are not in the least the same as those which Edmund would have uttered.

The silliness of Mrs. Palmer, with her final summary on the recreant Willoughby, "She was determined to drop his acquaintance immediately, and she was very thankful she had never been acquainted with him at all. She wished with all her heart Combe Magna was not so near Cleveland, but it did not signify for it was a great deal too far off to visit; she hated him so much that she was resolved never to mention his name again, and she should tell everyone she saw how good for nothing he was," is entirely different from the continuous weak outpourings of poor little Miss Bates. "And when I brought out the baked apples from the closet, and hoped our friends would be so very obliging as to take some, 'Oh,' said he directly, 'there is nothing in the way of fruit half so good, and these are the finest looking home-baked apples I ever saw in my life.' That, you know, was so very— And I am sure by his manner it was no compliment. Indeed, they are very delightful apples, and Mrs. Wallis does them full justice, only we do not have them baked more than twice, and Mr. Woodhouse made us promise to have them done three times; but Miss Woodhouse will be so good as not to mention it. The apples themselves are the very finest sort for baking beyond a doubt—" and so on and so on for a page or more.

The truth is that Jane Austen seized on qualities which are frequently found in human nature, and developed them with such fidelity that nearly all of us feel that we have at one time or another met a Miss Bates or a Mrs. Norris, or that we can see traits in others which resemble theirs; it is this which makes the appeal to all humanity. She did not take one person out of her acquaintance and depict him or her, but represented, in characters of her own creating, these salient traits which will ever revive perennially while men and women exist.

Lord Macaulay does not hesitate to speak of Jane in the same breath with Shakespeare. "Shakespeare has had neither equal nor second, but among the writers who have approached nearest to the manner of the great Master, we have no hesitation in placing Jane Austen, a woman of whom England is justly proud. She has given us a multitude of characters, all, in a certain sense, commonplace, all such as we meet every day, yet they are all as perfectly discriminated from each other as if they were the most eccentric of human beings." And Archbishop Whateley makes the suggestive remark, "It is no fool that can describe fools well."

Before the birth of Jane Austen, the novel, which had been hardly considered in England for many centuries, had suddenly found a quartette of exponents which had placed the country in the foremost rank of this branch.

It is rare indeed that four such men as Richardson, Fielding, Smollett, and Sterne, with powers of imagination which make their work classic, should be evolved at the same date. It would almost seem as if the theory which declares that the world, in its onward rush through space, passes through regions impregnated with certain forms of ether that affect men's minds, must have some grain of truth, when simultaneously there leaped forth four exponents and first masters of an art that hitherto can hardly have been said to exist. The united scope of their four lives ranged from 1689 to 1771, and between these dates England was enriched for all time.

With these four Jane Austen's work has little in common. It is to Richardson only that her novels owe anything, and they differ from Richardson's in many striking particulars.

Apart from the masters already mentioned, " A greater mass of trash and rubbish never disgraced the press of any country than the ordinary novels that filled and supported circulating libraries down nearly to the time of Miss Edgeworth's first appearance. There had been *The Vicar of Wakefield*, to be sure, before, and Miss Burney's *Evelina* and *Cecilia*, and Mackenzie's *Man of Feeling*, and some bolder and more varied fictions of the Misses Lee. But the staple of our novel market was beyond imagination despicable, and had consequently sunk and degraded the whole department of literature of which it had usurped the name." (Jeffrey, *Essays*, Ed. 1853.)

And Macaulay says: " Most of the popular novels

which preceded *Evelina* were such as no lady would have written, and many of them were such as no lady could without confusion own that she had read. The very name of novel was held in horror among religious people. In decent families which did not profess extraordinary sanctity, there was a strong feeling against all such works. Sir Anthony Absolute, two or three years before *Evelina* appeared, spoke the sense of the great body of sober fathers and husbands, when he pronounced the circulating library an evergreen tree of diabolical knowledge. This feeling on the part of the grave and reflecting, increased the evil from which it had sprung. The novelist, having little character to lose, and having few readers among serious people, took, without scruple, liberties which, in our generation, seem almost incredible."

The effect that Miss Burney's stories had upon contemporary readers may be judged from a letter of Mr. Twining, a country clergyman of education and standing, who wrote in 1782 to her father, Dr. Burney: "I need not tell you that I gobbled up *Cecilia* as soon as I could get it from my library. I never knew such a piece of work made with a book in my life. It has drawn iron tears down cheeks that were never wetted with pity before; it has made novel readers of callous old maiden ladies, who have not for years received pleasure from anything but scandal. Judge, then, what effect it has had upon the young and the tender hearted! I know two amiable sisters at Colchester, sensible and accomplished women, who were found blubbering at such a rate one morning! The tale had drawn them on till near the hour of an engagement to dinner, which they were actually obliged to put off, because there was not time to recover their red eyes and swelled noses."

Miss Burney's works are real enough, and not lightly to be dismissed; she understood the human heart, and especially the heart of a girl, her sentimental side is perfect, but beyond that she ceases to claim anything out of the common. Her society types are types only; the gay young man, a rake, but charming at heart, whose excesses were but the wildness of an ill-brought-up youth, had been drawn many times before. When she goes beyond affairs of the heart she at once caricatures; her Captain and Mrs. Duval are gross and overdrawn even according to the manners of the age.

Miss Burney preceded Jane Austen by several years; *Evelina* was published in 1778, when the sister-author was but three years old; *Cecilia* came out four years later, and *Camilla* in 1796, the same year in which *Pride and Prejudice* was written, though it was not published until 1813. There is no doubt that Jane Austen owed much to her rival and predecessor, but her gifts were incomparably the greater. Miss Burney's cleverness consisted in the portrayal of feeling in a young girl's sensitive mind, her stories are stories of fashion and incident; Jane Austen's are of country life, and simple everyday scenes. The one had its vogue, and, as an account of contemporary manners, the books have their value and delight now, especially *Evelina*, which stands high above its successors, each one of which is poorer than the preceding one; but none are to be compared with any of Jane Austen's novels, which are for all time.

"Miss Edgeworth indeed draws characters and details conversations such as occur in real life with a spirit of fidelity not to be surpassed; but her stories are most romantically improbable, all the important events in them being brought about by most providential coincidences." (Archbishop Whateley.)

It was a transition age from the conventional to the natural; as in the admiration of landscape, the love for natural gardens, the gradual disappearance of the formal and empty compliment to which women had hitherto been treated, we find taste changing, so in literature the conventional was giving way to the natural. Fielding and Smollett had broken down the barriers in this respect, they had depicted life as it was, not as convention had decreed it should be, hence their gigantic success; but the life they saw and rendered was the life of a man of the world, with all its roughness and brutality. Jane Austen was the first to draw exactly what she saw around her in a humdrum country life, and to discard all incident, all adventure, all grotesque types, for perfect simplicity. She little understood what she was doing, but herein lies her wonderful power, she was a pioneer. Jane's writing had nothing in common with Mrs. Radcliffe, whose style is mimicked in *Northanger Abbey*. It had absolutely no adventures. The fall of Louisa on the Cobb is perhaps the most thrilling episode in all the books, yet by virtue of its entire simplicity, its naturalness, its gaiety, her writing never fails to interest. Perhaps the most remarkable tribute to her genius lies in the fact that, though her books are simplicity itself, dealing with the love-stories of artless girls, they are read and admired not only by girls and women, but more especially by men of exceptional mental calibre. It has been said that the appreciation of them is a test of intellect.

Though her novels are novels of sentiment, they never drift into sickly sentiment, they are wholesome and healthy throughout. With tragedy she had nothing to do; her work is comedy, pure comedy from beginning to end. And as comedies well done are the most recreative of all forms of reading, it is no wonder that, slight as are her plots, hardly to be considered, minute as are the incidents, the attention of readers should ever be kept alive. In all her books marriage is the supreme end; the meeting, the obstacles, the gradual surmounting of these, and the happy ending occur with the regularity of clockwork. And yet each one differs from all the others, and she is never monotonous. Every single book ends well, and it is a striking fact that there is not a death in one of them. When, after a slight improvement, Marianne, in *Sense and Sensibility*, grows worse—

"The repose of the latter [Marianne] grew more and more disturbed; and her sister who watched with unremitting attention her continual change of posture, and heard the frequent but inarticulate sounds of complaint which passed her lips, was most wishing to rouse her from so painful a slumber, when Marianne, awakened by some accidental noise in the house, started hastily up, and, with feverish wildness cried out, 'Is mamma coming?' . . . Hour after hour passed away in sleepless pain and delirium on Marianne's side, and in the most cruel anxiety on Elinor's," we know that in most books we should expect the worst, but with Jane Austen we are sure that it will all turn out well, as indeed it does, and our feelings are not unduly harrowed.

One point which is obvious in all the books is the utter lack of conversation, except about the merest trivialities, among women. In *Sense and Sensibility* it is remarked of a dinner given by John Dashwood that "no poverty of any kind, except of conversation, appeared. . . . When the ladies withdrew to the drawing-room after dinner, this poverty was particularly evident, for the gentlemen had supplied the discourse with some variety—the variety of politics, enclosing land, and breaking horses—but then it was all over, and one subject only engaged the ladies till coffee came in, which was the comparative height of Harry Dashwood, and Lady Middleton's second son, William, who were nearly of the same age ... the two mothers though each really convinced that her own son was the taller, politely decided in favour of the other. The two grandmothers with not less partiality, but more sincerity, were equally earnest in support of their own descendant."

The Christian names of that date were plain, and, for women, strictly limited in number; it detracts something from a heroine to be called Fanny Price or Anne Elliot; and Emma Woodhouse and Elizabeth Bennet are little better; Elinor and Marianne Dashwood are the most fancy names applied by Jane to any of her heroines.

Another point which may be noticed in the novels is that the outward forms of religion, beyond the fact of a man's being a clergyman, are never mentioned, and that on all religious matters Jane is silent; but this does not signify that she was not herself truly religious at heart, for we have the testimony of those who knew her to the contrary, particularly that of her brother Henry in his preface prefixed to the first edition of *Northanger Abbey*, published after her death. But though actual religion does not appear in her pages, the lessons that the books teach are none the less enforced; had she been taking for her sole text the merit of unselfishness, she could not have done more, or indeed half so much, to further the spread of that virtue. To read the books straight through one after the other is to feel the petty meanness of self-striving, and the small gain that lies therein. The talk of the mammas, such as Mrs. Bennet, who are perfectly incapable of seeing their neighbours' interest should it clash with their own; the picture of the egregious Mrs. Norris with her grasping at the aspect of generosity and self-sacrifice, without any intention of putting herself to any inconvenience thereby; the weakness of such characters as Willoughby in *Sense and Sensibility*, who allow themselves to drift along the lines of least resistance without a thought of the after misery they may cause: each and all of these are more potent than a volume of sermons.

It may be noted that Jane Austen chose her characters from the class of life in which she herself lived, we meet in her pages no dukes or duchesses, and only a few slightly sketched labourers and gardeners, who are brought in when inevitable; the story itself is concerned with people of the middle classes, the squires and country gentlemen, the clergymen, and upper-class prosperous tradespeople. We have no inimitable rustics as in George Eliot's wonderful books, nor any disreputable knaves of the fashionable rich as in Miss Burney's works. It is, however, a remarkable fact that all the mankind are always at leisure to picnic and dance attendance on the ladies at any hour of the day; we have no business men; rides and excursions and picnics are always provided with a full complement of idle young men to match the young women. To this rule the clergymen are, of course, no exception.

There was a particular sort of country gentleman who seemed to flourish in those days, of the type of Mr. Knightley and Mr. Bennet. These men did not own enough land to call themselves squires, their farming was very slight, they owned a secure fortune in some safe investment, and apparently spent their lives in the insipid avocations which, until recently, were the lot of nearly all men who were neither rich nor poor. They played cards, and rode and saw their neighbours, and read the newspapers, without seeming to feel their time hang at all heavy on their hands. This breed seems almost extinct now, we are all too excitable, and live too rapidly to make it possible. A man with such an income as either of the two mentioned would almost certainly travel, or take up some special hobby; he would be a social reformer, or on his County Council, a J.P., a M.F.H., or something of the kind, with occupations varied enough to afford him some apology for his existence.

The lowest of what may be called Jane Austen's speaking parts are filled by well-to-do tradesmen, or people just emerging from trade, as the Gardeners in *Pride and Prejudice*, who still lived at the business house in Gracechurch Street; for it was a time when house and shop were not divided.

Her characters are all supposed to be gentlepeople, but there is a difference between those who are of better family than others, such as Bingley, who condescends in marrying Jane Bennet. There is one point on which I venture to disagree with Mr. Pollock, who, in his extremely suggestive and interesting book on *Jane Austen and her Contemporaries*, says—

"Comment has been made, and justly made, on the perfect breeding and manners of those people in Miss Austen's novels who are supposed and intended to be well-bred."

On the contrary, to go no further that *Pride and Prejudice*, Darcy himself passes every canon of gentlemanly conduct, and the Misses Bingley, who were supposed to be of irreproachable breeding, betray vulgarity and lack of courtesy in every sentence. The observations of Miss Bingley on Elizabeth and Darcy would disgrace a kitchen-maid. When Darcy has danced once with Elizabeth, Miss Bingley draws near to him, and observes of the society she is in—

"'You are considering how insupportable it would be to pass many evenings in this manner—in this society, and indeed I am quite of your opinion. I never was more annoyed. The insipidity and yet the noise—the nothingness and yet the self-importance of all these people! What would I give to hear your strictures on them!'

"'Your conjecture is totally wrong, I assure you. My mind was more agreeably engaged. I have been meditating on the very great pleasure which a pair of fine eyes in the face of a pretty woman can bestow!'

"Miss Bingley immediately fixed her eyes on his face, and desired he would tell her what lady had the credit of inspiring such reflections. Mr. Darcy replied with great intrepidity, 'Miss Elizabeth Bennet!'

"'Miss Elizabeth Bennet!' repeated Miss Bingley, 'I am all astonishment. How long has she been such a favourite? And pray when am I to wish you joy?'

"'That is exactly the question which I expected you to ask. A lady's imagination is very rapid; it jumps from admiration to love, from love to matrimony in a moment. I knew you would be wishing me joy.'

"'Nay, if you are so serious about it, I shall consider the matter as absolutely settled. You will have a charming mother-in-law indeed, and of course she will always be at Pemberley with you.'"

The insolence of Lady Catherine de Bourgh might be adduced as a second example from the same book. These people are well born and well bred, but their manners and conduct are impossible. It may be alleged that they were intended so to be. Probably; but that does not do away with the fact that the well-bred people in the books are not always free from vulgarity, which was the contention with which we started. They might have been made disagreeable in a hundred other ways, had Miss Austen so chosen, without violating all ordinary rules of conduct.

It is greatly to the author's credit, and speaks of her refinement of mind, that in an age when coarseness of every sort was rampant, her books should be free from a whisper of it. We of this present generation hardly realise how vice was countenanced in the days of the Georges; well indeed was it for England that males of that line died out, so that the heir to the throne was a girl-child, for during her long reign the example which the court set, and which the inferiors were quick to copy, was altered altogether. George the Third himself, who occupied the throne during the whole of Jane Austen's life, was a happy exception among the Hanoverian sovereigns, but the excesses of his sons were notorious.

Even the Duke of Kent, the best of them, accepts a left-handed alliance as inevitable, to say nothing of worse. In writing familiarly to Mr. Creevey after the death of Princess Charlotte, he says—

"The Duke of Clarence, I have no doubt, will marry if he can—he demands the payment of all his debts, which are very great, and a handsome provision for his ten natural children—God only knows the sacrifice it will be to make, whenever I shall think it my duty to become a married man. It is now seven and twenty years that Madame St. Laurent and I have lived together; we are of the same age, have been in all climates and all difficulties together, and you may well imagine, Mr. Creevey, the pang it will be to part with her." (*The Creevey Correspondence.*)

The irregular unions of princes of the blood are unfortunately an accepted fact, but the epoch in which such things were done in broad daylight was one in which libertinism of all kinds was rampant. It was an age also of excessive drunkenness, the Prince Regent frequently appeared in public hardly able to stand. Creevey records that the prince "drank so much as to be made very seriously ill by it"; he says also, as if it were a thing to wonder at, "It is reckoned very disgraceful in Russia for the higher orders to be drunk."

The books of Smollett and Fielding had inculcated the general belief that indecency and interest in a novel were inseparable, and it is greatly to the credit of Miss Burney and Miss Austen that their writings were of an entirely different tone.

Sir Walter Besant writes: " I do not wish to represent the eighteenth century as much worse than our own in the matter of what is called morality, meaning one kind of morality. The 'great' were allowed to be above the ordinary restraints of morality. A certain noble lord travelled with a harem of eight, which was, however, considered scandalous." (*London in the Eighteenth Century.*)

No whisper of these things stains Jane Austen's pages. And her clear, unaffected view of middle-class life in small towns and villages was true and not idealised, for these people were then, as they still are, the salt of the world, neither apeing the fantastic vices of the upper, nor the abandoned coarseness of the lower classes. They were respectable and sometimes humdrum. They suffered from monotony, not dissipation. That anyone should have been able to extract so much pure fun from such slight materials is ever matter for wonder. She did it by her marvellously close observation and power of selection, qualities which are a gift. She was far more true to human nature than the superficial reader knows, perhaps than she herself knew, for it is a trait of genius to do by the light of nature what other people must set about laboriously and ever fall short of attaining. When we notice Mr. Bennet's caustic humour reappearing in more genial form in his second daughter, there is one of those little touches that binds the characters together—the touch of heredity.

Another instance is in the case of Lady Middleton, who obviously had not married either for love or for suitability, but only for convenience; she is a cold woman, incapable of passion in the usual sense, but her nature breaks out in an adoration of her children which is neither for their benefit nor for hers. We see this again and again in real life; it is the cold, unloving wives who idolise their children because they are theirs, a feeling which is not real love but a kind of extended selfishness, an instinct which, in the case of animals, finds expression in licking their young. The books abound in similar true touches, put in apparently without effort, and almost without thought. When one considers that out of the mass of novels of that age, then, as now, circulated and read by the aid of libraries, such books as Hannah More's *Cœlebs in Search of a Wife* and Mackenzie's *Man of Feeling* and *Man of the World* were read and praised almost universally as being far superior to the usual run of novels, one gains some idea of the poverty of matter and manner that must have disgraced the ruck. Both these "masterpieces," so acclaimed as they were issued, are the dullest, driest stuff, without a gleam of humour, any attempt at a story, or any vivacity of expression or character. The general style is, "Mr. and Mrs. So-and-So are to-day expected. Mr. So-and-So is a pious, virtuous man, I am afraid I cannot say so much for his wife," and thereupon follows a long verbose description of the two, who when they appear on the scene do and say nothing to indicate any characteristics, but are mere dummies, pegs on which to hang the discourse that precedes their entry. A favourite device for filling up the pages that must be filled, is the narration by some

MISS BURNEY
(MADAME D'ARBLAY)

secondary character of all that has ever befallen them since their birth. Even Miss Burney is not free from this; in *Cecilia* at least the characters break into narration as easily as some persons do into song. With this kind of stuff to set the standard, the miracle of Jane's books becomes more admirable than ever, for anyone who has ever attempted to write knows how exceedingly difficult it is to resist the influence of the conventional canons in vogue.

Jane Austen seems to have been also as far ahead of her time in the use of simple direct English as she was in construction and effect. She is at least a generation in advance of average contemporary letters and journals, in which the phrasing is often ponderous; the sonorous roll of heavily-weighted sentences in the Johnsonian style, then so much admired, does not ever seem to have occurred to her.

Yet even in her lively, crisp narration there are a few phrases that strike on a modern ear as unaccustomed. Such is the use of the active for the passive tense, "tea was carrying round"; the elision of the final "n" in the infinitive, "but she said he seemed very angry at being spoke to"; the use of adjectives for adverbs (often reproved as a form of slang in the present day), "she must feel she has been acting wrong." The general use of men's surnames by women occurs in the earlier books, but we see an indication of change in this respect in the passage of Jane's lifetime, for in *Emma* it is considered vulgar of Mrs. Elton to address Mr. Knightley without the prefix. There are little ways of expressing things that are not now in vogue, men are "gentlemanlike," ladies "amiable," also "genteel and elegant"; one phrase which has now descended to the realm of the lady's-maid was then quite good English, "so peculiarly the lady in it." "Excessively" takes the place of our "awfully," we hear continually such expressions as "monstrous obliging," "prodigious pretty," and "vastly civil."

We have not hitherto noticed Miss Edgeworth's, Miss Ferrier's, or Miss Mitford's work, though they are generally considered as belonging to the clever group of women writers who illumined the end of the eighteenth and beginning of the nineteenth centuries, because in this chapter we are dealing only with Jane Austen's own novels, not with contemporary writers except as they affected her, and at the time when she wrote her first books none of these writers had published anything, and could not therefore possibly have influenced her. Miss Edgeworth's first novel, *Castle Rackrent*, came out in 1800, and Miss Ferrier's *Marriage* in 1818, after Jane was in her grave.

Jane Austen's own novels were written at such widely differing times, and the interval between writing and publication was so great in some cases, that the subject suffers from some confusion in the minds of those who have not looked into the question closely. As the order of writing is everything, and the order of publication a mere accident, we will take them as they were written. This was in two groups of three each. *Pride and Prejudice* was begun in October 1796 and finished the following August; *Sense and Sensibility* was begun in 1797 and finished in 1798, in which year *Northanger Abbey* was also written. Then there was a long gap, in which she produced only a fragment to be noted hereafter, and not until 1812 was *Mansfield Park* written; four years later, in 1816, came *Emma*, quickly followed by *Persuasion*. Of all these the first to be published was *Sense and Sensibility* in 1811, and the dates of publication will thereafter be noted in chronological order in the book as it progresses.

Besides these two distinct groups of three novels each, there is another of the unfinished fragments, which never became real stories. These consist of *Lady Susan*, a comedy in the form of letters, which is ended up hastily with a few paragraphs of explanation; and *The Watsons*, an unfinished tale, of which the end was told by Cassandra Austen from remarks that her sister had made. Both of these are included, as has been said, in Mr. Austen-Leigh's *Memoir*, and it seems a pity that they should not form a volume in one of the neat series of Jane Austen's novels now published, as to a real Austenite they contain much that is valuable, and are full of characteristic touches. Of the complete novels *Pride and Prejudice* is admittedly the best; there are several candidates for the second place, but the superiority of *Pride and Prejudice* is unquestioned. It was the earliest of the books written, under the title *First Impressions*, and as such it is referred to in Jane's correspondence: " I do not wonder at your wanting to read *First Impressions* again, so seldom as you have gone through it, and that so long ago;" this was to her sister in 1799, and later on she adds, with the playfulness never long wanting, " I would not let Martha read *First Impressions* again upon any account, and am very glad I did not leave it in your power. She is very cunning, but I saw through her design, she means to publish it from memory, and one more perusal must enable her to do it."

There has been great diversity of opinion as to the relative merit of the remaining books, but the concensus of opinion seems to declare for *Emma*, the last but one in point of time, which shows that the author's genius had not abated. This book is totally different from the first, it lacks the sparkle and *verve* which runs all through *Pride and Prejudice*, but it has perhaps more depth and is something softer and more finished also.

These two books, and all the others, will be dealt with in detail as they occur chronologically, for we are here only attempting to treat them generally, and to bring out those characteristics and excellencies common to all which made them such masterpieces, and gave their maker such a unique place in the hierarchy of authors.

Jane Austen is one of the three greatest among English women novelists; the other two being, of course, George Eliot and Charlotte Brontë, whose lives overlapped at a much later date. The genius of these three women is so entirely different in kind that the relative value of their gifts can never be put into like terms; so long as men and women read and discuss fiction, so long will each of the three styles have its partisans who will argue it to be the supreme one of the trio. Yet in spite of this, in spite also of a momentary fashion to decry the wonderful gifts of George Eliot, it is quite certain that in depth and breadth of feeling, and ability in its portrayal, she was unequalled by either her predecessor or contemporary. Her range far surpasses theirs. They each dealt with one phase of life or feeling: Jane Austen with English village life, Charlotte Brontë with the element of passion in man and woman, while George Eliot's works embrace many varieties of human nature and action. If her detractors are questioned, it will commonly be found that they do not deny her ability or her brain power, but her genius, which is of course a totally distinct thing. On further probing of the matter, it is usually discovered that the contention is based on the later works, such as *Middlemarch* or *Daniel Deronda*. To be quite fair, there are some appearances in these volumes to justify such an estimate, but the mistake is that the opinion is superficial and based on appearance only. In her later days George Eliot's tremendous ability, tremendous soul,—and tremendous is the only English word that can be fitly applied to it,—made her see so far round and over her own work, as well as allowing her such a wide survey as to the causes and nature of things, that even the productions of her genius were analysed, curbed, and held in channels. She could not let herself go; her subtle insight, her complete knowledge of her characters, made her qualify and account for their actions, perhaps more for her own satisfaction than for that of readers. She might safely have left this to her innate perception without fear, her genius would never have let her go wrong, but she could not, she must analyse even her own creations. No one in the world was more free from this tendency than Jane Austen, she was perfectly unconscious of her own mastery of her subject, as unconscious as the bee when it rejects all other shapes in its cells for the hexagonal. The marvellous precision with which she selected and rejected and grouped her puppets was almost a matter of instinct. She put in the little touches which revealed what was in the mind of her men and women without premeditation or any striving. It is the perfection of this gift which allows her books to be read again and again, for once the story is known, all the slight indications of its ultimate ending, which may have been overlooked while the reader is not in the secret, stand out vividly. We grant to George Eliot's detractors that in her later works her eyes were opened, and she analysed the work of her genius instead of writing spontaneously, but to her true admirers the genius is still there, though curbed and trammelled.

Every one of her men and women to the last are breathing human beings. Having granted, however, so much, we turn to the earlier works, which, amazing to say, are so often overlooked; here her gallery is full of realities, not analysed or thwarted, but moving as impelled by nature. Was there ever a boy-brother and girl-sister in all fiction to equal Tom and Maggie Tulliver? And what of that inimitable trio, Sisters Glegg and Tulliver and Pullet? Of its kind is there a scene that can beat Bob Jakin's twisting Mrs. Glegg round his finger with judicious management? And these are from the abundance of one book only. No, Jane cannot dispute precedence with George Eliot, but must yield the palm; her characters, true and admirable as they are, lack that living depth which George Eliot had the power to impart. But the two are so totally different that it is difficult to find any simile that will bring them into relation with one another. Perhaps the most expressive is that of instrumental music: Jane Austen's clear notes are like those which a skilful performer extracts from a good harp, sweet and ringing, always pleasant to listen to, and restful, but not soul stirring; while George Eliot's tones are like the deep notes of a violoncello, stirring up the heart to its core, and leaving behind them feeling even after the sound has ceased. The novels of Jane Austen were novels of character and manners, those of George Eliot of feeling. There is no intention in this comparison to minimise in any way the work of the earlier writer, she chose her style, and of its kind it is perfect; her subtle touches could only have been the result of the intuition which is genius, but the profounder emotions, the slow development of character by friction with those around, she did not attempt to depict.

We now turn to the third of the great trio. Charlotte Brontë's gift was a rush of strenuous passion that made her stories pour forth living and molten as from the furnace. Her best characters are admirable, but limited in number; we find the same timid heroine, who outwardly was herself, and inwardly was full of force and passion, appearing in more than one.

Charlotte's bitter indictment of Jane's work, though wholly untrue, can be made allowance for, seeing that her eyes viewed such a different section of the world of feeling. She says of *Pride and Prejudice:* "An accurate daguerreotyped portrait of a commonplace face; a carefully fenced, highly cultured garden, with neat borders and delicate flowers, but no glance of a bright vivid physiognomy, no open country, no fresh air, no blue hill, no bonny beck." And at another time, with much truth: "The passions are perfectly unknown to her; she rejects even a speaking acquaintance with that stormy sisterhood. What sees keenly, speaks aptly, moves flexibly, it suits her to study; but what throbs fast and full, though hidden, what the blood rushes through, what is the unseen seat of life, and the sentient target of death, this Miss Austen ignores."

Charlotte Brontë's own strongest point is her *story*, and as the teller of an interesting story, absorbing in its wild and strenuous action, she ranks very high, but character-drawing is not her forte. She herself fails in the point of which she accuses Jane, she could photograph those persons she knew intimately,—herself for instance, or her father's curates,—but directly she went beyond, she failed; what could be weaker than the society people in *Jane Eyre,*—the ringletted Blanche and the wooden young men?

A great many of her minor characters are mere dummies who do not remain in the mind at all. But one of her strong points is one entirely ignored by Jane, and that is the impression of scenery and the aspects of weather. Which of us has not felt a chill of desolation as he stood in fancy on the wet gravel-path leading up to Lowood? or not been sensible of the exhilaration of that sharp, clear, frosty night when Jane first encountered Mr. Rochester in the lane? In a few words, very few, Charlotte Brontë has a marvellous capability for making one feel the surroundings of her characters, and this is no mean gift. Adherents she will always have, and to them it may be granted that her whole theme was one totally ignored by Jane, whose men and women are swept by no mighty whirlwinds of their own generating. In fact it has been alleged against Jane that she had neither passion nor pathos, and perhaps, if we except one or two touches of the latter quality in dealing with forlorn little Fanny in *Mansfield Park*, this is true. The only simile that occurs as suitable to use in the comparison between Charlotte and Jane is that the soul of the one was like the turbulent rush of her own brown Yorkshire streams over the wild moorlands—streams which pour in cataracts and shatter themselves on great grey stones in a tumultuous frenzy, while that of the other resembled the calm limpid waters of her own Hampshire river, the Itchen, wending its way placidly between luscious green meadows.

> "A deeper sky, where stooping you may see
> The little minnows darting restlessly."

The preference between these two is all a matter of taste, and will be decided by the fact whether the admiration of clear incisive humour and comedy of manners outweighs that of fiery feeling and a rush of emotion.

CHAPTER VI

LETTERS AND POST

THE main source of information about Jane Austen is contained in her letters. The bulk of those that have been preserved are to be found in the two volumes edited by Lord Brabourne, her great-nephew. And these are only the remnant of what we might have had but for Cassandra's action. It could not matter to Jane or Cassandra now if those gay outpourings had been published in full, and we should have had a much more complete and true picture of one whom England holds among her three greatest women novelists. As it is, anything based on these letters must necessarily be subject to modification, the inferences drawn are imperfect, and there are long gaps in continuity, while many events of great moment to the writer herself are not so much as referred to in them. We owe it, however, to the fact that visits then really were visits, extending over weeks or months, to compensate for the difficulty and expense of travelling, that what remain are many in number; and also we have cause to be thankful that on account of Mrs. Austen and the household, the two sisters made a point of not leaving home together, generally taking turns, so that the letters are very much more numerous than they might otherwise have been.

Besides those written to Cassandra, there are a few

given by Lord Brabourne, which were written to his own mother as a girl, and these are by no means the least interesting in the book. A certain number also are addressed to Jane's other niece, Anna. Besides those in Lord Brabourne's book, there are one or two additional ones in the *Memoir* by Mr. Austen-Leigh, Jane's own nephew.

The first of the published letters is dated the beginning of 1796, when Jane was twenty-one. As the letters contain many comments on dress, food, daily occurrences of all sorts, the best method seems to be to use them as a thread on which to hang notes of the everyday life of the period, collating what the writer herself says with what is otherwise known, and in this way to gain a background against which her own figure will stand out.

One great characteristic of her correspondence is its extreme liveliness and humour. This is the more remarkable because in her age and time letters were, with a few brilliant exceptions, ponderous and laboured, written in the grand style, as was perhaps natural when the sending of a letter was a serious consideration.

The following is a good specimen of the style considered proper for a boy of sixteen, writing to his mother—

"I am extremely sorry to be thus troublesome to you, but I hope the time may come when I shall be able to say that I have in some small degree deserved the many cares and anxieties I have cost you, at least no effort shall be lost to attain that end. There are two objects (virtue and ability) constantly before my eyes; if I attain them I know myself sure of your approbation, in the possession of which I shall be happy, and without which I should be miserable, so that if selfish gratification was the only cause, I should proceed in my grand object. A more powerful cause, however, employs its influence upon my mind, a desire of doing good, which cannot operate without ability, cannot have effect without virtue."

If a fond mother of the present day got such a letter from a schoolboy son she would probably take the first train to see if he were ill!

The same stiffness was the rule in intimate family relations. This boy, who was no peculiar specimen, but a natural boy of his times, writes about his little sister: " I am very glad to hear that Anna Maria is such a nice girl. I hope she is clever both at her books and at her needle . . . at the former I am sure she is, if she always writes such nice letters as the last she sent to me. Is it asking too much, to beg her to write another before she returns to Kendal?"

How different these sentences are from the lively ones of Jane Austen to her sister: " Everybody is extremely anxious for your return, but as you cannot come home by the Ashe ball, I am glad I have not fed them with false hopes. James danced with Alithea, and cut up the turkey last night with great perseverance. You say nothing of the silk stockings, I flatter myself therefore that Charles has not purchased any, as I cannot very well afford to pay for them. . . . We received a visit from Mr. Tom Lefroy and his cousin George. The latter is really very well behaved now, and as for the other he has but one fault, which time will, I trust, entirely remove, it is that his morning coat is a great deal too light."

And again, " I am very much flattered by your commendation of my last letter, for I write only for fame and without any view to pecuniary emolument."

It was an age of letter writing, periodicals were expensive, and, in remote districts, difficult to get; even when obtained, the news was what we should deem at the present time scanty in the extreme. *The Times*, for instance, consisted of only a single folded sheet, of which the front page was occupied with advertisements. The foreign news was always some days old, as it was obtained by special packet-boats, which brought across the French papers. These boats being dependent on the wind and currents, were subject to many delays. The newspaper taxes were heavy and burdensome, and though even the poorest sheet of news must be considered wonderful in view of the difficulty and expense attendant on the procuring of news in pre-telegraph days, the fact remains that much was left out which could only be supplied by private correspondence. Horace Walpole, of course, stands out as the prince of letter-writers of his time; his published letters now amount to over two thousand, and deal with all the current questions of the day. Of course these letters are on an altogether different plane from the little batch of about two hundred, which are all we have of Jane's. Walpole's letters are read, not only for their style and manner, but for the light they throw on society and politics. Jane's can be of interest to none but those who are interested in her. And at the time they were published there were many voices raised in protest against the publication of such very "small beer," but in so far as they throw light on her own daily life they are certainly worth having.

Considered merely as private productions, it is wonderful, considering the expense of letter carriage and the delay of correspondence, that she wrote so much as she did.

Letters in those days consisted only of a single sheet without an envelope, which was formed by the last page of the sheet itself being folded over and fastened by a wafer. This did not leave much room for writing.

Jane wrote very small, and her lines are neat and straight, so that she got the largest amount possible into the available space. At that time a single sheet of paper, not exceeding an ounce in weight, varied in price from 4d. to 1s. 6d., according to the distance it was carried; if it exceeded an ounce, it was charged fourfold; any additional bit of paper made it into a double letter, which was charged accordingly. But the thing which would seem to us most intolerable of all, was that the recipient and not the sender paid for the missive, whereby many modest souls must have been prevented from ever writing to their friends lest the letter should not be considered worth the charge. Not until long after Jane had been in her grave did adhesive stamps come into use.

It is a commonly received idea that the Post Office as an institution dates from the establishment of universal penny post in the British Isles by Rowland Hill in 1840. But this is far from being the case; there was a postmaster in 1533, if not before. In 1680 a parcels post at a penny a pound was established in London by William Dockwra, who also suggested passing letters in London at the same rate.

The profits of the post-office at that time were, by a most flagrant abuse, the monopoly of the Duke of York, who vehemently resented Dockwra's improvements. In spite of this, however, Dockwra won his way. The London letters for the penny post were daily "Transmitted to Lyme Street, at the Dwelling House of the said Mr. Dockwra, formerly the Mansion House of Sir Robert Abdy, Kt.

"There are Seven sorting Houses proper to the seven Precincts into which the undertakers have divided London, Westminster, and the Suburbs, situated at equal Distances, for the better maintenance of mutual Correspondence.

There are about 400 or 500 receiving Houses, to take in letters, where the Messengers call every hour, and convey them as directed; as also *post letters*, the writing of which are much increased by this accommodation, being carefully conveyed by them to the general Post Office in Lombard Street."

These "post letters" are those for the country, still the monopoly of the Duke, who had been persuaded to yield to Dockwra's scheme as likely to further his own revenue.

Also, " By these [clerks, messengers, etc.] are conveyed Letters and Parcels not exceeding one Pound Weight, nor Ten Pound in Value, to and from all Parts at Seasonable Times, viz.: of the Cities of London and Westminster, Southwark, Redriff, Wapping, Ratcliff, Limehouse, Stepney, Poplar, and Blackwall, and all other places within the weekly Bills of Mortality, as also the four towns of Hackney, Islington, South Newington Butts, and Lambeth, but to no other towns, and the letters to be left only at the receiving offices of those towns, or if brought to their Houses a penny more."

Dockwra not only carried, but insured letters and parcels up to £10 in value. He was liberal in his deliveries. " To the most remote Places Letters go four or five times of the day, to other Places six or eight times of the day. To Inns of Court and Places of Business in Town, especially in term or Parliament time, ten or twelve times of the day." Stamps were also used to mark the hour when the letters were sent out to be delivered, an item only recently reintroduced into our postal service. Much wailing was heard at Dockwra's reforms from the porters of London, who had made a fine living by carrying correspondence, their outcries were much the same as those of the watermen, who afterwards wailed at the introduction of hackney coaches.

Dockwra was not long allowed to enjoy his idea, for his scheme was incorporated into the General Post Office, though he afterwards received a pension of £500 a year, and was made Comptroller of the London Post Office.

For anything outside of London, distance still counted in the cost, though we read in *The Times* of 1793 that a penny post had been established in Manchester. It was Rowland Hill who introduced the universal penny post in Great Britain, thus extending the Dockwra idea. In 1710 the postal system was reformed and improved, three rates were put in force, namely: threepence if under eighty miles; fourpence if above; and sixpence to Edinburgh or Dublin. This explains the custom of carrying letters for some distance and then posting them; Jane Austen says, "I put Mary's letter into the post office with my own hand at Andover," this was on the way to Bath. In 1720 cross-posts were introduced by the suggestion of Ralph Allen, a Bath postmaster; before that time every letter had to go round by London to be cleared, even supposing it to be intended for a town not far off from the sender. Allen offered to organise the whole thing, paying a fixed rent, and taking the profits. His plan succeeded so well that he cleared £10,000 a year. At his death in 1764 the Government took over the contract.

Up to 1784, letters were carried on horseback by post-boys, who were underpaid and undisciplined; if a boy got drunk, or entered into conversation with strangers who turned out to be well-mannered footpads, the bags never reached their destination. In 1783, John Palmer, manager of the Bath and Bristol Theatre, suggested the employment of regular coaches, which might at the same time carry passengers, hence the inauguration of mail-coaches, the first two of which started between London and Bristol in August 1784. The drivers and guards were armed, and if this did not altogether ensure the safety of the mails—as the weapons were often a mere farce, and the men themselves either chicken-hearted or in collusion with the robbers—it proved, at all events, productive of greater regularity in the delivery of letters.

> "Hark! 'Tis the twanging horn! O'er yonder bridge
> That with its wearisome but needful length
> Bestrides the wintry flood, in which the moon
> Sees her unwrinkled face reflected bright;
> He comes, the herald of a noisy world,
> With spattered boots, strapped waist, and frozen locks,
> News from all nations lumbering at his back.
> True to his charge the close packed load behind,
> Yet careless what he brings, his own concern
> Is to conduct it to the destined inn,
> And having dropped the expected bag—pass on." (COWPER.)

Hannah More remarks on the innovation: "Mail coaches, which come to others, come not to me; letters and newspapers now that they travel in coaches, like gentlemen and ladies, come not within ten miles of my hermitage."

The system of franking is one of those things that make us realise the difference between the ideas of our own time and those of the eighteenth century more than anything else; that such an abuse can have been permitted is incredible, monstrous. Of course as it was in force everybody availed themselves of it without scruple, few indeed are the persons whose private consciences are in advance of public rules; Jane writes frequently on the subject—

"As Eliza has been so good as to get me a frank, your questions shall be answered without much further expense to you.... On Thursday Mr. Lushington, M.P. for Canterbury, and manager of the lodge hounds, dines here and stays the night. If I can, I will get a frank from him, and write to you all the sooner."

"Now, I will prepare for Mr. Lushington, and as it will be wisest also to prepare for his not coming, or my not getting a frank, I shall write very close from the first, and even leave room for the seal in the proper place."

"Letters were sent when franks could be procured,
And when they could not, silence was endured." (CRABBE.)

Horace Walpole says, "I have kept this letter some days in my writing box till I could meet with a stray member of parliament, for it is not worth making you pay for."

"The franking of letters as an institution commenced as early as the year 1660, when it was resolved that members' letters should come and go free, during the sitting of the House. When the Bill was sent up to the Lords, it was thrown out because the privilege was not extended to them. When, however, the omission was supplied, the Bill passed. The privilege in course of time was grossly abused. Members signed large packets of envelopes at once, and either sold them, or gave them to their friends. It was worth the while of a house of business, when letters cost sixpence apiece, to buy a thousand franks at fourpence apiece; sometimes servants got them from their masters and sold them. In the year 1715, franked letters representing £24,000 a year passed through the post. In 1763 the amount was actually £170,000. Supposing that each letter would have brought in sixpence to the post office, this means nearly 7,000,000 letters, so that every member of the two Houses would have signed an average of 7000 letters a year. It was then enacted that no letter should pass free unless the address, as well as the signature, was in the member's handwriting. Lastly, it was ordered that all franks should be sealed and that they should be put into the post on the day of the date. Even with these precautions the amount of franks represented £84,000 a year. The privilege was finally abolished with the great reforms of 1841. It is needless to add that a system of wholesale forgery had sprung up long before." "Members of Parliament sold their privileges of franking sometimes for £300 a year." (Sir Walter Besant, *London in the Eighteenth Century*.)

In Joseph Brasbridge's *Fruits of Experience*, it is mentioned that a large firm of drapers used to buy their franks from the poor relations of M.P.'s at forty-eight shilling the gross.

The abuse of franking was called in question at various dates, and reforms advised. In reply to questions asked in Parliament, it was stated that various clerks in Government offices used to frank to any amount—not only their own correspondence but that of others; probably receiving large sums of money for doing so. In fact it was known that some persons whose salaries were £300 or £400 a year had been making incomes of £1000 and £1200 by this means! The celebrated bookseller Lackington had friends in one of the offices, and sent his catalogues free all over the country. A majority of twelve decided for the Question in the House.

The reforms practically meant the abolition of franks so far as private persons were concerned, as Hannah More put it, Pitt had murdered scribbling; while speaking of a friend she writes: " She will generously tell me she has postage in her pocket, but we have been used to franks, and besides the post is bewitched and charges nobody knows what for letters; two shillings and ninepence, I think Mrs. L. says she paid for a letter." And again, " The abolition of franks is quite a serious affliction to me, not that I shall ever regret paying the postage for my friends' letters, but for fear it should restrain them from writing. It is a tax upon the free currency of affection and sentiment, and goes nearer my heart than the cruel decision against literary property did, for that was only taxing the manufacture, but this the raw material."

These remarks were caused by the reforms of 1784.

But, as we have said, the whole system of franking was not abolished until 1841.

Of course there were no postmen to deliver letters as they do now. It was considered a great convenience to have a post-office at all, from which letters could be fetched. In 1787, Horace Walpole says there was no posthouse at Twickenham. The fetching of letters is one of the minor peeps we get into the times through the novels. In *Emma*, when Mr. Knightley meets Miss Fairfax he says—

"'I hope you did not venture far, Miss Fairfax, this morning, or I am sure you must have been wet. We scarcely got home in time. I hope you turned directly!'

"'I went only to the post-office,' said she, 'and reached home before the rain was much. It is my daily errand, I always fetch the letters when I am here. It saves trouble, and is a something to get me out. A walk before breakfast does me good.' . . .

"'The post-office has a great charm at one period of our lives. When you have lived to my age you will begin to think letters are never worth going through rain for.' . . .

"'You are speaking of letters of business; mine are letters of friendship.'

"'I have often thought them the worse of the two,' he replied coolly.

"'Ah! You are not serious now. . . . You have everybody dearest to you always near at hand. I probably never shall again; and therefore until I have outlived all my affections, a post-office, I think, must always have power to draw me out, in worse weather than to-day.'"

When we realise that every one of the letters preserved for us in Lord Brabourne's book must have cost on an average a shilling, we feel more strongly than before the tie between Jane and Cassandra, which demanded such constant communication, and the retailing of every minute affair.

We have nothing to tell us how letters came to Steventon, but can form some sort of conjecture for ourselves. There was of course no post-office in such a minute place; the letters would arrive at Winchester, and from thence be forwarded by the Basingstoke coach, and dropped at the inn which stands at Popham Lane End, about two miles away. It would be almost certainly impossible for Jane to walk, except in the driest weather, through lanes of which we are told they were impassable for carriages at certain seasons, and could only be traversed on horseback. The man-servant would therefore probably be detailed to go for the post-bag, possibly riding on one of the carriage horses; and Jane would wait in the damp mist of an autumn afternoon by the front door, dressed in a costume most unsuitable for the climate, according to our ideas, with thin heel-less slippers kept up by crossed elastic, and long clinging skirts, with bare arms and only a dainty chemisette not reaching to her neck. She would greet the man eagerly to see if there was a letter for her in the handwriting of her beloved sister,—a welcome break on the monotony of a grey day, when perhaps Mrs. Austen was in bed with one of her chronic complaints.

CHAPTER VII

SOCIETY AND LOVE-MAKING

THE first of the published letters was written in January 1796, a time of year when such a scene as that sketched at the end of the last chapter must often have taken place. The season was far from being a gloomy one, however, balls and entertainments were going on all round, and the Austens had guests of their own also. These were their cousins the Coopers, in regard to whom Lord Brabourne, who being himself a great-nephew ought to have known, makes a most curious blunder. In his notes previous to the letters he says, " The Coopers, whose arrival is expected in the first, and announced in the second letter, were Dr. Cooper, already mentioned as having married Jane Austen's aunt, Jane Leigh, with his wife and their two children, Edward and Jane, of whom we shall frequently hear." This was in 1796, but Dr. Cooper had died in 1792; he had held the livings of Sonning, in Berkshire, and Whaddon, near Bath, contemporaneously until his death. The Mr. Cooper whom the Austens were expecting, was Dr. Cooper's son Edward, of whom Lord Brabourne speaks as a child, with his wife and *their* two small children, Edward and Isabella, then both under two years old. The Coopers are mentioned a great deal in the entertaining Diary of Mrs. Philip Lybbe Powys, from which we have already quoted, for Edward

Cooper married her daughter Caroline. He, like his father, was in Orders, and was at first a curate at Harpsden under his non-residential grandfather, the Rev. Thomas Leigh, and was afterwards presented to the living of Hamstall Ridware, Staffordshire, by Mrs. Leigh, a relative of his mother's by whom he was connected with the Austens, Mrs. Austen having been a Miss Leigh. On January 21, 1799, Jane writes: "Yesterday came a letter to my mother from Edward Cooper to announce, not the birth of a child, but of a living; for Mrs. Leigh has begged his acceptance of the rectory of Hamstall Ridware in Staffordshire, vacant by Mr. Johnson's death. We collect from his letter that he means to reside there. The living is valued at one hundred and forty pounds a year, but it may be improvable."

The little boy mentioned above as coming with his parents to stay at Steventon, had been christened at Harpsden Church on December 3, 1794, and Henry Austen was one of the sponsors. At the christening of another little Cooper, named Cassandra, in 1797, Mrs. Austen stood sponsor. Jane remarks of the two elder children who came to Steventon, "the little boy is very like Dr. Cooper, and the little girl is to resemble Jane, they say." This probably gave rise to Lord Brabourne's mistake, but in reality Jane Austen was commenting on the child's likeness to its dead grandfather, not to its father, and the Jane the girl was to resemble, was Edward Cooper's sister Jane, who became Lady Williams, and was killed in a carriage accident in 1798.

Even Mr. Austen-Leigh, Jane Austen's own nephew, does not seem to have realised Dr. Cooper's plurality of livings, for he says, " The family lived in close intimacy with two cousins, Edward and Jane Cooper, the children of Mrs. Austen's eldest sister, and Dr. Cooper, the vicar of Sonning, near Reading. The Coopers lived for some years at Bath, which seems to have been much frequented in those days by clergymen retiring from work. I believe that Cassandra and Jane sometimes visited them there, and that Jane thus acquired the intimate knowledge of the topography and customs of Bath which enabled her to write *Northanger Abbey* long before she resided there herself."

The inference is not quite true, for if this had been so she must have acquired that knowledge before her seventeenth year, for she was that age when her uncle Dr. Cooper died, and it is probable that her aunt had predeceased him as she is never mentioned at all by Mrs. Lybbe Powys, who relates a tour she made with him, his son and daughter, to the Isle of Wight. But there is no need for any inference of the sort at all, for Jane had another uncle and aunt, Mr. and Mrs. Leigh-Perrot—her mother's brother having adopted the additional name of Perrot—who sometimes resided at Bath, and it is obviously to an invitation from this aunt she refers in a letter of 1799.

As we have said, it was the season of balls at Steventon; quiet as the rectory was there were many large houses of the country gentry around in various directions, and entertainments of all sorts were then perhaps even more in fashion than now; to all of these the rectory party received invitations. In the second paragraph of the first letter, Jane says, "We had an exceeding good ball last night," and later, "I am almost ashamed to tell you how my Irish friend and I behaved. Imagine to yourself everything most profligate and shocking in the way of dancing and sitting down together ... we had a very good supper, and the greenhouse was illuminated in a very elegant manner."

In another letter, written later, she gives the following account of a ball: "We were very well entertained, and could have stayed longer, but for the arrival of my list shoes to convey me home, and I did not like to keep them waiting in the cold. The room was tolerable full, and the ball opened by Miss Glyn. The Miss Lances had partners, Captain Dauvergne's friend appeared in regimentals, Caroline Maitland had an officer to flirt with, and Mr. John Harrison was deputed by Captain Smith, himself being absent, to ask me to dance. Everything went well, you see, especially after we had tucked Mrs. Lance's neckerchief in behind, and fastened it with a pin."

Mr. Austen-Leigh says: "There must have been more dancing throughout the country in those days than there is now, and it seems to have sprung up more spontaneously, as if it were a natural production, with less fastidiousness as to the quality of music, lights, and floor. Many country towns had a monthly ball throughout the winter, in some of which the same apartment served for dancing and tea-room."

People in the country were then more dependent on each other for entertainment, there was no looking upon the London season as a necessity, and people could not rush about from one end of England to another for a night or two as they now do. During the long winter months, when the bitter cold and the cumbersome methods of travelling made any journey out of the question for most, to say nothing of the expense, balls for those in the neighbourhood of Steventon were frequently given, and Jane and Cassandra Austen had their full share, and seem to have most heartily enjoyed it. Jane herself evidently loved dancing, balls are frequently mentioned in her novels, and the actual dancing itself, even without its enjoyable concomitant of flirtation, seems to have attracted her.

Customs, however, then differed very much from

those that now reign in ballrooms. In one way everything was more formal, in another more simple. The music, the wines, and the floor were less considered; young people got up an impromptu dance in a drawing-room very easily; and the champagne, without which no one would dare to ask their friends to a dance now, was then not considered necessary. On the other hand, the actual performance was more formal; there were no romps at lancers, no round dances such as waltzes at all; waltzes did not begin to be danced generally until 1814, and the polka not until 1844. In the beginning of 1814, when the waltz was just coming into fashion, Miss Mitford declaims against it, and calls it this "detestable dance." "In addition to the obvious reasons which all women ought to have for disliking it, I cannot perceive its much vaunted graces. What beauty can there be in a series of dizzying evolutions, of which the wearisome monotony banishes all the tricksy fancies of the poetry of motion, and conveys to the eyes of the spectators the idea of a parcel of teetotums set a-spinning for their amusement?" In Jane's time, minuets, cotillions, etc., were the staple of the programme, and toward the end of the evening country dances, no doubt danced with much precision and elegance. Deportment was then a necessary part of the curriculum at every girls' boarding-school; and the ways of getting in and out of a carriage, and much more of bowing and entering a reception room, were all taught as if the performer were to go upon the stage; every motion was regulated. It is true that the custom, so aptly illustrated in *Evelina*, when the lady was forced by politeness to accept the first man who asked her, and to remain his partner for the evening, a custom that must have been responsible for many sore hearts and spoiled evenings, had gone out in Jane's time. But it was the fashion, at what were called private dances, for any man to ask any girl he fancied to become his partner without previous introduction; at public balls the Master of the Ceremonies did the introducing. In Evelina's time, girls must have had many an exciting evening, many an anguished moment when the wrong man asked the honour of their hand while the right man had not come forward! Evelina made a terrible mess of things at her first dance. She refused the ridiculous little fop who first approached her, and afterwards accepted the handsome and engaging Lord Orville, who, it must be confessed, is a far superior man to Miss Austen's corresponding hero, Darcy. Evelina narrates her acceptance of him in a letter to her guardian—

"Well, I bowed, and I am sure I coloured; for indeed I was frightened at the thoughts of dancing before so many people, all strangers, and, which was worse, with a stranger; however, that was unavoidable; for, though I looked round the room several times, I could not see one person that I knew. And so he took my hand and led me to join in the dance."

Of course the fop was not one to take this considered insult quietly, he approached when Evelina and Lord Orville were sitting out between the dances, and asked, "'May I know to what accident I must attribute not having the honour of your hand?'

"'Accident, sir,' repeated I much astonished.

"'Yes, accident, madam,—for surely—I must take the liberty to observe—pardon me, madam,—it ought to be no common one—that should tempt a lady—so young a one too,—to be guilty of ill-manners.'

"A confused idea now for the first time entered my head, of something I had heard of the rules of an assembly, but I was never at one before—I have only danced at school—and so giddy and heedless I was, that I had not once considered the impropriety of refusing one partner, and afterwards accepting another. I was thunderstruck at the recollection . . .

"I afterwards told Mrs. Mirvan of my disasters, and she good-naturedly blamed herself for not having better instructed me, but she said she had taken it for granted that I must know such common customs."

There is no trace of such a custom in Jane's times, her partners were always numerous. At the dances at Basingstoke or in the neighbourhood, she probably knew almost everyone in the room on familiar terms; and she frequently had a brother with her to counterbalance the brothers of her girl friends. She danced well, with vivacity and grace; we can imagine her appearance without difficulty; her hair encircled by some neat bandeau or coquettish bow, her high-waisted simple frock of soft white muslin, her curls escaping in little ringlets on forehead and shoulders, her hazel eyes dancing as she parried the conversational thrusts of some too bold admirer, even as her own Elizabeth Bennet might have done. She certainly must have been popular; a girl who can talk wittily, dance well, and who is bright and sweet-tempered must always be in demand. And all the time her mind, half unconsciously, was storing up the little words and gestures of the persons around. Everything that was significant, everything that was amusing was noted, and from this storehouse she was to draw many a scene to delight unnumbered people yet unborn.

In her time, the acceptance of a dance still carried with it two dances, or the twice going up and down in the minuet.

Foolish Mrs. Bennet, overflowing with the events of the evening, on her return from the ball with her daughters, thus pours out her soul to her satirical husband—

"'Jane was so admired, nothing could be like it. Everybody said how well she looked; and Mr. Bingley thought her quite beautiful, and danced with her twice. Only think of that, my dear, he actually danced with her twice; and she was the only creature in the room that he asked a second time. First of all he asked Miss Lucas. I was so vexed to see him stand up with her, however, he did not admire her at all; indeed, nobody can, you know; and he seemed quite struck with Jane as she was going down the dance. So he inquired who she was, and got introduced, and asked her for the two next. Then the two third he danced with Miss King, and the two fourth with Maria Lucas, and the two fifth with Jane again, and the two sixth with Lizzy, and *the Boulanger*—'"

At another ball poor Elizabeth has Mr. Collins for a partner—

"The first two dances, however, brought a return of distress; they were dances of mortification. Mr. Collins, awkward and solemn, apologising instead of attending, and often moving wrong without being aware of it, gave her all the shame and misery which a disagreeable partner for a couple of dances can give."

In *Northanger Abbey* the hero and heroine first meet in the Lower Rooms at Bath at a ball, where they are introduced by the Master of the Ceremonies, but the subject of Bath is such an engrossing one that it must be treated separately in another chapter. In public ballrooms gentlemen wore swords, and ladies carried enormous fans; it must have required some practice to manage these respective weapons in a crowded room. Mr. Austen-Leigh says in a note, "Old gentlemen who had survived the fashion of wearing swords, were known to regret the disuse of that custom, because it put an end to one way of distinguishing those who had, from those who had not, been used to good society. To wear the sword easily, was an art which, like swimming or skating, required to be learned in youth."

As to the costumes worn, we get an idea of Catherine Morland's dress in her partner's jocose remark describing the "sprigged muslin robe with blue trimmings—plain black shoes." A few of the fashions we learn from contemporary newspapers, which thus filled their columns when foreign news was scarce.

The Times remarks facetiously,—for *The Times* had not learnt to take its high office seriously in those days,—"We are very happy to see the waists of our fair countrywomen walking downwards by degrees towards the hip. But as we are a little acquainted with the laws of increasing velocity in fashionable gravitation, we venture to express, thus early in their descent, a hope that they will stop there." (April 15, 1799.)

About this time fashion required ladies to wear an enormous pyramid of feathers on their heads, and many were the jests made about this extraordinary whim of fashion—

"At all elegant assemblies there is a room set apart for the lady visitants to put their feathers on, as it is impossible to wear them in any carriage with a top to it. The lustres are also removed on this account, and the doors are carried up to the ceiling. A well-dressed lady, who nods with dexterity, can give a friend a little tap upon the shoulder across the room without incommoding the dancers. The ladies' feathers are now generally carried in the sword case at the back of the carriage. (*The Times*, December 29, 1795.)

With the soft light of wax candles—even nowadays sometimes preferred to modern brilliancy—shining on the long, clinging muslin dresses, the arch head-dresses and nodding plumes, the swords and the fans, a ball-room must have presented a most animated spectacle; added to which the dress of the gentlemen was certainly far more picturesque and becoming than that of the present day. The gay satin coats and ruffles, the knee-breeches and silk stockings, must greatly have enlivened the scene. The subject of dress is too large to be treated in the middle of such a chapter, but to gain any idea of the balls which gave Jane Austen so much entertainment, these things must be at least indicated.

Apropos of the minuet, Mr. Austen-Leigh says: "It was not everyone who felt qualified to make this public exhibition, and I have been told that those ladies who intended to dance minuets, used to distinguish themselves from others by wearing a particular kind of lappet on their headdress. I have heard also of another curious proof of the respect in which this dance was held. Gloves immaculately clean were considered requisite for its due performance, while gloves a little soiled were thought good enough for a country dance; and accordingly some prudent ladies provided themselves with two pairs for their several purposes."

The lady of the greatest distinction in the room was chosen to open the ball. Modest Fanny in *Mansfield Park* was quite overwhelmed when she discovered that she was expected to do this, in the absence of her cousins, by taking the first part in the minuet, an idea that had never occurred to her before. "She found herself the next moment conducted to the top of the room, and standing there to be joined by the rest of the dancers, couple after couple as they were formed. . . . The ball began. It was rather honour than happiness to Fanny for the first dance at least; her partner was in excellent spirits, and tried to impart them to her; but she was a great deal too much frightened to have any enjoyment till she could suppose herself no longer looked at."

At balls there was generally a room set aside for the older people who preferred to play cards. Mrs. Lybbe Powys, in 1777, gives an account of a fashionable evening party—

"No minuets that night; it would have been difficult without a master of ceremonies among so many people of rank. Two card-rooms, the drawing-rooms and eating-room. The latter looked so elegant lighted up; two tables at loo, one quinze, one vingt-et-une, many whist. At one of the former large sums passed and repassed. I saw one lady of quality borrow ten pieces of Tessier within half an hour after she sat down to vingt-une, and a countess at loo, who owed to every soul round the table before half the night was over. The orgeat, lemonade, capillaire, and red and white negus with cakes, were carried round the whole evening. At half an hour after twelve the supper was announced, and the hall doors thrown open, on entering which nothing could be more striking, as you know 'tis so fine a one, and was then illuminated by three hundred coloured lamps round the six doors, over the chimney, and over the statue at the other end. . . . The tables had a most pleasing effect ornamented with everything in the confectionery way, and festoons and wreaths of artificial flowers prettily disposed; all fruits of the season as grapes, pines, etc., fine wines—ninety-two sat down to supper. . . . The once so beautiful Lady Almeria I think is vastly altered. She and Lady Harriot Herbert had the new trimmings, very like bell ropes with their tassels, and seemingly very inconvenient in dancing. After supper they returned to dancing, chiefly then cotillions, till near six."

Cotillions were later replaced by quadrilles. In 1816, Jane writes to her niece Fanny—

"Much obliged for the quadrilles which I am grown

to think pretty enough, though of course they are very inferior to the cotillions of my own day."

But balls were not the only recreations Jane and Cassandra had; people were very sociable in those days; the sketch of Sir John Middleton's horror of being alone, and his delight at gathering together in his house all the acquaintances whom he could persuade to come, is only slightly exaggerated from the prevailing spirit of his times. People were always running over to see each other, always spending long days at each other's houses; hospitality was taken for granted, and was too common to be reckoned a virtue. Jane and Cassandra in this way were continually in touch with their nearest neighbours at Deane and Ashe.

It is impossible to resist quoting the following malevolent description of Jane Austen, so unlike anything we know of her; it was given to Miss Mitford by a lady who, it is admitted, had every reason to dislike the Austens, for her brother-in-law was engaged in a lawsuit with Edward Austen (Knight), trying to get away from him one of his estates! This lady says that Jane had "stiffened into the most perpendicular, precise, taciturn piece of single blessedness that ever existed, and that, till *Pride and Prejudice* showed what a precious gem was hidden in that unbending case, she was no more regarded in society than a poker or a fire screen or any other thin upright piece of wood or iron that fills its corner in peace and quietness. The case is very different now, she is a poker, but a poker of whom everyone is afraid."

And Mrs. Mitford professes to recollect Jane in girlhood as being "the prettiest, silliest, most affected, husband hunting butterfly" she ever remembers.

The whole tone of Jane's own writings and letters redeems her memory from any possible reproach of affectation, and the evidence all points to the fact that, though not averse from a flirtation, she was the very last of all girls to desire a husband! But it is of interest to record contemporary impressions, so as to show both sides of the shield.

The first of the letters in Lord Brabourne's book contains suggestions of a subject much more interesting than mere dancing or visiting. In the case of an author like Jane Austen, who has become the world's property, it is impossible that there should be any concealment of those affairs of the heart usually reserved for private confidence only. To fail in discussing such a point would be to leave aside a whole aspect of her life and books. Jane must have been admired, her vivacity, her wit, her gaiety of heart, her pleasant person, and her keen enjoyment of life must have attracted attention; we know definitely she had at least two eligible offers, and probably others, as she was the very last person to boast of such things openly. It has sometimes happened that those most worth having have lived and died single, for they are too fastidious, too difficult to please, to mate readily, while a commonplace girl is made happy by the addresses of any ordinary man, and gladly persuades herself to be in love. Jane, who had a peculiar and deep knowledge of character, could not be easily blinded, she would have required much in a man, and men no doubt instinctively knew it. Her tongue, we know, was sharp, she had a knack of saying sharp things, and those who did not know her well may have been uneasy under her penetrating insight. Those who did know her may have gathered from her perfectly spontaneous manner and absence of any affectation that she was entirely heart whole, and been thus discouraged from trying their fate. The extract naming her Irish friend has already been quoted, this referred to the late Lord Chief Justice of

Ireland, at that time only Tom Lefroy, whose uncle was Rector of Ashe, adjoining Deane, and with whom Jane seems to have carried on a lively flirtation.

After telling Cassandra how much she had danced with him, she adds, " I can expose myself, however, only once more, because he leaves the country soon after next Friday, on which day we are to have a dance at Ashe after all. He is a very gentlemanlike, good looking, pleasant young man, I assure you. But as to our having ever met, except at the three last balls, I cannot say much ; for he is so excessively laughed at about me at Ashe, that he is ashamed of coming to Steventon, and ran away when we called on Mrs. Lefroy a few days ago . . . After I had written the above we received a visit from Mr. Tom Lefroy and his cousin George."

" I mean to confine myself in future to Mr. Tom Lefroy, for whom I don't care sixpence." . . . *Friday.* " At length the day is come on which I am to flirt my last with Tom Lefroy, and when you receive this it will be over. My tears flow as I write at the melancholy idea."

At this time she was twenty-one, and he twenty-three, but they do not seem to have been of such susceptible dispositions as many young men and women of their age.

We hear of Mr. Lefroy again in 1798, when his aunt has been calling at Steventon. The reference is a little perplexing. Jane says first, speaking of Mrs. Lefroy, " Of her nephew she said nothing at all, and of her friend very little," and a few sentences further on remarks, " She showed me a letter which she had received from her friend a few weeks ago, toward the end of which is a sentence to this effect, ' I am very sorry to hear of Mrs. Austen's illness. It would give me particular pleasure to have an opportunity of improving my acquaintance with

SOCIETY AND LOVE-MAKING

that family—with the hope of creating to myself a nearer interest. But at present I cannot indulge any expectation of it.' This is rational enough; there is less love and more sense in it than sometimes appeared before, and I am very well satisfied. It will go on exceedingly well, and decline away in a very reasonable manner. There seems to be no likelihood of his coming into Hampshire this Christmas, and it is therefore most probable that our indifference will soon be mutual, unless his regard, which appeared to spring from knowing nothing of me at first, is best supported by never seeing me."

It seems evident, therefore, that some friend who had been staying at Ashe previously had also shown symptoms of losing his heart to Jane, who did not take his affection seriously, and was in no danger of losing her own. Her prediction seems to have been verified, for we never hear of him again, unless he was the man to whom Mr. Austen-Leigh refers when he says—

"In her youth she had declined the addresses of a gentleman who had the recommendations of good character and connections, and position of life, of everything in fact except the subtle power of touching her heart."

The other offer above referred to was made to her in 1802 by someone described by her niece Anna as a "sensible pleasant man," but he also failed in the essential particular.

Mr. Austen-Leigh tells us further of "one passage of romance in her history with which I am imperfectly acquainted, and to which I am unable to assign name, or date, or place, though I have it on sufficient authority. Many years after her death, some circumstances induced her sister Cassandra to break through her habitual reticence and to speak of it. She said that, while staying at some seaside place, they became acquainted with a gentleman, whose charm of person, mind, and manners, was such that Cassandra thought him worthy to possess and likely to win her sister's love. When they parted he expressed his intention of soon seeing them again, and Cassandra felt no doubt as to his motives. But they never again met. Within a short time they heard of his sudden death."

This incident may seem too slight and unimportant even for reference, but in reality it may have had a deep significance. Those who have studied human nature, know that there are here and there among both men and women, minds that are satisfied with nothing less than the best. A temperament like Jane Austen's, where the whole nature was extremely sensitive, and the mind extremely clear-sighted, would have required qualities of the heart and mind in a man to be loved that are not to be found every day. In addition, it would have been quite impossible for her to marry any man from respect only or simple friendship. Nothing but love could have carried her fastidious nature over the bound of matrimony. Such natures as Jane's are not facile: not for them the willing self-deception which imagines love in any man who is an admirer; not for them the blindness which attributes qualities where they are not, nor the vanity which credits a man with every virtue merely because he has the taste to prefer them. Many marriages are made on these lines, and a proportion turn out well; but the higher natures, standing out here and there, require a sounder basis.

The incident above described is attributed by her niece (Anna Lefroy), writing many years later, to the year 1799 or 1800, when Jane was on a tour in Devonshire with her mother and sister, and other writers have drawn from it the inference that from this heart distress came the inability to create, and that it thus accounted for the long interval during which she wrote nothing at all. This hardly seems likely, or at all events there were many other causes equally likely, such as the impossibility of getting her MSS. published, which may have militated against her adding to them, and her own father's death may have been a shock from which she was slow to recover.

There is a cryptic sentence in the correspondence of 1808 which seems to show that her heart was at that time touched, and that she expected to meet someone who was an object of great interest to her. She was then staying at Godmersham, and writes—

"I have been so kindly pressed to stay longer here, in consequence of an offer of Henry's to take me back some time in September, that, not being able to detail all my objections to such a plan, I have felt myself obliged to give Edward and Elizabeth one private reason for my wishing to be at home in July. They feel the strength of it, and say no more, and one can rely on their secrecy. After this I hope we shall not be disappointed of our friend's visit; my honour as well as my affection will be concerned in it."

If these words had occurred some years earlier, they would seem to point directly to that visitor whose coming was hindered by death, but, according to the niece's account, they must have been written too long after this incident to have any bearing upon it. It may be, however, that Anna, being young at the time, and knowing of the affair only by hearsay, was mistaken; and in any case she does not authoritatively state the year as 1799, but believes it to have been about then. If, however, the first meeting had taken place in 1805 or 1806, this remark of Jane's might allude to it, for no one says that the death of the man in question took place immediately after she knew him, but only before there was a second meeting. Jane's own words, " my honour as well as my affection," point directly to some admirer, for she would feel that once having betrayed her own eagerness to her brother and sister-in-law, the fact of the visitor's not taking the trouble to come to see her would appear to them a direct slight. The reference can hardly have been to anything but a love-affair, and her own eagerness looks as if she were in earnest at last. If the words cannot be taken to refer to the known admirer, they must certainly have referred to some other; and as nothing more is heard of him, perhaps he did not come as she anticipated, and she, who had found it so difficult to take the proposals of others seriously, was herself mistaken when she was in earnest; but all this is mere conjecture.

Sir Walter Scott, in his review of *Emma* in the *Quarterly*, finds generally in Jane Austen's books a deficiency of what he considers romance, and he thus indicts her—

"One word, however, we must say in behalf of that once powerful divinity, Cupid, king of gods and men, who in these times of revolution, has been assailed, even in his own kingdom of romance, by the authors who were formerly his devoted priests. We are quite aware that there are few instances of first attachment being brought to a happy conclusion, and that it seldom can be so in a state of society so highly advanced as to render early marriages among the better classes acts, generally speaking, of imprudence. But the youth of this realm need not at present be taught the doctrines of selfishness. It is by no means their error to give the world, or the good things of the world, all for love; and before the authors of moral fiction couple Cupid indivisibly with calculating prudence, we would have them reflect that they may sometimes lend their aid to substitute more mean, more sordid, and more selfish motives of conduct, for the romantic feelings which their predecessors perhaps fanned into too powerful a flame. Who is it, that in his youth has felt a virtuous attachment, however romantic, or however unfortunate, but can trace back to its influence much that his character may possess of what is honourable, dignified, and disinterested?"

With due deference to the opinion of the greatest romancer in English fiction, he begs the question when he inserts the words "however unfortunate." An unfortunate love-affair in youth exercises without doubt a lasting good effect on any man who has grit in him, it is the fortunate ones that, paradoxically, are often so unfortunate.

Perhaps no word in the English language has ever been misused like poor "romance"; Jane was not devoid of it, in almost every case she distinguishes between the real and the false, Marianne's silly girlish admiration for Willoughby, and Emma's purely imaginary inclination toward Frank Churchill, are alike shown to be false, and founded only on that fleeting attraction which both men and women in early youth feel for the admirable person of one of the opposite sex. There are many persons still who think that this first flush of passion is real romance; that a young man who, at the most susceptible moment of his life, sees a pretty face, and falls a victim to it, perhaps even without ever having spoken to its possessor, has struck the real thing. This is to put love on the lowest basis of animalism. The beautiful girl, whatever the nature that lies beneath, is sought by a score of young men purely because she arouses in them their first instincts of manhood, but perhaps to no one of them is she the real mate. Love, that true deep attraction of the heart and mind, does not come so readily, nor is it induced by personal attractions without further knowledge, though it may well be enhanced by them.

Many and many a man takes a rash step into marriage, solely on the ground of external attraction, to gratify a youthful impulse, and having himself fitted the harness to his shoulders, spends the rest of his life in accommodating himself to it, without making the process of accommodation too patent to the eyes of the world. If he be a man at all, he realises that it was his own doing entirely, and he must bear the responsibility. Such marriages may, if the two be malleable and adaptable, turn out happily enough, especially if, as does sometimes happen, love comes after marriage, but the risk is a terrible one to take. The perpetuation of the race is the most urgent necessity, so nature takes care to secure it at all risks to the happiness of individuals; and certainly were it not for the indulgence of this momentary madness of youth, which oddly enough Sir Walter seems to regard as a form of unselfishness, the world would have fewer married couples in it.

When Jane depicted the slow growth of Emma's love for Knightley, she drew wisely. Lord Brabourne has remarked that he wished Emma had married Frank Churchill, and herein he shows his own superficial view of human nature. Emma was a strong character strongly developed. She must either have married, for her own happiness, a man who was her master, or one whom she could completely guide; the world usually accords the latter kind of marriage to such natures, and in the character of Elinor Dashwood, who in some ways resembles Emma, we see this alternative match, for she marries the hopelessly weak Edward Ferrars; but Emma's was the better match; for many a man has discovered for himself that when a strong nature finds its master it gives a far higher and nobler love and obedience than that given by a shallow one whose opinions and ideas are merely wisps of fancy. Emma recognised that Knightley was her master, his quiet audacity, his failure to join in the general pæan of flattery she received, his manliness in controlling his own feelings, appealed to her, and we may feel sure that her self-surrender just gave that finishing touch of softening to her nature which it needed; as a loving wife with full confidence in the judgment and principle of the man she had chosen, she would grow softer and kindlier every day of her life. She and Frank Churchill would very soon have been disgusted with each other, for he was not so weak as to have surrendered entirely to her authority, and constant friction would have been the result of their mating. Jane Austen does not make her ideal marriage a mere cementing of friendship, she recognises that to be perfect it must have that element of personal attraction which, to fastidious minds, alone makes marriage possible. Mr. Knightley was Emma's friend and adviser from the first, but not until her inclination for him was revealed in a lightning flash did the idea of marrying him enter her head. The difference between this personal inclination and the fantasy of youth is, that what is cause in the one is effect in the other. In the case of real love, the personal appearance is loved because of the personality behind it; in the spurious attraction the personal appearance is the first consequence, and the character behind it is idealised, with the constant result of woeful disillusionment. In one place Jane shows how fully she realised the difference between the true and the false by a little saying, "Three and twenty—a period when, if a man chooses a wife, he generally chooses ill."

In the softest and most tender of her books, *Persuasion*, she gives a beautiful picture of a girl's real love, a love which lasted through time and brought out what was best in the character, and in one of the most charming scenes in this novel, Anne Elliot, the heroine, gives her views on men's and women's constancy thus—

"'Your [men's] feelings may be the strongest,' replied Anne, 'but the same spirit of analogy will authorise me to assert that ours are the most tender. Man is more robust that woman, but he is not longer lived; which exactly explains my view of the nature of their attachments. Nay, it would be too hard upon you if it were otherwise. You have difficulties, and privations, and dangers enough to struggle with. You are always labouring and toiling, exposed to every risk and hardship. Your home, country, friends, all quitted. Neither time, nor health, nor life to be called your own. It would be too hard indeed if (with a faltering voice) woman's feelings were to be added to all this.'"

This, in spite of its somewhat glorified view of an ordinary man's career, is very touching, and still more so what follows—

"'We can never expect to prove anything upon such a point. It is a difference of opinion which does not admit of proof. We each begin probably with a little bias towards our own sex; and upon that bias build every circumstance in favour of it which has occurred within our own circle. . . . I hope to do justice to all that is felt by you—I believe you capable of everything great and good in your married lives. I believe you equal to every important exertion and to every domestic forbearance, so long as—if I may be allowed the expression—so long as you have an object. I mean while the woman you love lives and lives for you. All the privilege I claim for my own sex (it is not a very enviable one, you need not covet it) is that of loving longest, when existence or when hope is gone.'"

SOCIETY AND LOVE-MAKING

Natures which set their all on the chance of such a high throw as the demand for a marriage combining personal attraction and real suitability of character, know well that it is not likely that they will win; people who ask only for personal attraction, and risk all the rest, are in different case. But it is remarkable how the growing generation of men are learning to look below the surface and to take some trouble to find out the character of the girl who has attracted them before binding themselves; men, even young men, do not rush into marriage with the same lack of all self-control that a previous generation did. With the evaporation of the sentimentality of the Victorian period there has come also a far higher ideal of marriage, and a man demands more of his wife than evanescent personal attractions.

Though Jane set love at a high altitude, she was perfectly free from false sentiment or silly sentimentality. She says in one place of a man who loves hopelessly, "It is no creed of mine, as you must be well aware, that such sorts of disappointments kill anybody."

And her delightful sense of humour shows up in an inimitable light the foolish weakness of a girl suffering from a purely imaginary love-affair. The occasion is after the disillusionment of poor sentimental Harriet as to the real feelings of Mr. Elton, whom she had been encouraged by Emma to regard as an unexpressed lover. "Harriet came one morning to Emma with a small parcel in her hand, and after sitting down and hesitating thus began—

"'Miss Woodhouse, if you are at leisure, I have something that I should like to tell you; a sort of confession to make—and then you know it will be over.'

"Emma was a good deal surprised, but begged her to speak. . . .

"'How could I be so long fancying myself—,' cried Harriet warmly. 'It seems like madness! I can see nothing at all extraordinary in him now, I do not care whether I meet him or not, except that of the two I had rather not see him; and indeed I would go any distance round to avoid him, but I do not envy his wife in the least; I neither admire her nor envy her as I have done. She is very charming, I daresay, and all that, but I think her very ill-tempered and disagreeable; I shall never forget her look the other night. However, I assure you, Miss Woodhouse, I wish her no evil. No, let them be ever so happy together, it will not give me another moment's pang; and, to convince you that I have been speaking the truth, I am now going to destroy — what I ought to have destroyed long ago — what I ought never to have kept; I know that very well (blushing as she spoke). However, now I will destroy it all, and it is my particular wish to do it in your presence, that you may see how rational I am grown. Cannot you guess what this parcel holds?' said she with a conscious look.

"'Not the least in the world. Did he ever give you anything?'

"'No, I cannot call them gifts, but they are things that I have valued very much.'

"She held the parcel towards her and Emma read the words, 'Most precious treasures' on the top. Her curiosity was greatly excited. Harriet unfolded the parcel and she looked on with impatience. Within abundance of silver paper was a pretty little Tunbridge-ware box, which Harriet opened; it was well lined with the softest cotton; but excepting the cotton, Emma saw only a small piece of court-plaister.

"'Now,' said Harriet, 'you *must* recollect.'

"'No, indeed, I do not.'

"'Dear me! I should not have thought it possible that you could forget what passed in this very room about court-plaister, one of the very last times we ever met in it. . . . Do not you remember his cutting his finger with your new pen-knife, and your recommending court-plaister? But, as you had none about you, and knew I had, you desired me to supply him; and so I took mine out, and cut him a piece; but it was a great deal too large, and he cut it smaller, and kept playing some time with what was left before he gave it back to me. And so then, in my nonsense, I could not help making a treasure of it; so I put it by, never to be used, and looked at it now and then as a great treat.'

"'My dearest Harriet!' cried Emma, putting her hands before her face, and jumping up, . . . 'And so you actually put this piece of court-plaister by for his sake,' . . . and secretly she added to herself, 'Lord bless me! when should I ever have thought of putting by in cotton a piece of court-plaister that Frank Churchill had been pulling about! I never was equal to this.'

"'Here,' resumed Harriet, turning to her box again, 'here is something still more valuable,—I mean that *has been* more valuable,—because this is what did really once belong to him, which the court-plaister never did.'

"Emma was quite eager to see this superior treasure. It was the end of an old pencil, the part without any lead.

"'This was really his,' said Harriet. 'Do not you remember one morning? . . . I forget exactly the day . . . he wanted to make a memorandum in his pocket-book; it was about spruce beer . . . and he wanted to put it down; but when he took out his pencil there was so little lead that he soon cut it all away, and it would not do, so you lent him another, and this was left upon the table as good for nothing. But I kept my eye upon it; and, as soon as I dared, caught it up, and never parted with it again from that moment.' . . .

"'My poor dear Harriet! and have you actually found happiness in treasuring up these things?'

"'Yes, simpleton as I was!— but I am quite ashamed of it now, and wish I could forget as easily as I can burn them. It was very wrong of me, you know, to keep any remembrances after he was married. I knew it was—but had not resolution enough to part with them.'"

This is pure comedy!

In Jane Austen's day there certainly was an openness in the arrangements about marriage that jars on our more reticent minds. Of course it is undeniable that at that time a girl's only vocation, unless she happened to be a genius, was marriage, but the way in which suitability as to means and position were frequently considered as of all importance, and love merely as a secondary consideration, is slightly perturbing. Jane Austen's high ideal of marriage must have been rarer then than at the present time. Perhaps the best example of the shameless discussion of the *mariage de convenance* in the novels is the interview between Elinor Dashwood and her brother, when Colonel Brandon has shown some slight attention to her. Her brother begins by asking—

"'Who is Colonel Brandon? Is he a man of fortune?'

"'Yes, he has very good property in Dorsetshire.'

"'I am glad of it. He seems a most gentlemanlike

man; and I think, Elinor, I may congratulate you on the prospect of a very respectable establishment in life.'

"'Me, brother! what do you mean?'

"'He likes you. I observed him narrowly, and am convinced of it. What is the amount of his fortune?'

"'I believe about two thousand a year.'

"'Two thousand a year!' Then working himself up to a pitch of enthusiastic generosity, he added, 'Elinor, I wish with all my heart it were twice as much for your sake.'

"'Indeed, I believe you,' replied Elinor, 'but I am very sure that Colonel Brandon has not the smallest wish of marrying me.'

"'You are mistaken, Elinor; you are very much mistaken. A very little trouble on your side secures him. Perhaps just at present he may be undecided; the smallness of your fortune may make him hang back; his friends may all advise him against it. But some of those little attentions and encouragements which ladies can so easily give will fix him in spite of himself. And there can be no reason why you should not try for him. It is not to be supposed that any prior attachment on your side—in short you know, as to an attachment of that kind it is quite out of the question, the objections are insurmountable—Colonel Brandon must be the man; and no civility shall be wanting on my part to make him pleased with you and your family. It is a match that must give universal satisfaction.'"

The "prior attachment" was that to his own brother-in-law, Edward Ferrars, for whom his wife hoped to get a better match, and as a matter of fact the man in question, Colonel Brandon, was not in love with Elinor, but with her impulsive sister, Marianne, who was wasting away under the slights of Willoughby. Of her, her brother kindly remarks—

"'At her time of life, anything of an illness destroys the bloom for ever! Hers has been a very short one! She was as handsome a girl last September as ever I saw, and as likely to attract the men. There was something in her style of beauty to please them particularly. I remember Fanny used to say she would marry sooner and better than you did; she will be mistaken, however. I question whether Marianne now will marry a man worth more than five or six hundred a year at the utmost, and I am very much deceived if you do not do better.'

"Elinor tried very seriously to convince him that there was no likelihood of her marrying Colonel Brandon, but it was an expectation of too much pleasure to himself to be relinquished. . . . He had just compunction enough for having done nothing for his sisters himself to be exceedingly anxious that everyone else should do a great deal."

And John Dashwood's idea of the barter of women for so much, according to their attractions, though it differed not in essentials from that of a Circassian slave-dealer, was quite an ordinary one. The unblushing eagerness with which any heiress was literally pursued, the desperate devices to get portionless daughters married, doubtless have their counterparts now, but they are not so prominent; portionless daughters of wit and talent can make lives for themselves, independent of matrimony, and heiress hunters have at least the decency to pretend they are in love.

In view of the ideas of her times, Jane's ideal of marriage stands out conspicuously. She wanted all her heroines to have every probability of happiness in the marriage state, and though perhaps she did not consciously set to work to consider what would make them so in so many words, it is remarkable that certain points which, from her own observations of the human race, were the best foundations for married happiness, are to be found in every one of the marriages of her principal characters. The first essential which we have already touched upon was suitability of character. Poor Marianne Dashwood and the ardent Willoughby would have tried each other desperately with the vehemence of their enthusiasm; in six months they would have loathed each other as ardently as they had loved, therefore Marianne is not allowed to marry Willoughby, but mates with Colonel Brandon, the sort of man who would exercise an unconscious influence over her, teaching her self-control, and who would be kindly indulgent to her whims and wishes, not clashing with them on his own account.

The second essential, which is fulfilled in every case of the principal characters in the novels, is that the marriages are real unions, not those accidental associations which are based on imagination. Her men and women get to know each other thoroughly by constant intercourse, until the faults and virtues, the defects and abilities, are clear and plain. Jane knew that real love may begin by attraction, but must be built upon knowledge. In not a single case is a pretty face or a handsome person the reason for a man's or woman's falling in love. Darcy considers Elizabeth Bennet only "tolerable" when he first sees her, it is when he begins to care for her that he notes her "fine eyes." Though Catherine Morland was a pretty girl, it was not that which won Henry Tilney, but her naïve adoration of himself, and her sweet sincerity. Edmund Bertram runs after Miss Crawford for a time, but it is the excellence of Fanny's mind which gives him his life's happiness, and so on through all.

The third essential in Jane's mind was evidently that the love of the two should be mutual. In every case her heroine is genuinely in love before she gives her consent to marriage. Fanny Bertram of course knew her own love for Edmund long before his eyes were opened to the need he had for her. Anne Elliot had bitterly regretted for many weary years the fatal compliance with the wishes of her friends which had separated her from the man she loved, and when he returns only to pay attentions to another, and she imagines she has lost him for ever, she still never swerves in her loyalty to him. Poor Elinor has the mortification of hearing from the lips of a rival that Edward Ferrars is engaged to her, but still her choice never falters. For women of this kind, women of fine character, marriage without love is impossible; in the abstract it is not a necessity, as it often seems to be to a man; if they cannot have the one man they love, they will infinitely prefer to remain single. We must admit that, as Anne Elliot says, the power of loving longest remains with women, only we should amend to the extent of saying with the noblest women.

Many men hold that woman's love is not essential to a happy marriage, so long as they are in love with the woman they make their wife they think that her love is not necessary. This arises purely from want of imagination. They themselves, marrying a woman they passionately admire, start with all the glamour and glory which suffices to veil the difficult beginnings of a *menage à deux;* but the woman, who enters without this help, has to expend an immense amount of patience and self-control over wearisome domestic details, which would be transformed into pure joy if she also saw through a glorified atmosphere. A match where the woman does not love is very hard on her. It is, of course, perfectly true that the ardent love of a man has often won a woman's love in return; many a happy marriage has sprung from this beginning; but any man who is not more selfish than the rest of his sex, should try to assure himself that the love is there before marriage.

Of course to a man it is incredible that girls will consent to marry when they do not love; why should they? One knows it is not always the prospect of a home and maintenance, one would scorn to assess woman's nature at so low a rate. There is no real explanation, though possibly dense ignorance and girlish impulse toward the excitement, and the trivial accessories of a bride's position, may be the most usual contributory causes. If this is so, as woman increases in intelligence and reasonable knowledge, that is to say, as she becomes more fit to be a real mate to man, so will man find it increasingly difficult to persuade her into a one-sided-love marriage, oftentimes so disastrous to both, and at the best such a makeshift for what might be.

CHAPTER VIII

VISITS AND TRAVELLING

JANE AUSTEN'S life was very largely passed among her own relations, her visits away from home were nearly always to the houses of her brothers.

In the August of 1796 she went to stay with her brother Edward, at Rowling, a little place in Kent, near Goodnestone. Edward had been married for some time to Elizabeth Bridges, daughter of Sir Brook Bridges of Goodnestone. He had, as has been already stated, been adopted by his relative, Mr. Knight of Godmersham in Kent and Chawton in Hampshire, and had taken his name. This Mr. Knight had died two years previously, and left Edward his heir, subject to the widow's life-interest, but Mrs. Knight herself loved Edward like a son and retired from Godmersham in his favour. At this date, however, the family had not yet moved there, but continued to live at Rowling. Of the pleasant country life at Rowling we get several graphic touches. "We were at a ball on Saturday, I assure you. We dined at Goodnestone, and in the evening danced two country dances and the Boulangeries. I opened the ball with Edward Bridges; the other couples were Lewis Cage and Harriet, Frank and Louisa, Fanny and George. Elizabeth played one country dance, Lady Bridges the other, which she made Henry dance with her, and Miss Finch played the Boulangeries."

VISITS AND TRAVELLING

The Boulangeries seems to have been an innovation adopted from France, and occasionally formed the last figure of a quadrille, which had many variations, " either with a ' Chassecroise,' or with ' la boulangère,' ' la corbeille,' ' le Moulinet,' or ' la ste Simonienne.' "

Of the couples mentioned above, Lewis Cage had married Fanny Bridges; Harriet and Louisa were two young unmarried sisters; Frank and Henry, Jane's brothers. Henry Austen seems to have been of a very unsettled disposition; in Jane's first letter she says,—" Henry is still hankering after the Regulars, and as his project of purchasing the adjutancy of the Oxfordshire is now over, he has got a scheme in his head about getting a lieutenancy and adjutancy in the 86th., a new raised regiment, which he fancies will be ordered to the Cape of Good Hope."

Later on Henry became Receiver-General for Oxfordshire, afterwards he was partner in a bank, and when the bank broke in 1816, he took Orders, and on the death of his brother James he held the living of Steventon for a short time until one of his brother Edward's younger boys was ready for it.

After the impromptu evening's entertainment at Goodnestone the party walked home under the shade of two umbrellas. Another day they dined at Nackington, returning by moonlight in two carriages.

Visits were of long duration in days when getting about was so costly and difficult a process; Jane stayed on with her brother until October, and in September she records : " Edward and Fly went out yesterday very early in a couple of shooting jackets, and came home like a couple of bad shots, for they killed nothing at all. They are out again to-day, and are not yet returned. Delightful sport! They are just come home, Edward with his two brace, Frank with his two and a half.

What amiable young men!" She also records: "We are very busy making Edward's shirts and I am proud to say I am the neatest worker of the party"; and again, "Little Edward [her brother's eldest boy] was breeched yesterday for good and all, and was whipped into the bargain."

This is very small beer, but it suffices to give a sketch of the pleasant family life, where half the neighbours were related to each other and on cordial terms, where entertainments were simple and spontaneous, though it was an age that we are accustomed to regard as one of the most formal in social history.

Jane alludes to her difficulties of tipping. "I am in great distress. I cannot determine whether I shall give Richis half a guinea or only five shillings when I go away. Counsel me, most amiable Miss Austen, and tell me which will be the most."

We are accustomed to consider our own age as lying under the thraldom of tips, as none ever did before, but it is nothing to what the end of the eighteenth century was in this respect. When people went to dinner they were expected to tip the servants, who sometimes stood in long rows in the hall waiting the customary douceur.

As for hotels, they were worse than to-day, for it must be remembered money was of greater relative value. In a letter from a "Constant Reader" to *The Times* in October 1795, the vexed subject of tips is discussed—

"If a man who has a horse, puts up at an inn, besides the usual bill, he must at least give 1s. to the waiter, 6d. to the chambermaid, 6d. to the ostler, and 6d. to the jack-boot, making together 2s. 6d. At breakfast you must give at least 6d. between the waiter and Hostler. If the traveller only puts up to have a refreshment, besides paying for his horses standing he must give 3d. to the hostler, at dinner 6d. to the waiter and 3d. to the hostler; at tea 6d. between them, so that he gives away in the day 2s. 6d., which, added to the 2s. 6d. for the night, makes 5s. per day on an average to servants."

Jane did not expect to be able to return to Steventon until about the middle of October, but it was necessary to lay plans long before so as to arrange if possible for the escort of one of her brothers, as it was not thought at all the proper thing for a young lady to go by herself on a journey, and considering the changes at inn-yards and many stoppages, this is not to be wondered at. Just at this time Frank Austen received a naval appointment, and had to be up in town the next day, September 21, so Jane seized the opportunity to go with him. "As to the mode of our travelling to town, I want to go in a stage coach, but Frank will not let me." This means of course that they would have to travel post, a much more expensive performance.

The whole subject of travelling is one of the things that bring more vividly before us than any other the difference of the then and the now.

In 1755 an Act was passed compelling districts all over the country to make turnpike roads and charge toll accordingly; before this date the state of the roads had been too terrible for description, and even after it road-making progressed but slowly, for it was not until the beginning of the nineteenth century that Macadam's improvements were adopted.

Up to 1755 roads had been made certainly after a fashion, and many Acts had been passed with the object of improving them, but these had not had much effect. Even the great Act of 1755 seemed to be of little practical efficacy, for between 1760 and 1764 inclusive, upwards of four hundred and fifty Acts of Parliament were passed in order to effect the formation of new, and the repair and alteration of old, highways throughout the country, so Parliament certainly cannot be accused of regarding the matter with indifference. Many are the complaints of travellers. Arthur Young in his well-known *Tour* mentions the roads frequently: " Much more to be condemned is the execrable muddy road from Bury to Sudbury in Suffolk, in which I was forced to move as slow as in any unmended lane in Wales. For ponds of liquid dirt and a scattering of loose flints just sufficient to lame every horse that moves near them, with the addition of cutting vile grips across the road, under pretence of letting water off, but without the effect, altogether render at least twelve of these sixteen miles as infamous a turnpike as ever was travelled. Their method of mending the last mentioned road I found excessively absurd, for in parts of it the sides are higher than the middle, and the gravel they bring in is nothing more but a yellow loam with a few stones in it, through which the wheels of a light chaise cut as easily as in sand, with the addition of such floods of watery mud as renders the road, on the whole, inferior to nothing but an unmended Welsh lane. From Chepstow to the half way house between Newport and Cardiff they continue mere rocky lanes, full of hugeous stones as big as one's horse, and abominable holes."

Though the stones as " big as one's horse " must be allowed for as the pardonable exaggeration of a traveller's tale, it is true that the method of road mending previous to Macadam was nothing more than setting down enormous stones to be crushed in by passing wheels, but as they were not set close, the wheels went bumping into the mud between, and the force of the jolt instead of setting the stones pushed them out of position ever worse and worse. "Where they are mending, as they call it, you travel over a bed of loose stones none of less size than an octavo volume, and where not mended 'tis like a staircase."

As for the means of conveyance over these vile highways, before the making of turnpike-roads waggons had been the usual method, and flying coaches, as they were at first called, were considered a great improvement; however, coach fares were high, and even after the introduction of coaches many people who were unable to afford them still travelled by the slow-going waggon.

This mode of proceeding must have been inexpressibly wearisome; here is an account of a journey made by such means from London to Greenwich—

"We were twenty-four passengers within side and nine without. It was my lot to sit in the middle with a very lusty woman on one side, and a very thin man on the other. 'Open the window,' said the former and she had a child on her lap whose hands were all besmeared with gingerbread. 'It can't be opened,' said a little prim coxcomb, 'or I shall get cold.' 'But I say it shall, sir,' said a butcher who sat opposite to him, and the butcher opened it; but as he stood, or rather bent forward to do this, the caravan came into a rut and the butcher's head, by the suddenness of the jolt, came into contact with that of the woman who sat next to me, and made her nose bleed. He begged her pardon and she gave him a slap on the face that sounded through the whole caravan. Two sailors that were seated near the helm of this machine, ordered the driver to cast anchor at the next public house. He did so and the woman next to me called for a pint of ale which she offered to me, after she had emptied about a pint of it, observing, 'that as how she loved ale mightily.' I could not drink, at which she took offence. ... A violent dispute now arose between two stout-looking men, the one a recruiting sergeant, the other a gentleman's coachman, about the Rights of Man. . . . Another dispute afterwards was about politics, which was carried on with such warmth as to draw the attention of the company to the head of the caravan, where the combatants sat wedged together like two pounds of Epping butter, whilst a child incessantly roared at the opposite side, and the mother abused the two politicians for frightening her babe. The heat was now so great that all the windows were opened, and with the fresh air entered clouds of dust, for the body of the machine is but a few inches from the surface of the road."

If one can imagine this kind of thing continuing for hour after hour, while one's bones ached with the cramp, and one was stupefied with the noise and smell, one gains some idea of the delights of waggon travelling.

We find an account of the roads actually in Hampshire, Jane Austen's own county, in the correspondence of Lady Newdigate (*The Cheverels of Cheverel Manor*). In giving an account of going from Arbury (Warwick) to Stanstead near Portsmouth in 1795, she says: "The sisters were decidedly for going through Reading and Farnham, but Mr. Cotton, from consultation of maps and conversation with postillions, believed it would be full as good and pleasant and a much shorter road to go by Basingstoke and Alton. In the first of these places we found it 19 miles instead of 15, and were informed that instead of ten miles good turnpike to Alton there was not above three miles made, and the rest so cut as to be impassable for such a carriage as mine; in short that we had twelve miles across country road . . . the consequence was that we had eight miles bad road out of 16, and was an hour in the dark. But the poneys performed wonders."

Lady Newdigate also gives the cost of this journey, which is interesting: "We paid 14d. per mile great part of the way for the chaisehorses, and 6d. all the way for the saddle horse; the whole, baits and sleepings included, comes to above £24 to this place."

On the way to Brighton, two years later, she says, "I never saw this road so rotted, so heavy, or so deep. It was with difficulty my poor poneys could drag us."

We have therefore a tolerable notion of the fatigues attendant on a journey in those days.

Another drawback was, that if one wished to travel by coach instead of going post, one could not always be sure of a place unless booked beforehand. This kind of thing frequently happened—

"I was called up early—to be ready for the coach, but judge my disappointment and chagrin, when on my approach I found it chock-full. I petitioned, reasoned, urged and entreated, but all to no effect. I could not make any impression on the obdurate souls, who, proud and sulky, kept easy and firm possession of their seats, and hardly deigned to answer, when I requested permission to squeeze in. I was hoisted on the coach box as the only alternative; but on the first movement of the vehicle, had it not been for the arm of the coachman, I should have been instantly under the wheels in the street. I was chucked into a basket as a place of more safety, though not of ease or comfort, where I suffered most severely from the jolting, particularly over the stones; it was most truly dreadful and made one suffer almost equal to sea sickness." (Tate Wilkinson, *Memoirs*.)

This basket was actually a basket slung on for the purpose of carrying luggage, though it was also used for passengers, and sometimes filled with people in spite of its discomfort, because seats here were charged at a low price.

Richard Thomson, in *Tales of an Antiquary*, gives a very good word-picture of a stage coach: "Stage coaches were constructed principally of a dull black leather, thickly studded by way of ornament with broad black head nails tracing out the panels, in the upper tier of which were four oval windows with heavy red wooden frames or leathern curtains. The roofs of the coaches in most cases rose in a swelling curve. Behind the coach was the immense basket, stretching far and wide beyond the body, to which it was attached by long iron bars or supports passing beneath it. The wheels of these old carriages were large, massive, ill-formed and usually of a red colour, and the three horses that were affixed to the whole machine were all so far parted from it by the great length of their traces that it was with no little difficulty that the poor animals dragged their unwieldly burden along the road."

The accidents attendant on coach journeys were many and various, and the badness of the roads was the principal cause. In *Under England's Flag*, the autobiography of Captain Charles Boothby, R.E., we have this account of what happened to him in 1805 when he first left home—

"Down to Portsmouth then I went on the outside of the mail, in the highest health and the ardent spirits of youth, spirits that made, I suppose, even my body buoyant and elastic, for the Mail overturned in the night and threw me on the road without giving me so much as a scratch or a bruise. It was about twenty miles from London when we met a team of horses standing in a slant direction on the road, the night very foggy with misting rain, and the lamps not penetrating further into the mist than the rumps of the wheelers. The

FROM "A SUMMER'S EVENING"

coachman, to avoid the waggon, turned suddenly out of the way and ran up the bank. Finding the coach staggering, I got up, with my face to the horses, hardly daring to suppose it possible that the Mail could overturn, when the unwieldly monster was on one wheel, and then down it came with a terminal bang. During my descent I had just time to hope that I might escape with the fracture of one or two legs, and then found myself on my two shoulders, very pleased with the novelty and ease of the journey. I got up and spied the monster with his two free wheels whirling with great velocity, but quite compact and still in the body, and as soon as I had shaken my feathers and opened my senses I began to think of the one female and three males in the inside, whom I supposed to be either dead or asleep. I ran to open the door, when the guard, having thought of the same thing, did it for me, and we then took the folks out one by one, like pickled ghirkins or anything else preserved in a jar, by putting our hands to the bottom; we found that the inmates were only stupefied, though all had bruises of some kind, and one little gentleman complained that he was nipped in the loins by the mighty pressure of his neighbour, who had sat upon him some time after the door was opened to recollect himself or to give thanks for his escape."

Coaches did not as a rule run on Sundays, so passengers whose journeys were to extend over several days had to take care to start early in the week if they did not wish to pay expenses at an inn during the Sabbath.

This rule was, however, not stringently observed, as M. Grosley found when he landed in England on his tour of observation—

"The great multitude of passengers with which

Dover was then crowded, formed a reason for dispensing with a law of the police, by which public carriages are in England, forbid to travel on Sundays. I therefore set out on a Sunday with seven more passengers in two carriages called flying machines. These vehicles, which are drawn by six horses, go twenty-eight leagues in a day from Dover to London for a single guinea. Servants are entitled to a place for half that money, either behind the coach or upon the coach box, which has three places. A vast repository, under this seat, which is very lofty, holds the passengers' luggage, which is paid for separately. The coachmen, whom we changed every time with our horses, were lusty, well made men, dressed in good cloth."

Among the advantages of travelling on a Sunday when coaches were not expected, he enumerates that "we should meet none of those gentry who are called collectors of the highway, and of whom there is a great number upon the road; in fact we saw none of that sort, but such as were hanging upon gibbets at the road side; there they dangle, dressed from head to foot, and with wigs upon their heads."

The Austen women do not seem at any time to have travelled by coach, but always post, a much more comfortable method, ensuring privacy, though it also had its disadvantages, as when one arrived at an inn requiring change of horses only to find the Marquess of Carabbas had passed on before with a whole retinue of attendants, taking every horse in the stable, and the second comers were therefore compelled to wait until the return of the jaded steeds, and to use them again when the poor beasts had only had half the rest they deserved. The keeping of horses was a necessary branch of the business of every inn-keeper on the high-road, a branch which is now seldom called for,

TRAVELLERS ARRIVING AT 'EAGLE TAVERN,' STRAND

so that it is only at very large establishments, or those in the most out-of-the-way districts where trains come not, that "posting in all its branches" forms part of the landlord's boast.

Though one lady could not very well go alone on a journey, for two ladies to travel together was considered quite proper. In 1798, Jane and her mother returning from Godmersham managed for themselves very well. Jane says, "You have already heard from Daniel, I conclude, in what excellent time we reached and quitted Sittingbourne and how very well my mother bore her journey thither. . . . She was a very little fatigued on her arrival at this place, has been quite refreshed by a comfortable dinner, and now seems quite stout. It wanted five minutes of twelve when we left Sittingbourne, from whence we had a famous pair of horses, which took us to Rochester in an hour and a quarter; the postboy seemed determined to show my mother that Kentish drivers were not always tedious.

"Our next stage was not quite so expeditiously performed; the road was heavy and our horses very indifferent. However we were in such good time, and my mother bore her journey so well, that expedition was of little importance to us; and as it was, we were very little more than two hours and a half coming hither, and it was scarcely past four when we stopped at the inn. My mother took some of her bitters at Ospringe, and some more at Rochester, and she ate some bread several times. We sat down to dinner a little after five, and had some beefsteak and a boiled fowl, but no oyster sauce."

Though Jane refused to avail herself of the very present excitement of highwaymen in any of her novels, she might legitimately have done so, for these perils were by no means imaginary; the newspapers of the latter part of the eighteenth century are full of accounts of these pests, who were seldom caught.

Mrs. Lybbe Powys says—

"The conversation was for some time on a subject you'd hardly imagine—robbery. Postchaises had been stopped from Hodges to Henley, about three miles; but though the nights were dark we had flambeaux. Miss Pratt and I thought ourselves amazingly lucky; we were in their coach, ours next, and the chaise behind that, robbed. It would have been silly to have lost one's diamonds so totally unexpected, and diamonds it seems they came after, more in number than mine indeed."

The Duke of York and one of his brothers were robbed of watches, purses, etc., when they were returning late at night in a hackney coach along Hay Hill.

In 1786, Horace Walpole mentions, "The mail from France was robbed last night in Pall Mall, at half an hour after eight, yes! in the great thoroughfare of London, and within call of the guard at the Palace. The chaise had stopped, the harness was cut, and the portmanteau was taken out of the chaise itself."

The travellers who had to give up their valuables were numberless, and many ladies took to carrying secondary purses full of false money, which, with hypocritical tears they handed out on compulsion. There was really not much risk in the business of a highwayman, if a man had a good horse and good nerve. The poor citizens he robbed were not fighting men, and though the penalty of hanging was the award if my well-mannered and gallant gentleman were caught, yet his chances of escape were many. The wonder is not that highwaymen were so numerous, but that, with the cumbersome methods of capturing and dealing with them, any of them were ever caught at all.

CHAPTER IX

CONTEMPORARY WRITERS

THE end of the eighteenth century was an age when merit in literature was an Open Sesame to the very best society that the capital could supply. An author who had brought out a work a little above the average was received and fêted, not only by the literary set, who rapidly passed her or him on from one to another, but by the persons of the highest social rank also. London was so much smaller then, that there was not room for all the grades and sets that now run parallel without ever overlapping. When anyone was made welcome they were free of all the best society at once, and the ease with which some people slipped into the position of social lions on the strength of very small performance is little short of wonderful. When Hannah More first visited London, in 1774, she was plunged at once into the society of men of letters, of wit, of learning, and of rank. Her plays, which to our taste are intolerably stiff and dull, were accepted by Garrick, she became his personal friend, and he introduced her to everyone whose acquaintance was worth having. The Garricks' house became her second home, and she met Bishops by the half dozen, visited the Lord Chamberlain at Apsley House, and was on familiar terms with Sheridan, Johnson, Walpole, Reynolds, and many another whose name is still a household word in England.

In those days the same people met again and again at each other's houses, more after the fashion of a country town than of that of London at present. Indeed they seem to have spent the whole day and most of the night running after each other. There is one custom which we must all be thankful exists no longer, the intolerable fashion of morning calls. Calls are bad enough now as custom decrees, but we are at least free from the terror of people dropping in upon us before the day's work is begun. When staying in Northumberland Miss Mitford remarks, " Morning calls are here made so early, that one morning three different people called before we had done breakfast." Hannah More looked on a morning visit as an immorality, yet she breakfasted with a Bishop, afterwards going to an evening party with another on the same day! She, being of a sensible mind, soon grew tired of the ceaseless talk, though much of it may have been good stuff and worthy of preservation, and she rejoiced when she could get a day to herself, and deny herself to everyone.

After Garrick's death, when she came to stay with his brave but heart-broken widow she lived very quietly. " My way of life is very different from what it used to be. After breakfast I go to my own apartment for several hours, where I read, write and work; very seldom letting anybody in. At four we dine. We have the same elegant table as usual, but I generally confine myself to one single dish of meat. I have taken to drink half a glass of wine. At six we have coffee; at eight tea, when we have sometimes, a dowager or two of quality. At ten we have sallad and fruits."

This was in 1779, and two years previously her play *Percy* had been brought out with extraordinary success; she says of it herself, " far beyond my expectation," and it produced more excitement than any tragedy had done for many years. The author's rights, sale of copy, etc., amounted to near six hundred pounds, and "as my friend Mr. Garrick has been so good as to lay it out for me on the best security and at five per cent., it makes a decent little addition to my small income. Cadell gave £150, a very handsome price, with conditional promises. He confesses that it had had a very great sale and that he shall get a good deal of money by it. The first impression is near four thousand and the second is almost old."

It is customary to think of Hannah More as so quiet and Quakerish that the idea of her writing plays and living a gay society life is new to many people, but the seriousness and retirement came later.

Considering how easily the heights of celebrity were stormed at that time, and especially by a woman, it is most remarkable that Jane received no encouragement, and had no literary society, and not one literary correspondent in the whole of her lifetime. Of course her first novel was not published until 1811, and then anonymously, with the simple inscription "By a Lady" on the title-page, yet it sold well and became very popular, and though no effort was made to proclaim her the authoress certainly there was no rigid attempt to hide her personality. Before the publication of *Emma* her identity was known, for she was requested to dedicate this book to the Prince Regent, as will be related in due course. And this was the only recognition of any public sort she received. Many of her contemporaries were brought up in a sort of hotbed of intellect, and associated with men of talent and distinction from their cradles— what a wonderful quickening and impetus must this have brought with it! Jane had none of these advantages, her genius was her own entirely, and her material of the slightest; she had no contemporaries of original talent with which to exchange ideas, to strike out sparks or receive suggestions. She did not mingle with people of her own calibre at all. Herein Miss Burney had an immense advantage over her, from her babyhood she was surrounded by men and women of distinction. Her father, himself an author and possessing musical talent, drew to his house all sorts of persons. Macaulay says, "It would be tedious to recount the names of all the men of letters and artists whom Fanny Burney had an opportunity of seeing and hearing. Hundreds of remarkable persons had passed in review before her, English, French, German, Italian, lords and fiddlers, deans of cathedrals and managers of theatres, travellers leading about newly caught savages, and singing-women escorted by deputy-husbands." She was fêted, caressed and brought forward until she accepted the appointment at the court which condemned her to a weary round of dull duties, and must have made her life appear like a draught of ditch-water after the heady champagne to which she was accustomed.

But the London of 1811, when we have the first record of Jane's visiting it, was not what it had been thirty years before. Johnson was dead, Walpole was dead, Garrick was dead, Reynolds was dead, Sheridan living but sunk in debt and disease; of the brilliant band that Hannah More had known few were left. Doctor Johnson had died fourteen years previously, when Jane was only nine years old. Miss Burney had had not only his friendship but his help in the revision of her works—perhaps a doubtful privilege. To quote Lord Macaulay again: "When she wrote her early journals, and her novel of *Evelina*, her style was not indeed brilliant or energetic; but it was easy, clear, and free from all offensive faults. When she wrote *Cecilia* she aimed higher. She had then lived much in a circle of which Johnson was the centre; and she was herself one of his most submissive worshippers. . . . In an evil hour the author of *Evelina* took the *Rambler* for her model. She had her style. It was a tolerably good one; she determined to throw it away to adopt a style in which she could attain excellence only by achieving an almost miraculous victory over nature and over habit. In *Cecilia* the imitation of Johnson, though not always in the best taste, is sometimes eminently happy. There were people who whispered that Johnson had assisted his young friend and that the novel owed all its finest passages to his hand. This was merely the fabrication of envy."

But after the death of Johnson, "she had to write in Johnson's manner without Johnson's aid. The consequence was that in *Camilla* every passage which she meant to be fine is detestable; and that the book has been saved from condemnation only by the admirable spirit and force of those scenes in which she was content to be familiar."

After he had read *Camilla*, Walpole says of Miss Burney: "Alas! She had reversed experience which I have long thought reverses its own utility by coming at the wrong end of our life when we do not want it. This author knew the world and penetrated characters before she had stepped over the threshold; now she has seen so much of it she has little or no insight at all."

It was therefore, perhaps, lucky for Jane Austen that she was not so overshadowed by the direct personality of a mighty man as to lose her clear, bright English style. Her admiration for Miss Burney's work was decided and clearly expressed, and she was among the first subscribers to *Camilla* in 1796.

Though Jane never came into contact with the men and women who made literature in her day, she took a keen interest in their works, and was a great novel reader.

She says in one place, "As an inducement to subscribe (to her library) Mrs. Martin tells me that her collection is not to consist only of novels but of every kind of literature. She might have spared this pretension to our family, who are great novel readers and not ashamed of being so."

There are frequent references to novels in her letters: "We have got *Fitz-Albini*, my father has bought it against my private wishes, for it does not quite satisfy my feelings that we should purchase the only one of Egerton's works of which his family are ashamed."

In another place: "To set against your new novel, of which nobody ever heard before, and perhaps never may again, we have got *Ida of Athens* by Miss Owenson, which must be very clever because it was written the authoress says in three months. We have only read the preface yet, but her Irish girl does not make me expect much. If the warmth of her language could affect the body it might be worth reading this weather." [January.]

There were many writers thought highly of at the time of their writing, who have yet dropped into oblivion to all but the student; among these is Jane Porter, born a year later than Jane Austen, who published her first romance, *Thaddeus of Warsaw*, in 1803, this was a great success, and immediately ran through several editions; it was followed in 1810 by her *chef d'œuvre The Scottish Chiefs*. In 1809, when it had just come out, and was anonymous, Hannah More's *Cœlebs in Search of a Wife* came into Cassandra's hands.

Jane writes of it: "You have by no means raised my curiosity after Caleb. My disinclination for it before was affected but now it is real. I do not like the evangelicals. Of course I shall be delighted when I read it like other people, but till I do, I dislike it." And in her next letter she replies to her sister, "I am not at all ashamed about the name of the novel, having been guilty of no insult towards your handwriting; the diphthong I always saw, but knowing how fond you were of adding a vowel wherever you could, I attributed it to that alone, and the knowledge of the truth does the book no service; the only merit it could have was in the name of Caleb, which has an honest unpretending sound, but in Cœlebs there is pedantry and affectation. Is it written only to classical scholars?"

Cœlebs itself it must be admitted is dull, unqualifiedly dull. Jane Austen's own books are not novels of plot, but they radiate plot in comparison. In *Cœlebs* a procession of persons stalks solemnly through the pages; they never reveal themselves by action, but are described as by a Greek chorus by the other characters in conversation or by the author, while long dry disquisitions on religion fill half, or more than half, of the book, and Cœlebs himself is a prig of the first water. Yet there are certain little touches which indicate a knowledge of human nature, such as that of the man who has married a beauty, "Who had no one recommendation but beauty. To be admired by her whom all his acquaintance admired gratified his *amour-propre*."

A book called *Self Control*, which appeared in 1810, by Mary Brunton, the wife of a Scotch minister, had a fair measure of success, and was reprinted as lately as 1852. Jane speaks very slightingly of it: "I am looking over *Self Control* again, and my opinion is confirmed of its being an excellently meant, elegantly written work, without anything of nature or probability in it. I declare I do not know whether Laura's passage down the American river is not the most natural possible every-day thing she ever does." Miss Mitford in regard to this book quotes the opinions of two men, one of whom said it ought to be burnt by the common hangman and the other that it ought to be written in letters of gold, which shows that public opinion was as various in those days as it is in these. In 1807, Jane mentions *Clarentine*, a novel of Sarah Burney's, who was a younger sister of the famous Miss Burney; though the same author brought out another novel later, it was evidently only because she followed in her sister's wake, and not from any inherent ability. Jane says, "We are reading *Clarentine* and are surprised to find how foolish it is. I remember liking it much less on a second reading than at the first, and it does not bear a third at all. It is full of unnatural conduct and forced difficulties, without striking merit of any kind."

But these impressions of long-forgotten books are hardly worth recording, except as specimens of the quantities of worthless novels to be had at the libraries then.

Samuel Rogers says, "Lane made a large fortune by the immense quantity of trashy novels which he sent forth from the Minerva press. I perfectly well remember the splendid carriage in which he used to ride, and his footmen with their cockades and gold-headed canes. Now-a-days as soon as a novel has had its run, and is beginning to be forgotten, out comes an edition of it as a standard novel."

In Miss Mitford's *Life* is given a list of the books which she had from the circulating library in a month, and which she presumably read, when she was a girl just back from school. It is here quoted as, with one or two exceptions, the titles tell the style of work in vogue.

"St. Margaret's Cave; St. Claire of the Isles; Scourge of Conscience; Emma Corbett; Poetical Miscellany; Vincenza; A Sailor's Friendship and a Sailor's Love; The Castles of Athlin and Dumbayn; Polycratia; Travels in Africa; Novice of St. Dominick; Clarentina; Leonora; Count de Valmont; Letters of a Hindu Rajah; Fourth Vol. of Canterbury Tales; The Citizen's Quarter; Amazement; Midnight Weddings; Robert and Adela; The Three Spaniards; De Clifford."

In his *History of Eighteenth Century Literature* Edmund Gosse says: "The flourishing period of the eighteenth century novel lasted exactly twenty-five years, during which time we have to record the publication of no less than fifteen eminent works of fiction. The fifteen are naturally divided into three groups. The first contains *Pamela*, *Joseph Andrews*, *David Simple* (Sarah Fielding) and *Jonathan Wild*. In these books the art is still somewhat crude, and the science of fiction incompletely understood. After a silence of five years we reach the second and greatest section of this central period, during which there appeared in quick succession, *Clarissa*, *Roderick Random*, *Tom Jones*, *Peregrine Pickle*, *Amelia* and *Sir Charles Grandison* . . . there followed another silence of five years, and then were issued each on the heels of the other, *Tristram Shandy*, *Rasselas*, *Chrysal*, *The Castle of Otranto* and *The Vicar of Wakefield*—five years later still—*Humphrey Clinker*, and then, with one or two such exceptions as *Evelina* and *Caleb Williams*, no great novel appeared again in England for forty years until in 1811 the new school of fiction was inaugurated by *Sense and Sensibility*."

Though we may not agree entirely with Mr. Gosse's classification, this paragraph is suggestive.

As we have seen in her brother's record, Jane's favourites in prose and poetry respectively were Johnson and Cowper. These two are mentioned in one sentence of hers: "We have got Boswell's *Tour to the Hebrides*, and are to have his *Life of Johnson;* and as some money will yet remain in Burdon's hands, it is to be laid out in the purchase of Cowper's works."

She warmly admired Cowper, which is hardly wonderful, for, with some manifest differences, Cowper was trying to do in poetry what she did in prose. He was utterly lacking, of course, in her light vivacity of touch and sense of humour, but he did genuinely try to describe what he saw, not what he merely knew by hearing. The green fields and full rivers of the Olney country are depicted with fidelity to detail and clearness of line. Cowper was born in 1731, but his first volume of verse was not published until 1782, and it was not until *The Task* appeared a year or two later, with *John Gilpin* in the same volume, that he really came to his own.

In 1798, Jane writes: "My father reads Cowper to us in the morning to which I listen when I can." This implies no disparagement of the poet, but merely that her numerous household duties did not always allow her time to listen. In Morland's picture, "Domestic Happiness," we have a scene which helps us to realise the family group at these readings. The mother and daughter in their caps, with elbow-sleeves and white kerchiefs, are dressed as Jane and her mother must have been, and the plain simplicity of the part of the room shown is quite in accordance with the rectory environment.

Another of Jane's favourite poets was Crabbe. Crabbe and Cowper are both rather heavy reading, and of both it may be said that their poetry is not poetical, but they are honestly seeking after truth and thus they attracted Jane Austen. They were amongst the earliest of the natural school which used the method of realism. Crabbe had a bitter struggle to obtain a hearing, but his struggle was over before 1796. Burke had taken him up, and in those days much depended

DOMESTIC HAPPINESS

on a patron. In 1781 he had published *The Library*, two years after *The Village*, and two years later again came *The Newspaper*, and then he did not bring out anything more until 1807.

It is, of course, very difficult to give any picture of contemporary literature in Jane Austen's time without degenerating into mere strings of names. The fact that she herself came in contact with no one of the first rank in literature prevents any of the characters from being woven into her life. The books she mentions as having read are a mere drop in the ocean compared with the books which came out in her time, and which she probably, in some cases almost certainly, read. It was a brilliant age as regards writing. Perhaps the best way to give some general idea of those writers not already mentioned will be to divide the time into three sections; and, without any attempt at being exhaustive, to mention generally the leading names among the writers who lived on into her epoch, but whose best work had been published before her time; those who actually were contemporary in the sense that their books, by which their names are known, were published in her lifetime; and those whose names had not begun to be known when she died, though the owners were born in her epoch.

First, then, those whose work was done; foremost among these was Johnson, who has already been mentioned.

Walpole was considerably past middle-age at her birth, and died in 1797; Wesley's collected *Works* came out in 1771, and he died in 1791; Adam Smith preceded him by a year.

The seventies in the eighteenth century produced numerous brilliant men and women whose names still live; besides Jane Austen herself, we have Sir Walter

Scott, Hazlitt, Sydney Smith, Lamb, Sir Humphry Davy, Coleridge, Southey, Wordsworth, Hogg, Thomas Moore, and Thomas Campbell, who were all born in this decade, though, as the development of a writer differs enormously in growth, some of them were much later in making their appearance in print than others. Among the better known names of women novelists not already mentioned we have Miss Edgeworth, Jane Austen's senior by eight years, whose first novel, *Castle Rackrent*, was published anonymously in 1800. That Jane knew and admired her work is obvious from the fact that she sent her a copy of *Emma* for a present on its publication. Mrs. Inchbald, born in 1753, was at first known as an actress, her *Simple Story*, by which she is best remembered, was published in 1791. Mrs. Radcliffe, whose romances induced Jane Austen to write *Northanger Abbey* in mockery, was very busy between 1789 and 1797, during which time she published five novels, including her famous *Mysteries of Udolpho* in 1794. Joanna Baillie published a volume of verse in 1790, and her first volume of plays in 1798; though almost forgotten now, she was taken very seriously in her time, and her play *De Montfort* was produced at Drury Lane in 1800 by Mrs. Siddons and Kemble. Anna Seward, who was born in 1747, lived to 1809; she, like Hannah More, was far more praised and valued than any of her poor little productions warranted.

Sheridan brought out his famous play *The Rivals* in the year of Jane's birth; it was at first a dead failure, but, nothing daunted, he cut it about and altered it, and when reproduced two years subsequently it attained success at once. The same year saw *The School for Scandal*, and the following one *The Critic*. In this year also the first volume of Gibbon's great History appeared.

Burns, who had written some of his best work while

Jane was still a child, died in 1796, and the brilliant Burke the succeeding year.

Just to give some general idea of the wonderful fruitfulness of this epoch it may also be mentioned that Samuel Rogers' *Pleasures of Memory* came out in 1792; *Lyrical Ballads*, including Coleridge's *Ancient Mariner* and some of Wordsworth's poems, in 1798; Campbell's *Pleasures of Hope* in 1799.

Byron was thirteen years younger than Jane, yet his precocity was so great that his first book, *Hours of Idleness*, was produced in 1807. The first two cantos of *Childe Harold* followed in 1812, but the whole poem was not completed until Jane was in her grave; the *Giaour*, *Corsair*, etc., she must have known as new books a year or two before her death.

Southey's *Thalaba* came out in the first year of the new century, and Thomas Moore published the first of his *Irish Melodies* in 1807.

Scott's literary career began with the publication of a translation of Burger's "Lenore" in 1799, between that date and 1814 his poems appeared at intervals, and in 1814 his first great novel *Waverley*. Though it was anonymous, Jane seems to have discovered the secret of the authorship, for she writes: "Walter Scott has no business to write novels, especially good ones. It is not fair. He has fame and profit enough as a poet and ought not to be taking the bread out of other people's mouths. I do not mean to like *Waverley* if I can help it, but I fear I must." But she was not the only one to make such a conjecture, for Miss Mitford having read *Waverley* also imputes it unhesitatingly to him, she says, "If there be any belief in internal evidence it must be his." Judging by these two specimens, the secret of Scott's anonymity was not the great mystery it is generally imagined to have been.

The third period, that of the great men who were actually contemporary with Jane Austen, though she was unconscious of their existence, as they did not win their laurels until after her death, is of course much less interesting, and may be quickly dismissed, such names as those of Lingard and Hallam among historians; Mill, Hazlitt, and De Quincey belong by right of birth to an earlier epoch, though their works place them in this.

Miss Ferrier and Miss Mitford, too, were not much younger than Jane Austen, but neither had brought out anything noticeable before her death. Miss Ferrier's first novel, *Marriage*, made its appearance in 1818; and though Miss Mitford had written poems, her *Our Village* first appeared in the *Lady's Magazine* only in 1819. As we have seen, Miss Mitford was a scholar at the same school as Jane Austen, though many years later. She was also a native of Jane's county, Hants.

In the last decade of the eighteenth century were born among poets: Shelley, Keats, Hood, Keble, and Mrs. Hemans; among historians, Grote, Alison, Napier, Carlyle, and Thirlwall; among men of science, Faraday and Lyell; and among novelists, Marryat.

In the beginning of the nineteenth century we have a string of great names; a trio of poets: Tennyson, Longfellow, and Browning; men of science such as Darwin; historians such as Macaulay; novelists in numbers, such as Dickens, Thackeray, Charles Reade, Harrison Ainsworth, Bulwer Lytton, and Trollope; statesmen such as Gladstone and Disraeli.

Perhaps no forty years that could have been chosen at any period of English history would have covered such a variety of talent, and that of such a high order, as was given to the world during Jane Austen's brief life.

And if she did not know personally the men whose names have lived with her own, at all events she drew from their works inspiration and knowledge, and she herself was not by any means the least among so mighty a company.

CHAPTER X

A TRIO OF NOVELS

WHEN Jane returned home in October, after her pleasant visit to Godmersham, she began her first real novel. She was then nearly twenty-one, and the girlish scribblings in which she had delighted began to be shaped into something more coherent. This very visit, with all its bright intercourse, all its pleasant variety,—for she had been thrown among a set of county people of better social standing than those she usually saw,—may have quickened the germ, and been the cause of her development. The book was at first called *First Impressions*, and under this title she herself frequently refers to it; but some time later she re-christened it by the name under which it was published.

The idea that the name *Pride and Prejudice* was suggested by some sentences at the end of *Cecilia* has been mooted, and though arguments against this supposition have been found, it appears extremely probable. For in *Cecilia* it is declared, " The whole of this unfortunate affair has been the result of PRIDE AND PREJUDICE," which last words are repeated twice on the same page, each time in large type so that they catch the eye. *Cecilia* itself might well have borne this title in reference to the pride and prejudice of the Delvile family. The book was published in 1786, and we know that Jane had a great admiration for Miss Burney's work. In re-

reading it some time subsequently it may very easily have struck her that "Pride and Prejudice" was an improvement on her own more common-place title, and there was nothing to prevent her adopting it. The repetition of two striking qualities and the alliteration may further have given rise to *Sense and Sensibility*, which also replaced an earlier title of *Elinor and Marianne*.

Pride and Prejudice was apparently written solely to gratify the instincts of the writer, without any thought of publication. But after it was completed, a year later, November 1797, Jane's father wrote for her to the well-known publisher Cadell as follows:—

"SIR,—I have in my possession a manuscript novel comprising 3 vols. about the length of Miss Burney's *Evelina*. As I am well aware of what consequence it is that a work of this sort should make its first appearance under a respectable name, I apply to you. I shall be much obliged therefore if you will inform me whether you choose to be concerned in it, what will be the expense of publishing it at the author's risk, and what you will venture to advance for the property of it, if on perusal it is approved of. Should you give any encouragement I will send you the work."

This proposal, modest as it is, was rejected by return of post. One would have thought that the success of Miss Burney's books would have made a leading publisher anxious to look at a work on similar lines, but no—*Pride and Prejudice* was destined not to be published until 1813, sixteen years later!

As we have said, it is unanimously accorded the premier place amongst Jane Austen's novels, partly because it is full of that brilliancy and sparkle which are its author's greatest characteristics, and partly because of the inimitable character of Elizabeth Bennet, whose combined archness and intelligence captivate everyone. Elizabeth is the embodiment of the heroine so many authors have tried to draw. Witty without being pert, having a reasonable conceit of herself without vanity, and a natural gaiety of heart that makes her altogether lovable. Whether she is repelling the patronage of Lady Catherine de Bourgh, or chaffing the sombre Darcy, she is equally delightful. Her first scene with Lady Catherine embodies much character—

"'Are any of your younger sisters out, Miss Bennet?'

"'Yes, Ma'am, all.'

"'All! What, all five out at once? Very odd! And you only the second. The younger ones out before the elder are married! Your younger sisters must be very young?'

"'Yes, the youngest is not sixteen. Perhaps she is full young to be much in company. But really, Ma'am, I think it would be very hard upon younger sisters that they should not have their share of society and amusement, because the elder may not have the means or inclination to marry early. The last born has as good a right to the pleasures of youth as the first. And to be kept back on such a motive! I think it would not be very likely to promote sisterly affection or delicacy of mind.'

"'Upon my word,' said her Ladyship, 'you give your opinion very decidedly for so young a person. Pray what is your age?'

"'With three younger sisters grown up,' replied Elizabeth, smiling, 'your Ladyship can hardly expect me to own it.'"

And again, when Lady Catherine comes to ask if the report of her nephew's engagement to Elizabeth is true.

"'If you believed it impossible to be true,' said Elizabeth, colouring with astonishment and disdain, 'I wonder you took the trouble of coming so far. What could your Ladyship propose by it?'

"'At once to insist on having such a report universally contradicted.'

"'Your coming to Langbourn to see me and my family,' said Elizabeth coolly, 'will be rather a confirmation of it; if, indeed, such a report is in existence.'

"'If! Do you then pretend to be ignorant of it? Has it not been industriously circulated by yourselves? Do you not know that such a report is spread abroad?'

"'I never heard that it was.'

"'And can you likewise declare there is no foundation for it?'

"'I do not pretend to possess equal frankness with your Ladyship. You may ask questions which I shall not choose to answer.'

"'This is not to be borne, Miss Bennet, I insist on being satisfied. Has he, has my nephew, made you an offer of marriage?'

"'Your Ladyship has declared it to be impossible.'"

Her verbal encounters with Darcy are equally characteristic.

"Elizabeth turned away to hide a smile.

"'Your examination of Mr. Darcy is over, I presume?' said Miss Bingley, 'and pray what is the result?'

"'I am perefctly convinced by it that Mr. Darcy has no defect. He owns it himself without disguise.'

"'No,' said Darcy, 'I have made no such pretension. I have faults enough, but they are not, I hope, of understanding. My temper I dare not vouch for. It is, I believe, too little yielding; certainly too little for the convenience of the world. I cannot forget the follies and vices of others so soon as I ought, nor their offences against myself. My feelings are not puffed about with every attempt to move them. My temper would perhaps be called resentful. My good opinion once lost is lost for ever.'

"'*That* is a failing indeed,' cried Elizabeth. 'Implacable resentment *is* a shade in a character. But you have chosen your fault well. I really cannot *laugh* at it. You are safe from me.'

"'There is, I believe, in every disposition a tendency to some particular evil, a natural defect, which not even the best education can overcome.'

"'And *your* defect is a propensity to hate everybody.'

"'And yours,' he replied with a smile, 'is wilfully to misunderstand them.'"

Darcy, by the way, is one of the least attractive of the principal men characters. It is inconceivable that any man with the remotest pretension to gentlemanly feeling should say, even to himself, much less aloud in a ball-room, on having his attention called to a young girl sitting out: "'Which do you mean?' and, turning round, he looked for a moment at Elizabeth, till, catching her eye, he withdrew his own, and coldly said,— 'She is tolerable; but not handsome enough to tempt me; and I am in no humour at present to give consequence to young ladies who are slighted by other men.'"

Indeed, Darcy's whole character is so averse from anything usually associated with the word gentleman, that one wonders where Miss Austen found her prototype. Possibly he was one of the few characters for which she drew entirely on her imagination. In saying this there is no innuendo that in other cases she drew straight from the life; it is, I believe, very few novelists who ever wish to do such a thing, but it is certainly true, and everyone who has attempted fiction knows it, that nearly every character in a life-like book has some prototype in real life, some man or woman who gave the first indication of a certain character; the personality may be altered entirely, it may be only one small quality which is derived from the prototype, but it is nevertheless that person who brought that particular character into existence. So far as we know there was no haughty, self-satisfied man of the world in Jane Austen's list of acquaintances.

It is true that Darcy is represented as behaving much better when his pride has been bitterly stung by Elizabeth's rejection of him, but it is hard to believe that a man, such as he is at first represented, could have had sufficient good in him to change his character completely as the effect of love.

To show how entirely opinions differ it is amusing to quote some of the remarks of Miss Mitford, who wrote in 1814, the year after the publication of *Pride and Prejudice*: "The want of elegance is almost the only want in Miss Austen. I have not read her *Mansfield Park* but it is impossible not to feel in every line of *Pride and Prejudice*, in every word of Elizabeth, the entire want of taste which could produce so pert, so worldly a heroine as the beloved of such a man as Darcy. Wickham is equally bad. Oh, they were just fit for each other, and I cannot forgive that delightful Darcy for parting them. Darcy should have married Jane. He is of all the admirable characters the best designed and the best sustained. I quite agree with you in preferring Miss Austen to Miss Edgeworth. If the former had a little more taste, a little more perception of the graceful, as well as of the humorous, I know not indeed anyone to whom I should not prefer her. There is none of the hardness, the cold selfishness, of Miss

Edgeworth about her writings; she is in a much better humour with the world; she preaches no sermons; she wants nothing but the *beau ideal* of the female character to be a perfect novel writer!"

Miss Mitford would no doubt have preferred as a heroine the elegant languishing female, without any of the savour of originality about her, who was the stereotyped heroine of most works of fiction at that time.

Sir Walter Scott in the *Quarterly Review* of 1815 makes the base insinuation that Elizabeth having refused Darcy "does not perceive that she has done a foolish thing, until she accidentally visits a very handsome seat and grounds belonging to her admirer."

We are sure from what we know of Lizzie, that this is quite unfounded. Had she been liable to any undue influence of that sort, she would have accepted Darcy at the first, for she knew very well all about his position and estates from the beginning. That she had the courage and good sense to snub him speaks much more forcibly for her character than a like action on the part of any girl similarly circumstanced would do now. For then a position gained by marriage was the only one a woman could hope for, and such chances were few and far between when, as we have seen, men were desperately prudent in their matrimonial affairs, and looked on marriage more as a well considered and suitable monetary alliance than as a love match, though perhaps the actual person of the woman was not always such a matter of perfect indifference to them as it seems to have been to the writer of the following contemporary letter:—

"I thank you with ye utmost Gratitude for ye good offices you was to have done me; and though I cannot now for Reasons above specifyd accept of them, yet I hope they will still continue in Reversion: not that I have any schemes for ever resuming my Designs upon

Miss A.: (on ye contrary I should be very loth she should wait so long) but because whenever my Time is come You are ye first person I should apply to, as having a good Number of Friends and Correspondents; and none who are priviledged with ye Intimacy of Mrs. Jennings can fail of Accomplishments to render them highly agreable to your most obedient servant." (*A Kentish Country House.*)

The character of the solemn, pompous, thick-skinned Mr. Collins is the best of the kind Jane ever drew; he is a creation whose name might signify a quality of " collinesqueness."

Perhaps within the limits possible for quotation there is nothing which in so short a space sums up so well his inimitable character as the letter of condolence he sends to Mr. Bennet on the occasion of Lydia's having eloped with the weak and untrustworthy Wickham.

" I feel myself called upon by our relationship and my situation in life, to condole with you on the grievous affliction you are now suffering under, of which we were yesterday informed by a letter from Hertfordshire. Be assured, my dear sir, that Mrs. Collins and myself sincerely sympathise with you, and all your respectable family, in your present distress, which must be of the bitterest kind, because proceeding from a cause which no time can remove. No arguments shall be wanting on my part, that can alleviate so severe a misfortune; or that can comfort you under a circumstance that must be of all others, most afflicting to a parent's mind. The death of your daughter would have been a blessing in comparison of this. And it is the more to be lamented, because there is reason to suppose, as my dear Charlotte informs me, that this licentiousness of behaviour in your daughter has proceeded from a faulty degree of indulgence; though, at the same time, for the consolation of yourself and Mrs. Bennet, I am inclined to think that her own disposition must be naturally bad, or she could not be guilty of such an enormity, at so early an age. This false step in one daughter will be injurious to the fortunes of all the others; for who, as Lady Catherine herself condescendingly says, will connect themselves with such a family? And this consideration leads me to reflect, with augmented satisfaction on a certain event of last November, for had it been otherwise I must have been involved in all your sorrow and disgrace. Let me advise you then, my dear sir, to console yourself as much as possible, to throw off your unworthy child from your affection for ever, and leave her to reap the fruits of her own heinous offence."

Jane's own impressions of *Pride and Prejudice* are given in a letter to her sister, written many years later, on the publication of the book—

"Miss B. dined with us on the very day of the book's coming, and in the evening we fairly set at it and read half the first vol. to her. . . . She was amused, poor soul! *That* she could not help you know, with two such people to lead the way, but she really does seem to admire Elizabeth. I must confess that I think her as delightful a creature as ever appeared in print, and how I shall be able to tolerate those who do not like *her* at least, I do not know. There are a few typical errors; and a 'said he' or a 'said she' would sometimes make the dialogue more immediately clear; but 'I do not write for such dull elves' as have not a great deal of ingenuity themselves. . . . Our second evening's reading to Miss B. had not pleased me so well, but I believe something must be attributed to my mother's too rapid way of getting on: though she perfectly understands the characters herself, she cannot speak as they ought. Upon the whole, however, I am quite vain enough and well satisfied enough. The work is rather too light and bright and sparkling; it wants shade, it wants to be stretched out here and there with a long chapter of sense if it could be had; if not, of solemn specious nonsense, about something unconnected with the story; an essay on writing, a critique on Walter Scott or the history of Buonaparte or something that would form a contrast, and bring the reader with increased delight to the playfulness and epigrammatism of the general style." And later, in reference to the same subject, she writes—

"I am exceedingly pleased that you can say what you do, after having gone through the whole work, and Fanny's praise is very gratifying. My hopes were tolerably strong of *her*, but nothing like a certainty. Her liking Darcy and Elizabeth is enough. She might hate all the others if she would." (Mr. Austen-Leigh's *Memoir*.)

The fact that Jane felt the extreme brilliancy and lightness of her own work shows that the critical faculty was active in her, but as for wishing to do away with it in order to bring the book more into conformity with the heavily padded novels of the time, that of course is pure nonsense.

After only the lapse of a month or two from the completion of *First Impressions,* Jane began on *Sense and Sensibility*, which she at first called *Elinor and Marianne*, and which, in the form of letters, had been written long before; probably, if the truth were known, this might be called her first long story, and it was in any case the first published. The story in letters has been wittily described as the "most natural but the most improbable" form; and certainly, though this style of novel had a brief renewal of popularity a year or two ago, it is one that is aggravating to most readers, and requires many clumsy expedients to fill in gaps in order to make the story hang together connectedly. Miss Burney had employed it with good effect in *Evelina*, but even here the story would have run much better told straightforwardly. In any case Jane was well advised to abandon this form. The novel was finished in 1798 but not published until 1811.

Sense and Sensibility, though it has never been placed first in position among Jane Austen's novels, has been accounted second by many people. The two sisters, Elinor and Marianne, who represent Sense and excessive Sensibility, are finely sketched. In this book the fact that Jane Austen's leading men are not equal to her leading women is clearly exemplified. Mr. Austin Dobson speaks of the "colourless Edward Ferrars and stiff-jointed Colonel Brandon," and the epithets are well deserved. We might add the selfish and unchivalrous Willoughby, for here may be noted a defect not uncommon in women-writers, an inability to grasp the code belonging to gentlemanly conduct. This is noticeable in the behaviour ascribed to Darcy in *Pride and Prejudice* already mentioned, but it is worse in the case of Willoughby, who is supposed to be brilliant, charming, and a gentleman, even though he acts badly by Marianne. His long explanation with Elinor, when Marianne lies on a sick-bed, and he himself is married, is supposed to atone for his bad behaviour; at all events it is made to exonerate him in Elinor's eyes, whereas, far from exonerating him in the eyes of any ordinary person, it shows him in a worse light than anything that has preceded.

It is only a scoundrel or cad of the weakest sort who speaks slightingly of his wife, though unfortunately the code for women is different, and many a woman "gives away" her husband on small enough grounds. Yet in spite of one of the most stringent and least frequently infringed rules of manly conduct, we find Willoughby saying, apparently without any debasement in his creator's eyes—

"'With my hand and heart full of your sister, I was forced to play the happy lover to another woman, . . . Marianne, beautiful as an angel, on one side . . . and Sophia, jealous as the devil, on the other hand.'" He then goes on to say that the letter sent in his name, which had cut poor Marianne to the heart, was dictated by his wife. "'What do you think of my wife's style of letter writing?—delicate—tender—truly feminine—was it not?'" and in excuse for his marriage, "'In honest words her money was necessary to me.'"

After this even Elinor feels bound to rebuke him, saying: "'You have made your own choice. It was not forced on you. Your wife has a claim to your politeness, to your respect, at least.'

"'Do not talk to me of my wife,'" he replies. "'She does not deserve your compassion. She knew I had no regard for her when we married.'"

In this book also there is a serious blot of another sort, a violation of probabilities, which suffices to score a heavy mark against it. In *Pride and Prejudice* there is certainly improbability in the fact that two portionless girls like Jane and Elizabeth Bennet should find such husbands as Bingley and Darcy, but the improbability is lessened by the fact that the pair of men were friends, and so one match contributes to the other; but in *Sense and Sensibility* the weak subterfuge for getting rid of Lucy Price, to whom Edward holds himself in honour bound, is hardly credible. There is no rational explanation of the obliging conduct of Robert Ferrars, Edward's brother; to make a man so vain and selfish marry a woman who could bring him nothing, and whose charms were not great, is a poor means of escaping from an undesirable deadlock.

There remain a few other points for comment. We have in Mrs. Dashwood one of the silly though fond mothers that Jane Austen delights to describe. In Mrs. Jennings we have the comic relief, not so clever as that supplied by Mr. Collins in *Pride and Prejudice* or by Miss Bates in *Emma*. A little too coarse for many people, but still true enough to the times, when the fact of a man's paying any attention to a girl at all was sufficient to make the gossips discuss their marriage and settlement in life with all openness.

The second chapter, often quoted, is one of the finest scenes in the whole book; here John Dashwood, mindful of his promise to his dying father, suggests giving each of his sisters a portion of one thousand pounds out of the magnificent estate which has come to him under the entail, but by the insidious arguments of his wife he at last settles it with his conscience to afford them such assistance "as looking out for a comfortable small house for them, helping them to move their things, and sending them presents of fish and game and so forth, whenever they are in season."

The cottage in which the Dashwoods were installed at Barton seems greatly to have resembled the cottage at Chawton. "As a house, Barton Cottage, though small, was comfortable and compact; but as a cottage it was defective, for the building was regular, the roof was tiled, the window-shutters were not painted green, nor were the walls covered with honeysuckles. A narrow passage led directly through the house into the garden behind. On each side of the entrance was a sitting-room about sixteen feet square and beyond them were the offices and the stairs. Four bedrooms and two garrets formed the rest of the house. It had not been built many years and was in good repair." But as *Sense and Sensibility* was written long before Jane went to live at Chawton, it is possible this account of the cottage was interpolated later, perhaps when she revised the book for publication in 1811.

On the whole, though interesting enough, *Sense and Sensibility* does not take very high rank among the novels. *Northanger Abbey* was begun in 1798, soon after the completion of *Sense and Sensibility*, and, unlike its predecessors, it does not seem to have been based on existing MSS., but to have been written as we now have it, though the writing was spread over a long period. It is the one of all Miss Austen's novels about which opinions differ most. It was written avowedly as a skit on the romantic school, whose high priestess was Mrs. Radcliffe; but, as Mr. Austin Dobson says: "The ironical treatment is not always apparent, and there are indications that, as often happens, the author's growing interest in the characters diverts her from her purpose." This is true enough, and the book certainly improves in consequence as it goes on, for at first it is sententious, and the author talks aside to her readers and explains her characters in a way that she does nowhere else. Archbishop Whateley remarks that it is "decidedly inferior to her other works—yet the same kind of excellences that characterise the other novels may be perceived in this to a degree which would have been highly creditable to most other writers of the same school, and which would have entitled the author to considerable praise had she written nothing better."

The scene of *Northanger Abbey* is laid in Bath, and it is easy to see how very well acquainted not only with the topography, but with the manners of Bath, Jane was. The chattering and running to and fro from Pump rooms to Upper or Lower Assembly rooms, the continual meetings, and the saunterings in the streets, with all the affected or real gaiety, and the magnifying of trifles, are cleverly sketched in the earlier part of the book. The sincere but foolish little heroine, with her contrast to and intense admiration for her silly and selfish friend, Isabella Thorpe, is a life-like figure. Her mother is one of the very few elderly ladies who are allowed to be sensible in Jane's books, and she comes in so little as to be a very minor figure.

The account of Bath society is one of the principal features of the book, another is that it abounds, perhaps more than any of the rest, in those three or four line summaries which express so admirably reflections, situations, and characters. Mrs. Thorpe's "eldest daughter has great personal beauty; and the younger ones by pretending to be as handsome as their sister, imitating her air, and dressing in the same style, did very well." "Mrs. Allen was now quite happy, quite satisfied with Bath. She had found some acquaintance—and as the completion of good fortune, had found these friends by no means so expensively dressed as herself." "Her [Catherine's] whole family were plain matter of fact people, who seldom aimed at wit of any kind; her father at the utmost being contented with a pun, and her mother with a proverb."

"The advantages of natural folly in a beautiful girl have been already set forth by the capital pen of a sister author, and to her treatment of the subject I will only add, in justice to men, that though, to the larger and more trifling part of the sex, imbecility in females is a great enhancement of their personal charms, there is a portion of them too reasonable, and too well informed themselves to desire anything more in woman than ignorance."

The rattle-pate Miss Thorpe is sketched with particular care, and if we may judge from other contemporary novels, including *Cecilia*, this was by no means an uncommon type at that day. Her conversation with Catherine on the novels she had read is worth giving at length. She asks: "'Have you gone on with *Udolpho*?'

"'Yes, I have been reading it ever since I woke; and I am got to the black veil.'

"'Are you indeed? How delightful! Oh, I would not tell you what is behind the black veil for the world! Are not you wild to know?'

"'Oh yes, quite! what can it be? But do not tell me, I would not be told on any account. I know it must be a skeleton, I am sure it is Laurentina's skeleton! Oh! I am delighted with the book! I should like to spend my whole life in reading it, I assure you; if it had not been to meet you I would not have come away from it for all the world.'

"'Dear creature! How much I am obliged to you; and when you have finished *Udolpho* we will read the *Italian* together; and I have made out a list of ten or twelve more of the same kind for you.'

"'Have you indeed? How glad I am! Where are they all?'

"'I will read you their names directly, here they are in my pocket-book. *Castle of Wolfenbach, Clermont, Mysterious Warnings, Necromancer of the Black Forest, Midnight Bell, Orphan of the Rhine,* and *Horrid Mysteries.* Those will last us some time.'

"'Yes, pretty well; but are they all horrid, are you sure they are all horrid?'

"'Yes, quite sure; for a particular friend of mine—a Miss Andrews—a sweet girl, one of the sweetest creatures in the world, has read every one of them. I wish you knew Miss Andrews, you would be delighted with her. She is netting herself the sweetest cloak you can conceive. I think her as beautiful as an angel, and

I am so vexed with the men for not admiring her! I scold them all amazingly for it.'

"'Scold them! Do you scold them for not admiring her?'

"'Yes, that I do. There is nothing I would not do for those who really are my friends. I have no notion of loving people by halves, it is not my nature. My attachments are always excessively strong. I told Captain Hunt at one of our assemblies this winter, that if he was to tease me all night, I would not dance with him unless he would allow Miss Andrews to be as beautiful as an angel. The men think us incapable of real friendship you know, and I am determined to show them the difference.'"

And shortly after she exclaims, "'For Heaven's sake! let us move away from this end of the room. Do you know there are two odious young men who have been staring at me this half hour. They really put me quite out of countenance! Let us go and look at the arrivals, they will hardly follow us there.'

" In a few moments Catherine with unaffected pleasure assured her that she need not be any longer uneasy, as the gentlemen had just left the Pump room.

"'And which way are they gone?' said Isabella, turning hastily round. 'One was a very good-looking young man.

"'They went towards the churchyard.'

"'Well, I am amazingly glad I have got rid of them! And now, what say you to going to Edgar's Buildings with me and looking at my new hat? You said you should like to see it.'

"Catherine readily agreed. 'Only,' she added, 'perhaps we may overtake the two young men.'

"'Oh! never mind that! If we make haste we shall

COWPER

pass by them presently, and I am dying to show you my hat.

"'But if we only wait a few minutes there will be no danger of our seeing them at all.'

"'I shall not pay them any such compliment, I assure you. I have no notion of treating men with such respect. That is the way to spoil them.'

"Catherine had nothing to oppose against such reasoning, and therefore to show the independence of Miss Thorpe and her resolution of humbling the sex, they set off immediately as fast as they could walk in pursuit of the two young men."

Perhaps *Northanger Abbey* may be described as the book which real Austenites appreciate most, but which the casual reader does not admire. The story is not interesting, the simplicity of Catherine rather irritating than attractive, and it is the form and the flashes of insight in the book that make it so enjoyable.

The writing, though begun in 1798, spread over a long period, for the book was not finished until 1803, by which time Jane herself was settled in Bath. It was then offered to a Bath bookseller, the equivalent of a publisher in our day. He gave ten pounds for it, probably because of the local colour, but evidently after reading it he found it lacked that melodramatic flavour to which he was accustomed; and it is also highly probable that he did not at all comprehend the delightful flavour of irony. The book remained with him, luckily in safety, until thirteen years had passed, when it was bought back by Henry Austen on his sister's account for the same sum that had been given for it. When the transaction had been completed he told the bookseller that it was by the author of *Sense and Sensibility*, which had attracted much attention, whereat the man must have experienced the regret he deserved to feel, as he had missed the honour of introducing Jane to the public, an honour that would have linked his name with genius.

The book did not appear until 1818, when the author was in her grave, and it was the first to bear her name on the title-page. It was published in one volume with the last of her writings, *Persuasion*. In a preface written before her death, she says of *Northanger Abbey*—Thirteen years have made it "comparatively obsolete, places, manners, books, and opinions have undergone considerable changes." It is evident, therefore, she did not attempt to bring it up to date. This preface is prefixed to the first edition, as is also the biographical Memoir by her brother which has already been referred to.

The few closing years of the eighteenth century, the last spent at Steventon, while these three works were in hand, must have been bright ones to Jane; she had found an outlet for all the vivacious humour that was in her, and must have lived in the world of fancy with her characters, which were all very real to her, quite as much as in the material world.

At this time her eldest brother James was living not far off, and on November 8, 1796, his wife had become the mother of a boy, named Edward. It was he who afterwards took the additional name of Leigh, affixed to that of Austen, and who published the Memoir of Jane Austen from which we have already drawn so much interesting detail. How little could Jane have dreamt that night when her brother sent over a note to tell her of the child's safe arrival in the world, that more than a hundred years later the work of that boy, describing her as one of the world's famous authoresses, would be read eagerly. It was only the preceding month that she had begun to work on the first of her delightful books. When she went to see the new baby she was allowed a glimpse of him while he was asleep, and was told that his eyes were "large, dark, and handsome." What a subject for a picture! She in her girlishness, quaintly dressed, bending over the cot of the infant, quite as unconscious of all that was to come as even the baby itself!

CHAPTER XI

THE NAVY

THE last few years of the century which passed so quietly at Steventon were times of continual change and stir in the larger world, a world in which both Francis and Charles Austen were taking an active part. But except for the personal matters that affected them, Jane does not refer to these events. It is true that from September 1796 to October 1798 we have no letters of hers, which may be due to the fact that she and her sister were not much parted then. This is one of the disadvantages of a correspondence carried on with such a near relation. But subsequently to this break the allusions to her brothers' promotions and prospects are fairly frequent.

"Admiral Gambier, in reply to my father's application writes as follows:—'As it is usual to keep young officers in small vessels, it being most proper on account of their inexperience, and it being also a situation where they are more in the way of learning their duty, your son has been continued in the *Scorpion*, but I have mentioned to the Board of Admiralty his wish to be in a frigate, and when a proper opportunity offers and it is judged that he has taken his turn in a small ship, I hope he will be removed. With regard to your son, now in London, I am glad I can give you the assurance that his promotion is likely to take place very soon, as Lord

Spencer has been so good as to say he would include him in an arrangement that he proposes making in a short time relative to some promotions in that quarter.'

"There, I may now finish my letter and go and hang myself, for I am sure I can neither write or do anything which will not appear insipid to you after this."

Again, "Frank is made. He was yesterday raised to the rank of Commander, and appointed to the *Petterel* sloop now at Gibraltar. . . . As soon as you have cried a little for joy you may go on, and learn further that the Indian House have taken Captain Austen's petition into consideration, and likewise that Lieutenant Charles John Austen is removed to the *Tamar* frigate."

Nearly a month later—

"Charles leaves us to-night, the *Tamar* is in the Downs and Mr. Daysh advises him to join her there directly, as there is no chance of her going to the westward. Charles does not approve of this at all, and will not be much grieved if he should be too late for her before she sails, as he may then hope to get into a better station."

And two days after, "I have just heard from Charles, who is by this time at Deal. He is to be second lieutenant, which pleases him very well. He expects to be ordered to Sheerness shortly as the *Tamar* has never been refitted."

Frank apparently remained on the *Petterel* until he received promotion in the beginning of 1801, for his sister writes jestingly: "So Frank's letter has made you very happy, but you are afraid he would not have patience to stay for the *Haarlem*, which you wish him to have done as being safer than the merchantman. Poor fellow, to wait from the middle of November to the end of December, and perhaps even longer, it must be sad work; especially in a place where the ink is so abominably pale. What a surprise to him it must have been on October 20, to be visited, collared, and thrust out of the *Petterall* by Captain Inglis. He kindly passes over the poignancy of his feelings in quitting his ship, his officers, and his men. What a pity it is that he should not be in England at the time of his promotion, because he certainly would have had an appointment, so everybody says, and therefore it must be right for me to say it too. Had he been really here, the certainty of the appointment, I dare say, would not have been half so great, but as it could not be brought to the proof, his absence will always be a lucky source of regret."

The real name of the ship was evidently the *Petrel*, but it is very variously spelt by other writers beside Jane, for orthography was not considered of great moment in the eighteenth century.

Captain Francis Austen had done good service on board and had well earned his promotion; in William James's *Naval History of Great Britain*, his name is mentioned with praise. On the 20th March, 1800, in the evening, while the *Mermaid*, a twelve-pounder thirty-two gun frigate, under Captain R. D. Oliver, and the ship sloop *Petrel*, under Captain Francis William Austen, were cruising together in the Bay of Marseilles, the *Petrel*, which was nearer the coast than the *Mermaid*, came into action with three armed vessels; two escaped by running on shore, but the third, the *Ligurienne* of " fourteen long six pounders two thirty-six pounder carronades all brass" and with one hundred and four men on board to the *Petrel's* eighty-nine,—for the first lieutenant and some of the crew were absent on prizes,—began to fight. They kept up a running fight of an hour and an half's duration, within two hundred and fifty yards, and sometimes half that distance. Then the *Ligurienne* struck her colours, her commander being shot. The *Petrel* was at that time only six miles from Marseilles. No one was hurt on the *Petrel*, though four of her twelve pounder carronades were upset, and the sails riddled with shot holes. The *Mermaid* apparently stood in the offing, giving moral support throughout. The *Ligurienne* was a fine vessel, only about two years old, and her capture must have meant good prize-money into the pockets of the captain and crew of the *Petrel*. After describing this action, Mr. James continues—

"Before quitting Captain Austen we shall relate another instance of his good conduct; and in which, without coming to actual blows, he performed an important and not wholly imperilous service." On the thirteenth of August, the *Petrel* being then attached to Sir Sydney Smith's squadron on the coast of Egypt, he was the means of burning a Turkish ship so as to prevent the French from stealing her guns, and for this service the Captain Pacha presented him with a handsome sabre and rich pelisse. Though his service seems to have landed the Turkish vessel "out of the frying-pan into the fire."

Charles Austen had seen active service when only a lad of fifteen, and both brothers frequently took part in the small actions which were continually occurring on the seas.

There was, as we have seen, six years' difference in age between them, but they were both at sea during some of the most glorious years in the whole annals of England. In spite of bad provisions, bad quarters, bad discipline, all of which will be again referred to, the English seamen at this time showed pluck and energy that was limitless. Britain was absolutely supreme on the seas. In 1794, Tobago, Martinique, St. Lucia, and Guadaloupe were all taken in less than a month. In the same year, Lord Howe, encountering twenty-six ships which the French by great exertions had sent to sea, manœuvred for three days, but on the "glorious first of June" bore down upon them and broke their line, captured six, and dispersed the rest, while 8000 men were killed or wounded on the French side against 1158 of the English. On September 16 of the following year, the Cape of Good Hope was taken by the English under Sir James Craig. The Dutch made an attempt to retake the Cape in 1796, but the whole of the armament they sent was captured by Admiral Elphinstone. In 1797 the Spaniards, who had declared war against Great Britain, put forth their full naval strength to attempt to raise the blockade which bound the ports of France. They were met by Sir John Jarvis, who had only fifteen ships of the line against their twenty-seven, and half the number of frigates.

By the well-known manœuvre the Admiral broke the Spanish line, cutting off a number of their ships, and when three of the largest wore round to rejoin their comrades, they were met by Nelson and Collingwood. Two of these Spanish ships got entangled with each other, and Nelson, driving his own vessel on board of one of them, carried both sword in hand, and received the sword of the Spanish Rear-Admiral in submission; this was afterwards awarded to him for his own possession. The Spaniards were totally routed and comparatively few ships were taken; the battle, which earned its commander the title of Lord St. Vincent, is considered one of the most important in the whole history of England.

In October of the same year, the battle of Camperdown was gained by Admiral Duncan, and these two victories together, by making the British complete masters of the home seas allayed for a while the terror of a French invasion. The mezzotint by James Ward from

Copley's famous picture, given in illustration, shows the variety of costume adopted by the British seamen at that time, the style of the officers' dress, and gives a very good idea of the appearance of the picturesque old wooden sailing-ships in which such heroic services were performed.

The most amazing part of this splendid series of victories, all of which contained much boarding and hand-to-hand fighting, demanding personal pluck and endurance, is, that the sailors, as a mass, were either unwilling men pressed into a service which they disliked, or the very off-scourings of the country. On board there was bad food, bad water, wretched accommodation, and often rank brutality. There was the discipline of terror not of respect, and insubordination was only held down by fear.

The officers fared a little better than the men in regard to comfort, but it speaks well for young Charles Austen that he followed in his brother's steps when he must have known by word of mouth of all the discomforts, to speak of nothing worse, which must be his lot on board ship.

For the sons of gentlemen, the first entrance into the navy was a most precarious venture, and the system, if system it can be called, so haphazard, that one marvels men should have been found to let their sons attempt it. A boy first obtained interest of some sort from an admiral or captain on board a ship, and was taken by him in any odd capacity for a voyage. He might go as " boy " or even as servant, and though nominally a midshipman, was in reality without a position or standing save what his patron allowed to him. He could not go in for an examination until he had served on board for six years, then he might do so to qualify for a lieutenancy. Once a lieutenant his position was secured, and he had authority and consequently a very different life. Captain

Edward Thompson, writing in the middle of the eighteenth century to a young relative who thought of following the sea for a trade, says, " Besides, the disagreeable circumstances and situations attending a subaltern officer in the navy, are so many and so hard, that, had not the first men in the service passed the dirty road to preferment, to encourage the rest, they would renounce it to a man. It is a most mistaken notion that a youth will not be a good officer unless he stoops to the most menial offices, to be bedded worse than hogs, and to eat less delicacies. In short, from having experienced such scenes of filth and infamy, such fatigues and hardships, that are sufficient to disgust the stoutest and bravest, for alas there is only a little hope of promotion sprinkled in the cup to make a man swallow more than he digests the rest of his life."

The wonder is that such boys as went to sea picked up enough seamanship to pass any but the most practical examination. Navigation was in those days even more difficult than at present, owing to the dependence on the wind and the necessity for understanding the exact management of sails. There were no engineers who could make the vessel go in any direction the captain thought best at a moment's notice; and the man on the bridge had a heavy responsibility.

That matters in regard to the service were improving is evident, for the same writer quoted above continues—

" The last war, a chaw of tobacco, a ratan, and a rope of oaths were sufficient qualities to constitute a lieutenant, but now education and good manners are the study of all."

Yet the surroundings on board ship were enough to prevent any but the most earnest and determined youth from studying; food and accommodation were alike revolting. "At once you resign a good table for no table, and a good bed for your length and breadth. Nay, it will be thought an indulgence too to let you sleep where day ne'er enters; and where fresh air only comes when forced. You must get up every four hours, and they never forget to call you, though you may forget to rise.

"Your light for day and night is a small candle which is often stuck on the side of your platter at meals for want of a better convenience. Your victuals are salt and often bad; and if you vary the mode of dressing them you must cook yourself ... in a man-of-war you have the collected filth of jails; condemned criminals have the alternative of hanging or entering on board. There is not a vice committed on shore but is practised here, the scenes of horror and infamy on board a man-of-war are so many and so great, that I think they must rather disgust a good mind than allure it."

Smollet's pictures of life on board are too well known to quote.

The between decks, where the men slept, had not been ventilated at all up to the middle of the eighteenth century, when a hand-pump was invented to expel the foul air, the fresh air being left to find its own way in. The noisome smells, the cramped space, the continual darkness and disorder, must have bred sickness and debility in many, which all the open-air life on deck could not counteract.

As for the food served for the men, it seems to have been loathsome. In *Tracts relating to the Victualling of the Navy*, we read of "sour tainted pickled meat. If such can be called food—human food—when dogs that I have offered it to have flaged their tails, ran away, and would not even smell to it;" of "rotten, musty, weevily flour," and "as for the butter, cheese, oil, raisins, they might have been expended, the cheese into ammunition, cast into cannon balls, the raisins as wadding, the butter and oil to grease their tackle with, for which it may be thought very fit—stinking slush. It is no longer a wonder at the pursers being tormented with execrations and bitter wrath from remediless, aggrieved, and tortured men on board."

It is said that any man who had been long a sailor, got into the habit of tapping his biscuit on the table to knock the weevils out before he ate it, a trick that old salts were seen to do at the tables of their friends on shore!

As for the state of the hospitals in India and elsewhere, the following story tells a tale. "Soon after the last action with the French fleet, I observed a wounded seaman, who had lost part of his hand by a shot, climbing up the side with one hand, and holding his bread bag in his teeth. I asked why he had left the hospital. He answered they were so much in want of provisions that he had come on board to beg some biscuit (which was full of maggots) for his messmates. At that time I understood Government was charged a rupee a day for every man in the hospital (about 1000 or 1500) but I believe seven or eight pence was all it cost the contractor for their provisions, and it was reported that he was obliged to share the profits with the admiral and his secretary, said to amount to about £70 a day."

We have had some revelations of official corruption recently, but there is nothing to compare with the openly recognised stealing of the eighteenth century, when, so late as 1783, a minister could say in earnest to a purser who had been a commissary and complained of poverty, "You had your hand in the bag, sir, why did you not help yourself?" And help themselves everyone apparently did, from the highest to the lowest. Enquiry first began to be made by Lord St. Vincent, who set himself to clean this Augean stable.

There being a prospect of a vacancy in the office of the Admiralty, a satirical correspondent to the *Morning Chronicle* in 1792 forwarded the following list of qualities essential for any candidate applying:—

He should know nothing of a ship.
He should never have been to sea.
He should be ignorant of geography.
He should be ignorant of naval tactics.
He should never attend office until four in the afternoon.
He should be unfit for business every day.
He should be very regular in keeping officers waiting for orders.
He should not know a bumboat from a three decker.
His hair should always be well dressed,
And his head should be empty!

Though matters were bad enough for the officers they were fifty times worse for the men, and it is not at all singular that men should have been procured with difficulty to enter a service where they were liable to all sorts of hardships; to great risk of life; where they were at the mercy of an irresponsible commander, who could order them to be strung up on the slightest provocation, and given any number of lashes he thought fit; where they could be hanged for disobeying or manifesting the smallest revolt to this tyrant; where prize-money, which was freely distributed to officers, sometimes never reached the men. There were instances of prize-money fairly due to the men being held over for a year or more as "not worth distributing."

The deficiency of men was, as we have seen, supplied by using the criminals of the gaols. Bounty money was also liberally offered, the authorities realising that a few pounds ready money were likely to be a valuable bribe to a man out of luck. The *St. James's Chronicle* remarks at the beginning of the war, "Five pounds bounty, and two pounds extra from the Corporation of London; surely no tars can be found backward."

In 1770 the Government had offered thirty shillings a head, which was augmented by various towns; London offering forty shillings additional, and Edinburgh forty-two shillings. In 1788 a prohibition forbidding seamen to serve in foreign navies was issued, and in 1791 the bounty money of London rose to two pounds for an ordinary seaman, and sixty shillings for an able seaman. The city added twenty shillings to the one, and forty shillings to the other at the beginning of the war in 1793. And in 1795 the total bounties in some places even amounted to thirty pounds a head!

In 1795 an Act was passed demanding levies of men from the whole country, the proportions varying according to the size of the county or port; from Yorkshire more than a thousand were demanded. In addition to this the pressgang was hard at work, and the monstrous injustice perpetrated by it makes one wonder how, even in times of greatest stress, it could have been allowed.

The difference between an ordinary press and a "hot press" was that in the latter all protection was disregarded, and men of every sort, even apprentices usually protected by law, were seized and carried off to serve, utterly regardless of mercy. The odd part of it is that, when it was found to be inevitable, the men who had been taken against their will plucked up spirit and performed their duties well.

John Ashton in *Old Times* quotes a number of cuttings from *The Times* of 1793 and 1794 giving details of these presses. "The press in the river Thames for the three last days has been very severe. Five or six hundred seamen have been laid hold of." (February 18, 1793.)

"A hot press has, for the last two nights, been carried on from London Bridge to the Nore; protections are disregarded, and almost all the vessels in the river have been stripped of their hands." (April 26, 1793.)

"Sailors are so scarce that upwards of sixty sail of merchant's ships bound to the West Indies, and other places, are detained in the river, with their ladings on board; seven outward bound East Indiamen are likewise detained at Gravesend, for want of sailors to man them." (January 7, 1794.)

"That part of Mr. Pitt's plan for manning the navy, which recommends to the magistrates to take cognizance of all idle and disorderly people, who have no visible means of livelihood, may certainly procure a great number of able-bodied men who are lurking about the Metropolis." (February 11, 1795.)

"There was a very hot press on the river on Friday night last, when several hundred able seamen were procured. One of the gangs in attempting to board a Liverpool trader, were resisted by the crew, when a desperate affray took place, in which many of the former were thrown overboard, and the lieutenant who boarded them killed by a shot from the vessel." (June 9, 1795.)

In 1798 all protection from the operations of the pressgang was suspended, even in the case of the coal trade, for one month!

To counterbalance all the manifold disadvantages of service in the navy, for the officers at least, there were some attractions; that of prize-money was very great, for a man might literally make his fortune at sea in a few years by lucky captures, and the spirit of gambling and adventure to which this gave rise must have had a very strong effect in attracting young officers.

The account of the sums received in prize-money is perfectly amazing; the best haul of all was perhaps the *Hermione*, a Spanish ship taken long before the Austens' day, in 1762. The treasure was conveyed to London in twenty waggons with the British colours flying over those of Spain, a sight that would confound those of our own time, who seem to think the true way to celebrate a victory is to give compensation to those who have provoked war, and brought defeat upon themselves! The share of one ship alone, the *Active*, amounted to over £250,000; and the proportion given to the ships of the same squadron not actually present amounted to nearly £67,000. The value of the *St. Jago*, taken in 1793, as adjudged to the captors was £935,000, of which about £100,000 went to Admiral Gell. (*The Times*, February 4, 1795.) Each captain got nearly £14,000.

In 1801, Jane tells us that "Charles has received £30 for his share of the privateer and expects ten pounds more, but of what avail is it to take prizes if he lays out the produce in presents to his sisters? He has been buying gold chains and topaz crosses for us. He must be well scolded."

After this it does not seem so strange to read in *Persuasion* that in only seven years Anne's lover, Wentworth, "had distinguished himself, and early gained the other step in rank, and must now, by successive captures, have made a handsome fortune," which otherwise strikes oddly on our ears.

The abuses in the navy included those of interest, which in those days honeycombed every branch of professional life. Lord Rodney made his son John a

VICTORY OF LORD DUNCAN (CAMPERDOWN) 1797

post captain after he had been a midshipman little over a month, and when he was just over fifteen years old. But this, at a time when boys of fourteen held commissions in the Guards, must have seemed a trifle. Mrs. Lybbe Powys, speaking of her brother-in-law, says—

"Our young officer is what I fear too generally young men in the army are, gay, thoughtless, and very handsome; but what boy of fourteen, having a commission in the Guards, can be otherwise?"

The Times of 1797 speaks of the "baby officers," and says—

"Some of the sucking colonels of the Guards have expressed their dislike of the short skirts. They say they feel as if they were going to be flogged."

A peculiar feature of the end of the eighteenth and beginning of nineteenth centuries was the tendency to mutiny, induced doubtless by the terrible hardships and injustices undergone by the men on board. And the wonder is, not that the men did mutiny, but that they endured so long and fought so splendidly without doing so.

Some of the mutineers on board the *Téméraire*, in the beginning of the nineteenth century, are thus described by an eye-witness. "They were the noblest fellows, with the most undaunted mien, I ever beheld—the beau ideal of British sailors; tall and athletic, well-dressed, in blue jackets, red waistcoats, and trousers white as driven snow. Their hair like the tail of the lion, hung in a queue down their back. At that time this last article was considered, as indeed it really was, the distinguishing mark of a thoroughbred seaman. Unfortunately, these gallant fellows were as ignorant as they were impatient, and the custom of the time was to hang everyone who should dare to dispute the orders of his superior officers."

Of the mutinies the most serious were those at Spithead and the Nore, which followed closely upon one another. After the first, concessions in regard to pay and various improvements in commissariat were granted; and both mutinies were put down firmly and sharply, but they were followed from time to time by lesser outbreaks.

All these excitements, and the constant changes in the pay of officers, must have been watched with interest by the Austen family, whom they touched so nearly. Jane certainly understood the best type of naval officer, and had no little admiration and affection for him.

The officers in her novels may easily be divided into two sorts, they are the officers of the old school, of which Admiral Crawford, in *Mansfield Park*, to whom his nephew and niece were indebted for their bringing up, is a prominent example. Here is the aforesaid niece's account of the type, when Edmund Bertram asks her whether she has not a large acquaintance in the navy. "'Among admirals, large enough, but,' with an air of grandeur, 'we know very little of the inferior ranks. Post captains may be very good sort of men, but they do not belong to us. Of various admirals I could tell you a great deal; of them and their flags, and the gradation of their pay, and their bickerings and jealousies. But in general, I can assure you that they are all passed over and all very ill-used. Certainly my home at my uncle's brought me acquainted with a circle of admirals. Of Rears and Vices I saw enough. Now, do not be suspecting me of a pun, I entreat.'"

Mr. Price, Fanny's father, who is in the Marines, with his noise, and his oaths, and his coarseness and ill-temper, is a terrible revelation to his gentle daughter.

On the other side of the scale we may set Admiral Croft in *Persuasion*, a polished and delightful man, " rear-admiral of the white. He was in the Trafalgar action, and has been in the East Indies since; he has been stationed there, I believe, several years."

The younger generation of sailors is represented charmingly in the novels from Fanny's admirable, straightforward, single-minded brother William, who, when he came to Mansfield Park shortly after getting promoted to his lieutenancy, " would have been delighted to show his uniform there too, had not cruel custom prohibited its appearance except on duty. So the uniform remained at Portsmouth, and Edmund conjectured that before Fanny had any chance of seeing it, all its own freshness, and all the freshness of its wearer's feelings must be worn away; for what can be more unbecoming or more worthless than the uniform of a lieutenant who has been a lieutenant a year or two, and sees others made commanders before him."

Captain Wentworth, Anne's lover, who had been treated so cruelly in deference to the wishes of her family, is gallant, handsome, charming, a man of the world, without having lost his freshness, and a man who has won his way and yet been unspoiled by flattery; he is one of the best of Jane Austen's heroes.

CHAPTER XII

BATH

AT the end of 1800, Mr. Austen made up his mind to put his son James into the rectory at Steventon as *locum tenens*, and himself retire to live at Bath. In those days parents were not quite so communicative to their children as they are now; many things were decided without being discussed in full family conclave, as propriety dictates at present, and the change of plan does not seem to have been mooted to the girls at all, so that, " coming in one day from a walk, as they entered the room their mother greeted them with the intelligence : 'Well, girls, it is all settled. We have decided to leave Steventon and go to Bath.' To Jane, who had been from home, and who had not heard much before about the matter, it was such a shock that she fainted away . . . she loved the country, and her delight in natural scenery was such that she would sometimes say it must form one of the delights of heaven." (From Family MSS. quoted by Constance Hill, in *Jane Austen, Her Homes and Her Friends.*)

The break up of the home of one's childhood is no trifling matter, and it often carries with it removal from many friends and neighbours whose society has become an integral part of life. It is no wonder that the blow was severe, yet Jane was of a cheerful disposition, a disposition that could make its own happiness anywhere, and it was not long before she entered with alacrity into all the needful preparations.

She wrote not long after, "I get more and more reconciled to the idea of our removal. We have lived long enough in this neighbourhood; the Basingstoke balls are certainly on the decline; there is something interesting in the bustle of going away, and the prospect of spending future summers by the sea or in Wales is very delightful. For a time we shall now possess many of the advantages which I have often thought of with envy in the wives of sailors or soldiers. It must not be generally known, however, that I am not sacrificing a great deal in quitting the country, or I can expect to inspire no tender interest in those we leave behind."

Mr. Austen was perfectly justified in his decision to stop work; he was then seventy, and had held the two livings for thirty-six years, his son James was ready to take them up, he was living in the neighbourhood, and had been of assistance to his father for some time past. We learn this from many casual sentences in the letters, such as the following: "James called by my father's desire on Mr. Bayle to enquire into the cause of his being so horrid. Mr. Bayle did not attempt to deny his being horrid, and made many apologies for it; he did not plead his having a drunken self, he talked only of a drunken foreman, etc., and gave hopes of the tables being at Steventon on Monday se'nnight next."

Mr. Austen died in 1805, only four years after the removal, which shows that he had not withdrawn from active life at all too soon. In giving up country life he had to give up also many of the hobbies in which he had taken delight; his pigs and his sheep could not accompany him to Bath. References to these animals often occur in his daughter's lively letters. " My father furnishes him [Edward] with a pig from Cheesedown; it is already killed and cut up, but it is not to weigh more than nine stone; the season is too far advanced to get him a larger one. My mother means to pay herself for the salt and the trouble of ordering it to be cured, by the spareribs, the souse, and the lard."

" Mr. Lyford gratified us very much yesterday by his praises of my father's mutton, which they all think was the finest that was ever ate."

" You must tell Edward that my father gave twenty-five shillings apiece to Seward for his last lot of sheep."

In Bath, pigs, poultry, and a garden would be impossible, but there would be compensating advantages. The country life had but narrow interests, and trifles had to be made the most of.

Jane's letters for the last few years before leaving Steventon show some of the decadence due to trivial surroundings, and her remarks are apt to be spiced with unkindness. Evidently her sister-in-law, James's wife, was not a favourite; she objected to her husband's being so much at Steventon, though Jane notes that he persevered in coming " in spite of Mary's reproaches." But Jane's sharpness is also extended to her remarks on her acquaintances. " The Debaries persist in being afflicted at the death of their uncle, of whom they now say they saw a great deal in London."

Poor Debaries, it is quite possible that his death had showed them how much they had cared for him, at all events, after his death they could have had nothing to gain by any display of affection !

After a small ball Jane writes : " There were very few beauties, and such as there were were not very handsome. Miss Iremonger did not look well, and Mrs. Blount was the only one much admired. She appeared exactly as she did in September, with the same broad face, diamond bandeau, white shoes, pink husband, and fat neck. The two Miss Coxes were there; I traced in one the remains of the vulgar, broad-featured girl who danced at Enham eight years ago; the other is refined into a nice composed-looking girl like Catherine Bigg. I looked at Sir Thomas Champneys and thought of poor Rosalie; I looked at his daughter, and thought her a queer animal with a white neck." And later she adds: "I had the comfort of finding out the other evening who all the fat girls with long noses were that disturbed me at the 1st H. ball." It is obvious that a wider horizon would do the writer of these remarks no harm.

The income which the family would have is indicated in the following remark of Jane's made about this time: "My father is doing all in his power to increase his income, by raising his tithes, etc., and I do not despair of getting very nearly six hundred a year."

Once the great fact of the removal was settled, there remained the minor difficulty as to which part of Bath would be the best to live in; of this Jane writes: "There are three parts of Bath which we have thought of as likely to have houses in them—Westgate Buildings, Charles Street, and some of the short streets leading from Laura Place or Pulteney Street. Westgate Buildings, though quite in the lower part of the town, are not badly situated themselves. The street is broad and has rather a good appearance. Charles Street, however, I think is preferable. The buildings are new, and its nearness to Kingsmead Fields would be a pleasant circumstance. Perhaps you may remember, or perhaps you may forget, that Charles Street leads from the Queen's Square Chapel to the two Green Park Streets. The houses in the streets near Laura Place I should expect to be above our price. Gay Street would be too high, except only the lower house on the left hand side as you descend. Towards that my mother has no disinclination; it used to be lower rented than any other house in the row, from some inferiority in the apartments. But above all others her wishes are at present fixed on the corner house in Chapel Row which opens into Prince Street. Her knowledge of it, however, is confined only to the outside, and therefore she is equally uncertain of its being really desirable as of its being to be had. In the meantime she assures you that she will do everything in her power to avoid Trim Street, although you have not expressed the fearful presentiment of it, which was rather expected. We know that Mrs. Perrot will want to get us into Oxford Buildings, but we all unite in particular dislike of that part of the town, and therefore hope to escape." This was from Steventon in January 1801.

The Mrs. Perrot is the aunt, Mrs. Leigh-Perrot, before mentioned, she was sister-in-law to Mrs. Austen, and her husband had taken the additional name of Perrot. It was from him that Mr. Austen-Leigh inherited the additional name of Leigh when he came into the estate. The Austen family seem to have been almost as much in the habit of changing their names as of marrying twice.

The topography of the letter can only be appreciated by those who know Bath, and requires little comment. The various streets mentioned are still existing, and we can pass through the despised Trim Street, survey the house in Gay Street lower rented than the others, or cross over the river to Laura Place to see the neighbourhood Jane feared would be too expensive, just as well now, as she could then.

In May of 1801, Jane, with her father and mother, went to Bath and stayed with Mr. and Mrs. Leigh-Perrot at Paragon, in order to hunt for a house,

Paragon remains unchanged, the doorways enclosed by pent-house and pilasters remain the very type of late eighteenth-century architecture.

It is easy to imagine the difficulties that had to be encountered by the Austens in their quest.

"In our morning's circuit we looked at two houses in Green Park Buildings, one of which pleased me very well. We walked all over it except into the garret; the dining-room is of a comfortable size, just as large as you like to fancy it; the second room about fourteen feet square. The apartment over the drawing-room pleased me particularly, because it is divided into two, the smaller one, a very nice sized dressing-room which upon occasion might admit a bed. The aspect is south-east. The only doubt is about the dampness of the offices, of which there were symptoms."

"Yesterday morning we looked into a house in Seymour Street which there is reason to suppose will soon be empty; as we are assured from many quarters that no inconvenience from the river is felt in those buildings, we are at liberty to fix on them if we can. But this house was not inviting; the largest room downstairs was not much more than fourteen feet square, with a western aspect."

"I went with my mother to look at some houses in New King Street, towards which she felt some kind of inclination, but their size has now satisfied her. They were smaller than I expected to find them; one in particular out of the two was quite monstrously little; the best of the sitting-rooms not as large as the little parlour at Steventon, and the second room in every floor about capacious enough to admit a very small single bed."

"Our views on G.P. Buildings seem all at an end; the observation of the damp still remaining in the offices of a house which has only been vacated a week, with reports of discontented families and putrid fevers, has given the *coup-de-grace*. We have now nothing in view."

Anyone who has ever been house-hunting will sympathise with the difficulties sketched in these remarks. It was finally decided that the family should go to 4 Sydney Place, and later they removed to the despised Green Park Buildings after all.

The sale of the effects at Steventon had begun before the family left, and continued after.

"My father and mother, wisely aware of the difficulty of finding in all Bath such a bed as their own, have resolved on taking it with them; all the beds, indeed, that we shall want are to be removed. . . . I do not think it will be worth while to remove any of our chests of drawers, we shall be able to get some of a much more commodious sort, made of deal, and painted to look very neat . . . we have thought at times of removing the sideboard, or a Pembroke table, or some other piece of furniture, but on the whole it has ended in thinking that the trouble and risk of the removal would be more than the advantage of having them at a place where everything may be purchased."

In another letter she imagines that the appraisement of the furniture for sale will amount to about two hundred pounds, and when actually at Bath she sends the following details:—

"Sixty-one guineas and a half for the three cows gives one some support under the blow of only eleven guineas for the tables. Eight for my pianoforte is about what I really expected to get." "Mr. Bent seems bent upon being very detestable, for he values the books at only seventy pounds. Ten shillings for Dodsley's Poems, however, please me to the quick, and I do not care how often I sell them again for as much."

Sydney Place is on the east side of the River overlooking Sydney Gardens, which had been opened for public entertainment in 1795; the following description of the Gardens is given in a guide contemporary with Jane's residence in Bath. "The Kennet and Avon Canal runs through the garden, with two elegant cast-iron bridges thrown over it, after the manner of the Chinese. There are swings, bowling greens, and a Merlin's swing in the labyrinth. During the summer are public nights, with music, fireworks, and superb illuminations." Before Jane herself lived here, while she was staying in Queen Square with her brother and his family, she had been to a grand gala in Sydney Gardens, with illuminations, and fireworks which "surpassed" her expectations. It was a pleasant part of Bath, and probably the Austens were comfortable enough here. The house is still standing; it is one of a solid uniform row facing nearly due east, and bears a plate stating "Here lived Jane Austen from 1801–1805," an inscription not quite accurate as the Austens left in 1804. It is one great charm of Bath that, electric trams and modern buildings notwithstanding, the place is so very much the same as it was when Jane knew it. The narrow intricate streets, the little courts and passages, and jutting houses are everywhere to be seen. The town is essentially late eighteenth century, and the modern buildings are mere additions that do not in any way interfere with its character.

The beautiful abbey had in her time been more or less repaired, and the choir was used as a parish church. But the pinnacles were added to the spire only in 1834, and the complete restoration took place in 1874. The Pump Room, near at hand, was built in 1796, replacing one which had existed for forty-five years. If we except a few trifles, such as electric pendants to the great central chandelier, we see it as it was in Jane's day. The fluted pilasters running up to the ceiling are very characteristic of the florid Georgian taste. In a print of the interior of the Pump Room, dated 1804, we see all the women, even the attendants, with bare arms and necks, quite uncovered,—a fashion revived in 1905,—and some of the women wear a kind of modified poke-bonnet with "coquelicot" plumes. In the alcove at the end is a statue of fat little Beau Nash, who was the regenerator and in some sense the maker of Bath.

But Nash's name is associated even more with the Assembly Rooms than the Pump Room. The Assembly Rooms are some distance from the Pump Rooms and the Baths, being situated not far from the famous crescent. In Jane's time there were two sets of Assembly Rooms, upper and lower, governed by two different masters of the ceremonies, positions which were much coveted. In 1820 the Lower Rooms were burnt down and not rebuilt, but the Upper are still used, and the names over the doors of the rooms, Card-room, Tea-room, etc., recall many a scene in Jane Austen's novels.

Bath really began to be fashionable in the early part of Queen Anne's reign, but it was Nash who consolidated its attractions, and brought it up to its highest pitch of popularity.

When he went there "the amusements of the place were neither elegant nor conducted with delicacy. General society among people of rank or fortune was by no means established. The nobility still preserved a tincture of Gothic haughtiness, and refused to keep company with the gentry at any of the public entertainments of the place. Smoking in the rooms was permitted; gentlemen and ladies appeared in a dis-

FAÇADE OF THE PUMP ROOM, BATH, IN THE EIGHTEENTH CENTURY

respectful manner at public entertainments in aprons and boots. With an eagerness common to those whose pleasures come but seldom, they generally continued them too long, and thus they were rendered disgusting by too free an enjoyment. If the company liked each other they danced till morning. If any person lost at cards he insisted on continuing the game till luck should turn. The lodgings for visitants were paltry, though expensive, the dining-rooms and other chambers were floored with boards coloured brown with soot and small beer to hide the dirt; the walls were covered with unpainted wainscot, the furniture corresponded with the meanness of the architecture; a few oak chairs, a small looking-glass, with a fender and tongs, composed the magnificence of these temporary habitations. The city was in itself mean and contemptible, no elegant buildings, no open streets, no uniform squares."

Thither Nash came in 1705. He was the man of all others to organise fashionable entertainments. Under his severe, yet fatherly rule, the place sprang quickly into popularity. Houses were built, streets repaved, balls and entertainments followed each other in quick succession. An Assembly Room was built, and good music engaged; but it was not until 1769, eight years after Nash's death, that the present building was erected. Nash's code of rules continued in force for long after his death, before which he had sunk from the position of esteem which he had once enjoyed. His rules throw some light on the conduct of these delightful assemblies, and are worth quoting—

1. That a visit of ceremony at first coming, and another at going away, are all that are expected or desired by ladies of quality and fashion—except impertinents.

2. That ladies coming to the ball appoint a time for their footmen coming to wait on them home, to prevent disturbance and inconvenience to themselves and others.

3. That gentlemen of fashion never appearing in a morning before the ladies in gowns and caps show breeding and respect.

4. That no person take it ill that anyone goes to another's play or breakfast and not theirs; except captious by nature.

5. That no gentleman give his ticket for the balls to any but gentlewomen. N.B.—Unless he has none of his acquaintance.

6. That gentlemen crowding before the ladies at the ball show ill manners; and that none do so for the future except such as respect nobody but themselves.

7. That no gentleman or lady takes it ill that another dances before them; except such as have no pretence to dance at all.

8. That the elder ladies and children be content with a second bench at a ball, as being past or not come to perfection.

9. That the younger ladies take notice how many eyes observe them.

10. That all whisperers of lies or scandal be taken for their authors.

11. That all repeaters of such lies and scandal be shunned by the company; except such as have been guilty of the same crime.

Nash's rigour in regard to appearances in the case of top-boots is elsewhere mentioned, he disliked quite as much the aprons which smart ladies then wore on many occasions, and when the Duchess of Queensberry entered one evening in one of these, he snatched it off and flung it over the back benches among the ladies' maids.

The rules for balls were probably very much the same when Jane Austen attended them as when Nash was living. Everything was to be performed in proper order. Each ball was to open with a minuet danced by two persons of the highest distinction present. When the minuet concluded the lady was to return to her seat, and Mr. Nash was to bring the gentleman a new partner. The minuets generally continued two hours. At eight the country dances began, ladies of quality according to their rank standing up first. About nine o'clock a short interval was allowed for rest, and for the gentlemen to help their partners to tea, the ball having begun, it must be remembered, about six. The company pursued their amusements until the clock struck eleven, when the music ceased instantly; and Nash never allowed this rule to be broken, even when the Princess Amelia herself pleaded for one dance more.

Among other rules was one mentioned by Mr. Austen-Leigh, that ladies who intended to dance minuets were requested to wear lappets to distinguish them. Also, in order that every lady may have an opportunity of dancing, gentlemen should change their partners every two dances. We see in this last rule how the transition from one partner for the whole evening to the continual change of partners came to pass.

After returning from Lyme Regis in the autumn of 1804, the Austens left Sydney Place, and went to Green Park Buildings, which had been among the houses first considered. They were here when Mr. Austen's death occurred in January 1805; and then Mrs. Austen and her daughters moved into lodgings in Gay Street.

Mrs. Lybbe Powys gives us a lively word-picture of Bath in 1805—

"The Dress Ball, Upper Rooms immensely crowded at ten; but the number of card parties quite spoilt the balls, as 'tis fashionable to attend five or six before you go to the room. It was endeavoured to alter these hours, but fortunately for the old people, and those who drink the waters, it was not permitted, and at eleven, if in the middle of a dance, the music stops. But I suppose 'tis reckoned vulgar to come early, one sees nothing of the dancing or company for the crowds. The rooms are not half so agreeable as they were some years ago, when the late London hours were not thought of; and how prejudicial must they be to the health of all, is very visible in the young as in the old. . . . Sixteen thousand strangers at Bath in the season 1805!"

Of Bath itself we hear in the satirical skit called *The New Guide*—

> "Of all the gay places the world can afford,
> By gentle and simple for pastime adored,
> Fine balls, and fine concerts, fine buildings and springs,
> Fine walks and fine views and a thousand fine things,
> Not to mention the sweet situation and air,
> What place, my dear mother, with Bath can compare?"

There is little reason to doubt that Jane would thoroughly enjoy the change afforded by such constant opportunity for diversion, such delightful mingling with a crowd in which her bright humour must have found frequent opportunities for indulgence.

As we have seen, she had written her first Bath book, *Northanger Abbey*, many years before, and while she sat in the Pump Room, awaited a partner in the Assembly Rooms, or shopped in Milsom Street, she must have recalled her own creations, Catherine Morland and Isabella Thorpe, Henry Tilney and Mrs. Allen, quite as vividly as if they were real persons of her acquaintance.

The second Bath book, *Persuasion*, was not written until many years after, yet these two, chronologically so far apart, topographically so near each other, have always been, owing to conditions of length, bound together.

This is Jane's own account of her first ball after coming to live at Bath: "I dressed myself as well as I could, and had all my finery much admired at home. By nine o'clock my uncle, aunt, and I entered the Rooms, and linked Miss Winstone on to us. Before tea it was rather a dull affair; but then tea did not last long, for there was only one dance, danced by four couple, think of four couple surrounded by about an hundred people dancing in the Upper Rooms at Bath! After tea we cheered up; the breaking up of private parties sent some scores more to the ball, and though it was shockingly and inhumanly thin for this place, there were people enough, I suppose, to have made five or six very pretty Basingstoke assemblies."

It is interesting to compare this with her account of her heroine, Catherine Morland's first appearance: "Mrs. Allen was so long in dressing, that they did not enter the ball-room till late. The season was full, the room crowded, and the two ladies squeezed in as well as they could. As for Mr. Allen he repaired directly to the card-room and left them to enjoy a mob by themselves. With more care for the safety of her new gown than for the comfort of her protegée, Mrs. Allen made her way through the throng of men by the door, as swiftly as the necessary caution would allow; Catherine, however, kept close at her side, and linked her arm too firmly within her friend's to be torn asunder by any common effort of a struggling assembly. But to her utter amazement she found that to proceed along the room was by no means the way to disengage themselves from the crowd; it seemed rather to increase as they went on; whereas she had imagined that when once fairly within the door, they should easily find seats, and be able to watch the dances with perfect convenience. But this was far from being the case; and though by unwearied diligence they gained even the top of the room, their situation was just the same; they saw nothing of the dancers, but the high feathers of some of the ladies. Still they moved on, something better was yet in view; and by a continued exertion of strength and ingenuity they found themselves at last in the passage behind the highest bench. Here there was something less of crowd than below; and hence Miss Morland had a comprehensive view of all the company beneath her, and of all the dangers of her late passage through them. It was a splendid sight, and she began, for the first time that evening, to feel herself at a ball, she longed to dance, but she had not an acquaintance in the room. . . . Everybody was shortly in motion for tea, and they must squeeze out like the rest . . . and when they at last arrived in the tea-room . . . they were obliged to sit down at the end of a table, at which a large party were already placed, without having anything to do there, or anybody to speak to except each other. . . . After some time they received an offer of tea from one of their neighbours; it was thankfully accepted, and this introduced a light conversation with the gentleman who offered it, which was the only time that anybody spoke to them during the evening, till they were discovered and joined by Mr. Allen when the dance was over.

"'Well, Miss Morland,' said he directly, 'I hope you have had an agreeable ball.'

"'Very agreeable indeed,' she replied, vainly endeavouring to hide a great yawn."

But poor Catherine was much more fortunate in her second essay, being introduced to Henry Tilney, the hero, who captivated her girlish admiration, and who at last, struck by her *naïveté* and earnest affection for himself, fell in love with her and made her his wife.

In *Northanger Abbey*, Jane places the Thorpes in Edgar Buildings, which she always spells "Edgar's," the Tilneys in Milsom Street, and Catherine Morland with the Allens in Pulteney Street. Her topography is always very exact and unimpeachable. Milsom Street also plays a large part in *Persuasion*. It is here that Anne comes across Admiral Croft looking into a print shop window, from whence he accompanies her back to Camden Place where her father and sister are, and in the course of the walk Anne learns, to her infinite relief, that Louisa Musgrove is engaged to Captain Benwick, so that the terrible thought that she might hear any day of her engagement to Captain Wentworth is dispelled for ever. In Milsom Street also, while sheltering in a shop from the rain, she first sees Captain Wentworth after his arrival in Bath, and on his coming accidentally into the same shop with some friends, both he and she are unable to hide their signs of perturbation. But it is at a concert in the Upper Rooms that Anne goes through far worse disquietude, while, with the tormenting uncertainty of an undeclared love, she sits wondering whether he will come to speak to her or not.

It is at the White Hart Inn, which overlooked the entrance to the Pump Room Arcade, that the real crisis of the book takes place. Here Anne, on coming to spend the day with her sister Mary, Mrs. Charles Musgrove, who is staying there with her husband, finds Captain Harville and Captain Wentworth. It is her conversation with the former that reveals to the latter her own unchanged feelings, and gives him the courage to write her a letter declaring once more his own love, after the lapse of many years. Anne is thereby rewarded for her gentle loyalty, and when in going up Union Street with her brother-in-law she is overtaken by Captain Wentworth, and handed over to his charge, mutual explanations are made and mutual happiness reached.

Certainly to the lovers of Jane Austen's books these characters people the streets quite as vividly as any flesh-and-blood persons who have ever lived in them.

CHAPTER XIII

DRESS AND FASHIONS

JANE AUSTEN had a lively and natural interest in dress, and her letters abound in allusions to fashions, new clothes, and contrivances for bringing into the mode those that had fallen behind it. She cannot have had much chance of seeing new fashions at Steventon, but when she went to a town her instincts revived. During her visit to Bath, 1799, when she was staying with her brother Edward and his wife Elizabeth, and some of their children, she writes—

"My cloak is come home, I like it very much, and can now exclaim with delight, like J. Bond at hay harvest, 'This is what I have been looking for these three years.' I saw some gauzes in a shop in Bath Street yesterday at only fourpence a yard, but they were not so good or so pretty as mine. Flowers are very much worn, and fruit is still more the thing. Elizabeth has a bunch of strawberries, and I have seen grapes, cherries, plums, and apricots. There are likewise almonds and raisins, French plums, and tamarinds at the grocers', but I have never seen any of them in hats. A plum or greengage would cost three shillings; cherries and grapes about five, I believe, but this is at some of the dearest shops."

The fashion to which she refers was soon carried to excess; Hannah More in her Diary says that she met women who had on their heads "an acre and a half of shrubbery, besides slopes, grass-plats, tulip beds, clumps of peonies, kitchen-gardens, and green-houses," and she "had no doubt that they held in great contempt our roseless heads and leafless necks."

"Some ladies carry on their heads a large quantity of fruit, and yet they would despise a poor useful member of society who carried it there for the purpose of selling it for bread."

This fashion continued to increase until it was mimicked by Garrick, who appeared on the stage with a mass of vegetables on his head, and a large carrot hanging from each side, and ridicule killed the folly. It seems quite certain that fashion, which never reached such grotesque monstrosities as in the lifetime of Jane Austen, hardly touched, in its extremer modes, herself and her sister, who kept to the simpler styles with good taste. In fact the jest about the grocers shows that Jane herself saw the humour of the thing even when living in the very midst of it, a most unusual acuteness. She describes her own hat in the same letter as being "A pretty hat,—a pretty style of hat too. It is something like Eliza's, only, instead of being all straw, half of it is narrow purple ribbon," which seems simple enough.

What one would like to get is some mental picture of Jane as she appeared indoors and out of doors, and this is extremely difficult. In the illustration "Dressing to go Out," by Tomkins, we get some idea of everyday fashions. The simple style of a plain material, with perhaps a little spot or sprig upon it, of soft muslin, made with a flowing skirt, and a chemisette folded in, and with sleeves reaching only to the elbow, was doubtless the most ordinary kind of indoor dress for women; add to this a cap, and this is as near as we can get to Jane's usual appearance. The caps, however, varied

DRESSING TO GO OUT

DRESS AND FASHIONS

greatly, being worn both indoors and also for driving. Mr Austen-Leigh remarks that Jane and her sister took to wearing caps earlier in life than was generally the custom, but, on the contrary, caps were worn by very young girls at this period, for Mrs. Papendick says in her Journal, which is contemporary, that no young girl of eighteen was seen in public without some head-covering of this description. We learn many particulars of the different kinds of cap worn by Jane from her own letters.

"I have made myself two or three caps to wear of evenings since I came home, and they save me a world of torment as to hairdressing which at present gives me no trouble beyond washing and brushing, for my long hair is always plaited up out of sight, and my short hair curls well enough to want no papering."

"I took the liberty a few days ago of asking your black velvet bonnet to lend me its caul, which it readily did, and by which I have been enabled to give a considerable improvement of dignity to the cap, which was before too *nidgetty* to please me.... I still venture to retain the narrow silver round it, put twice round without any bow, and instead of the black military feather shall put in the coquelicot one as being smarter, and besides coquelicot is to be all the fashion this winter. After the ball I shall probably make it entirely black."

"I am not to wear my white satin cap to-night after all; I am to wear a mamalouc cap instead, which Charles Fowle sent to Mary, and which she lends me. It is all the fashion now, worn at the opera, and by Lady Mildmay at Hackwood balls."

The word "mamalouc" was used at this time to describe many articles of dress; it had come into fashion after Nelson's great victory in Egypt, and there were mamalouc cloaks as well as caps, but whether these articles of attire bore the most distant resemblance to those worn in Egypt, or whether the word was tacked on to them merely for the purpose of advertisement, I do not know. Another cap Jane mentions seems to have been much more pert: " Miss Hare had some pretty caps and is to make me one like one of them, only white satin instead of blue. It will be satin and lace and a little white flower perking out of the left ear, like Harriot Byron's feather. I have allowed her to go as far as one pound sixteen." " My cap has come home, and I like it very much, Fanny has one also, hers is white sarsenet and lace, of a different shape from mine, more fit for morning carriage wear, which is what it is intended for, and is in shape exceedingly like our own satin and lace of last winter, shaped round the face exactly like it, with pipes and more fulness and a round crown inserted behind. My cap has a peak in front. Large full bows of very narrow ribbon (old twopenny) are the thing. One over the right temple perhaps, and another at the left ear."

Some ladies used to hang at the back of their turban-like caps four or five ostrich feathers of different colours. But apparently a bow or a bit of ribbon sometimes was worn instead of a cap, and supposed to represent it, just as a bit of wire and gauze a few years ago was supposed to be a toque. In one place Jane says—

"I wore at the ball your favourite gown, a bit of muslin of the same round my head bordered with Mrs. Cooper's band, and one little comb."

The fashion of caps for middle-aged ladies has so recently gone out that it is well remembered, but the fashion of night-caps, which belongs to a much older generation, seems to us now curious. They were then an essential part of a wardrobe; Henry Bickersteth, afterwards Lord Langdale, writes to his mother in 1800, "I must give you my thanks for the supply of linen you have sent me; it was indeed seasonable, as that which I had before was completely worn out. I am still obliged to solicit some night-caps." He was then only a boy of sixteen, and the vision of all the boys in a school going to bed in night-caps is a funny one.

Head-dresses reached their climax of absurdity at the end of the eighteenth century, but the styles varied so much that almost everyone could please themselves. At a famous trial only a few ladies were dressed in the French taste. "All the rest, decked in the finest manner with brocades, diamonds, and lace, had no other head-dress, but a ribband tied to their hair, over which they wore a flat hat, adorned with a variety of ornaments. It requires much observation to be able to give full account of the great effect produced by this hat; it affords the ladies who wear it that arch and roguish air, which the winged hat gives to Mercury." And Sir Walter Besant says: "The women wore hoods, small caps, enormous hats, tiny milkmaid's straw hats; hair in curls and flat to the head; 'pompoms,' or huge structures two or three feet high, with all kinds of decorations—ribbons, birds' nests, ships, carriages and waggons in gold and silver lace—in the erection."

"Nothing can be conceived so absurd, extragavant, fantastical, as the present mode of dressing the head. Simplicity and modesty are things so much exploded, that the very names are no longer remembered. I have just escaped from one of the most fashionable disfigurers; and though I charged him to dress me with the greatest simplicity, and to have only a very distant eye upon the fashion, just enough to avoid the pride of singularity without running into ridiculous excess, yet in spite of all these sage didactics, I absolutely blush at myself and turn to the glass with as much caution as a vain beauty, just risen from the small-pox, which cannot be a more disfiguring disease than the present mode of dressing." (H. More, 1775.)

But in 1787 a great change occurred in the mode of hair-dressing, the huge cushions disappeared and the main part of the hair was gathered together at the back in a chignon from which one or two loose curls were allowed to escape.

The long feathers, which have already been commented on, varied in number from three to one, and continued to be worn well on into the nineteenth century. These feathers appeared in turbans, bonnets, and head-dresses of all kinds, and hardly a picture of the period representing ladies at a card-table does not show one or more of these ludicrous quivering monstrosities.

Samuel Rogers says that he had been to Ranelagh in a coach with a lady who was obliged to sit on a stool on the floor of the coach on account of the height of her head-dress.

Fantastic headgear was not in Jane's line, all the accounts of her hats and bonnets are simple. "My mother has ordered a new bonnet and so have I; both white strip trimmed with white ribbon. I find my straw bonnet looking very much like other people's and quite as smart. Bonnets of cambric muslin are a good deal worn, and some of them are very pretty, but I shall defer one of that sort until your arrival."

In the last ten years of the century, poke bonnets and Dunstable hats were much in evidence, and with flowing curls, and flowing ribbons tied in a large bow under the chin, were sometimes not unbecoming to a pretty face.

But in Jane's lifetime the strangest fashion, that ever caused discomfort to a whole nation, gradually died down, that is to say the use of wigs. Yet that they were worn so late as 1814 is shown by Jane's remark in one of the letters. "My brother and Edward (his son) arrived last night. Their business is about teeth and wigs."

Nothing quickened the departure of the wig so much as the tax put on hair powder by Pitt in 1785; people argued that they did not mind the money, but they thought it so iniquitous to tax powder that they left off wearing powdered wigs to spite the Government, and probably, once having discovered the comfort of doing without these hideous evils, they would never return to them. Yet that the wig, even in its heyday, was not universally worn is shown by the fact that King George III. himself refused to wear one. The king's "hair, which is very thick, and of the finest light colour, tied behind with a ribband, and dressed by the hand of the queen, is one of his most striking ornaments. Notwithstanding this, the peruke makers have presented an address to the king, requesting His Majesty that, for the good of their body and the nation, he would be pleased to wear a wig." (Grosley.)

No one has given a better account of the wig than Sir Walter Besant, he says: "The wig was a great leveller . . . with the wig it mattered nothing whether one was bald or not. Again the wig was a great protection for the head; it saved the wearer from the effects of cold draughts; it was part of the comfort of the age like the sash window and the wainscoted wall. And the wig, too, like the coat and the waistcoat, was a means of showing the wealth of its owner, because a wig of the best kind, new, properly curled and combed, cost a large sum of money. Practically it was indestructible, and with certain alterations descended. First it was left by will to son or heir; next it was given to the coachman;

then, with alterations, to the gardener; then it went to the second-hand people in Monmouth Street, whence it continued a downward course until it finally entered upon its last career of usefulness in the shoeblack's box. There was lastly an excellent reason why in the eighteenth century it was found more convenient to wear a wig than the natural hair. Those of the lower classes who were not in domestic service wore their own hair. Their heads were filled with vermin—these vermin were very easily caught—now the man who shaved his head and wore a wig was free of this danger." (*London in the Eighteenth Century.*)

We know that Dr. Johnson's wigs were a constant source of trouble, for they were not only dirty and unkempt, but generally burnt away in the front, for being very nearsighted, he often put his head into the candle when poring over his books. Whenever he was staying with the Thrales therefore the butler used to waylay him as he passed in to dinner, and pull off the wig on his head, replacing it with a new one.

Ladies rarely appeared without head-dresses of some kind, be it only a bow or an ornamental comb, they seemed to think that a woman should be seen with her head covered in every place as well as in church. Near the end of *Cecilia* the flighty Lady Honoria cries, "'Why you know sir as to caps and wigs, they are very serious things, for we should look mighty droll figures to go about bareheaded,'" which shows how entirely custom dictates what appears "mighty droll" or quite ordinary.

Wigs were sometimes the cause of ludicrous incidents, as when in the House of Commons Lord North suddenly rising from his seat and going out bore off on the hilt of his sword the wig of Welbore Ellis who happened to be stooping forward.

Many people, when wigs began to go out of fashion,

powdered their own hair, and of this Besant gives us also an unpleasant but speaking picture: "Among the minor miseries of life is to be mentioned the slipping and sliding of lumps of the powder and pomatum from the head down to the plate at dinner."

Even boys at school wore queues. Of a master at Eton it is said that his management of the boys, excellent in other respects, was in some things amiss, for "he burnt all their ruffles, and cut off their queues."

The Times of April 14, 1795, mentions that: "A numerous club has been formed in Lambeth called the Crop Club, every member of which, on his entrance, is obliged to have his head docked as close as the Duke of Bridgewater's old bay coach horses. This assemblage is instituted for the purpose of opposing, or rather evading, the tax on powdered heads."

The use of powder is mentioned in Jane Austen's story *The Watsons*, and is one of the very few touches she gives that carry us backward in time. Mrs. Robert Watson is speaking to her sisters-in-law, "'I would not make you wait,' said she, 'so I put on the first thing I met with. I am afraid I am a sad figure. My dear Mr. W. (addressing her husband) you have not put any fresh powder in your hair.'

"'No, I do not intend it, I think there is powder enough in my hair for my wife and sisters.'

"'Indeed, you ought to make some alteration in your dress before dinner when you are out visiting, though you do not at home.'

"'Nonsense!'

"Dinner came, and except when Mrs. Robert looked at her husband's head she continued gay and flippant."

Later, when Tom Musgrave arrives, "Robert Watson, stealing a view of his own head in an opposite glass, said with equal civility, 'You cannot be more in deshabille than myself. We got here so late that I had not time even to put a little fresh powder in my hair.'"

The powders used were very various.

"And now we are upon vanities, what do you think is the reigning mode as to powder? only tumerick, that coarse dye that stains yellow. It falls out of the hair and stains the skin so, that every pretty lady must look as yellow as a crocus, which I suppose will come a better compliment than as white as a lily." (Mrs. Papendick.)

Flour was frequently used for powdering heads, and in 1795 flour was very scarce and enormously valuable. In the same year when the powder tax was passed, the Privy Council " implored all families to abjure puddings and pies, and declared their own intention to have only fish, meat, vegetables, and household bread, made partly of rye. It was recommended that one quarter loaf per head per week should be a maximum allowance. The loaf was to be brought on the table for each to help himself, that none be wasted. The king himself had none but household bread on his table. In 1801 the Government offered bounties on the importation of all kinds of grain and flour, and passed the Brown Bread Act (1800) forbidding the sale of wheaten bread, or new bread of any kind, as stale bread would go further (Mary Bateson in *Social England*). This scarcity and dearness of bread is a thing never felt in the present day, when lumps of the best white bread are flung in heaps in the squares and streets of London, and disdained even by tramps and beggars, and when boys in the North Country go round with sacks begging bits of bread which they afterwards use for feeding ponies or horses!

Many epigrams and *bon mots* were made on the new powder tax; a tax on dogs had at that time been generally expected, so one wit wrote—

> "Full many a chance or dire mishap,
> Ofttimes 'twixt the lip and the cup is;
> The tax that should have hung our dogs,
> Excuses them, and falls on puppies."

Of the inconveniences attending the use of powder the following anecdote is an instance—

"At one of Lady Crewe's dinner parties, Grattan, after talking very delightfully for some time, all at once seemed disconcerted, and sunk into silence. I asked his daughter, who was sitting next to me, the reason of this. 'Oh,' she replied, 'he has just found out that he has come here in his powdering coat.'" (Samuel Rogers, *Table Talk*.)

The Act claimed one guinea a year from every user of powder, and was calculated to bring in about £400,000 per annum. The Royal Family, clergymen whose incomes were under a hundred pounds, subalterns and all below that rank in the army, officers in the navy under the rank of commander, and all below the two eldest unmarried daughters of a family were exempt.

Walter Savage Landor was the first of undergraduates at Oxford to do without powder, and was told he would be stoned for a republican.

"The regular academic costume, so late as 1799, consisted of knee breeches of any colour, and white stockings. The sun of wigs had not even then set; they covered the craniums of nearly all dons and heads of houses. The gentlemen wore their hair tied up behind in a thin loop called a pigtail; footmen wore their hair tied up behind in a thick loop called a hoop." (Sydney, *England and the English*.)

In regard to the rest of the costume of ladies, the most noticeable points of the mode were the high waists and long flowing skirts clinging tightly to the figure. This, if not carried to excess, was certainly becoming, but fashion cannot be content with mediocrity, it must be extravagant. Consequently, "With very low bodices and very high waists, came very scanty clothing, with an absence of petticoat, a fashion which left very little of the form to the imagination. I do not say that our English belles went to the extent of some of their French sisters, of having their muslin dresses put on damp—and holding them tight to their figures till they dried—so as absolutely to mould them to their form . . . . but their clothes were of the scantiest, and as year succeeded year, this fashion developed, if one can call diminution of clothing development." (John Ashton, *Old Times*.)

It is difficult to give any consecutive account of fashions extending over such a long period, for they varied as frequently then as they do now, however, here are a few notes.

Coquelicot, that is poppy colour, was very fashionable, Jane as we have seen adopted it; at one time no lady's dress was considered complete without a dash of coquelicot in sash or trimmings.

Jane frequently mentions her cloak; this would not be what ladies call a cloak now, but more what would be described as a fichu or tippet, covering the shoulders and having long ends which fell like a stole in front, some of the modern fur stoles are in fact made very much on the same pattern; no lady's wardrobe seems to have been complete without at least one black silk cloak of this sort. Dresses were cut low in front, either in V shape or curved, and even in winter this custom was followed; a silk handkerchief was sometimes folded crosswise over the opening, but very generally, though warmly dressed in other respects, a lady had her neck quite uncovered. The short sleeves which went with low necks necessitated the use of long gloves, which reached above the elbow and were tied there with ribbon. The high waists made the bodice of the dress so small that it was of very little consequence, and sometimes was formed merely by a folded bit of material like a fichu. This was covered by that fashionable and characteristic garment, the pelisse. It was not considered proper for very young girls to wear pelisses, they wore cloaks, but the pelisse did not really differ very greatly from the cloak, for it was like a long open coat, fitting closely to the arm, but falling straight in long ends from the armholes, thus leaving the front of the dress exposed in a panel; later, pelisses became more voluminous and completely covered the dress, fastening in front.

Mrs. Papendick says, "The outdoor equipment in those days, when pelisses and great-coats of woollen were not worn by girls, was a black cloak of a silk called 'mode,' stiff, glossy, wadded, armholes with a sleeve to the wrist from them, a small muff, and a quaker-shaped bonnet all of the same material."

Huge muffs were very common, and this is one of the features of the dress of that date which is generally remembered because of its singularity.

The small girls were dressed in long skirts plainly made, and their robes must have precluded any possibility of romping; the short skirts and long stockinged legs of our present mode would have made them stare indeed.

As for the materials for dresses, they were of course much less varied than the inventions of printing and machinery allow women to use nowadays. Plain muslins, or muslins embroidered at the edge, were most common, though there were other materials such as taffeta, sarsenet, and bombazine. We must realise also that any lace used in trimming must have been real lace, there was no machine-made stuff at $2\tfrac{3}{4}$d. a yard with which every servant girl could deck herself as she does now. India muslins were extremely popular, and seemed to have been worn quite regardless of the climate, which according to accounts, our grandmothers notwithstanding, does not seem to have changed remarkably.

When Lady Newdigate was at Brighton in 1797 she writes to her husband: " Do ask of your female croneys if they have any wants in the muslin way. Nothing else is worn in gowns by any rank of people, but I don't know that I can get them cheaper here, but great choice there is, very beautiful and real India."

In January 1801, Jane writes from Steventon, " I shall want two new coloured gowns for the summer, for my pink one will not do more than clear me from Steventon. I shall not trouble you, however, to get more than one of them, and that is to be a plain brown cambric muslin, for morning wear; the other, which is to be a very pretty yellow and white cloud, I mean to buy in Bath. Buy two brown ones, if you please, and both of a length, but one longer than the other—it is for a tall woman. Seven yards for my mother, seven yards and a half for me; a dark brown, but the kind of brown is left to your own choice, and I had rather they were different as it will be always something to say, to dispute about, which is the prettiest. They must be cambric muslin."

Ten years later muslins are still fashionable. " I am sorry to tell you that I am getting very extravagant [she was at this time in London] and spending all my money, and what is worse for you, I have been spending all yours too; for in a linendraper's shop to which I went for checked muslin, and for which I was obliged to give seven shillings a yard, I was tempted by a pretty coloured muslin and bought ten yards of it on the chance of your liking it; but, at the same time, if it should not suit you, you must not think yourself at all obliged to take it. It is only three and six per yard, and I should not in the least mind taking the whole. In texture it is just what we prefer, but its resemblance to green crewels I must own is not great, for the pattern is a small red spot."

That silly and affected nomenclature for the dress fabrics was in use then as it is still, is apparent from Hannah More's remark, " One lady asked what was the newest colour; the other answered that the most truly fashionable silk was a *soupçon de vert*, lined with a *soupir etouffée et bradée de l'espérance ;* now you must not consult your old-fashioned dictionary for the word *espérance* for you will there find that it means nothing but hope, whereas *espérance* in the new language of the time means rose-buds."

The most particular description of a dress Jane ever gives is almost minute enough to be followed by a dressmaker : " It is to be a round gown, with a jacket and a frock front, to open at the side. The jacket is all in one with the body, and comes as far as the pocket holes —about half a quarter of a yard deep, I suppose, all the way round, cut off straight at the corners with a broad hem. No fulness appears either in the body or the flap, the back is quite plain—and the side equally so. The front is sloped round to the bosom and drawn in, and there is to be a frill of the same to put on occasionally when all one's handkerchiefs are dirty, which frill must fall back. She is to put two breadths and a half in the tail, and no gores—gores not being so much worn as they were. There is nothing new in the sleeves; they are to be plain, with a fulness of the same falling down and gathered up underneath. Low in the back behind, and a belt of the same."

It is of course most obvious that the ludicrous fashions and enormous erections, which were carried by the leaders of fashion, did not affect quiet country girls; just as in our own time the distorted sleeves or ever-changing skirts, and all the vagaries of the smart set, are known and seen by hundreds who daily go about in perfectly simple clothes which yet can not be called unfashionable because they conform in main points to the dictates of the fashion of the moment without going to excess.

Two more characteristic quotations from the letters must be given—

"How do you like your flounce? We have seen only plain flounces. I hope you have not cut off the train of your bombazine. I cannot reconcile myself to giving them up as morning gowns; they are so very sweet by candlelight. I would rather sacrifice my blue one for that purpose; in short I do not know, and I do not care," and in the following year, "I have determined to trim my lilac sarsenet with lilac satin ribbon just as my chine crape is. Sixpenny width at bottom, threepenny or fourpenny at top. Ribbon trimmings are all the fashion at Bath. With this addition it will be a very useful gown, happy to go anywhere."

In one small point the lady of the eighteenth century resembled her successor of to-day.

The Times of November 9, 1799, notes: "What is still more remarkable is the total abjuration of the female pocket . . . every fashionable fair carries her purse in her workbag, and she has the pleasure of laying everything that belongs to her upon the table wherever she goes."

Hoops were worn in Court dress long after they were abandoned elsewhere, someone describes them as the "excrescences and balconies with which modern hoydens overwhelm and barricade their persons." Apart from this survival at Court, dress was generally long and clinging.

At one of the Drawing Rooms of 1796 crape was all the fashion; Princess Augusta was dressed in "a rich gold embroidered crape petticoat in leaves across, intersected with blue painted foil in shaded spots, having the appearance of stripes from top to bottom; ornamented with a rich embroidered border in festoons of blue shaded satin and gold spangles. Pocket holes ornamented with broad gold lace, and blue embroidered satin bows; white and gold body and train." There are many other costumes described at the same Drawing Room, from which we gather that the hair was dressed very full and high, and quite off the ears, and that bandeaus of gold or silver lace, or black velvet embroidered with gold, were run through it. Gold and silver artificial flowers were also very commonly worn, and some ladies had plumes. There were also a few caps. "The ladies all wore full dress neckerchiefs with point lace, sufficiently open to display irresistible charms."

Men's dress of the same period was most magnificent, and perhaps the feature of it that would strike one most in contrast with modern fashions, would be its variety of colour; coats and waistcoats were always coloured, black was only donned for mourning. Gold and silver lace and figured brocades, with lace cuffs and ruffles, were essential to a beau. Horace Walpole notes at the wedding of a nephew that, except for himself, there wasn't a bit of gold lace anywhere in the dress of the men, and he considered it altogether as a very poor affair.

A fairly good idea of the different degrees of plainness and ornament in the clothes worn by gentlemen may be gathered from Reynold's portrait group of Inigo

Jones, Hon. H. Fane, and C. Blair which was done at this time.

The following is the wordrobe of a fashionable man of the time. " My wardrobe consisted of five fashionable coats full mounted, two of which were plain, one of cut velvet, one trimmed with gold, and another with silver lace; two frocks, one of which was drab with large plate buttons, the other of blue with gold binding; one waistcoat of gold brocade, one of blue satin, embroidered with silver, one of green silk trimmed with broad figured gold lace; one of black silk with fringes; one of white satin, one of black cloth and one of scarlet; six pairs of cloth breeches, one pair of crimson, and another of black velvet; twelve pair of white silk stockings, as many of black silk, and the same number of fine cotton; one hat laced with gold Point d'Espagne; another with silver lace scalloped, a third gold binding, and a fourth plain; three dozen of fine ruffled shirts, as many neckcloths; one dozen of cambric handkerchiefs, and the like number of silk. A gold watch with a chased case [it was the fashion to wear two watches at one time during the century], two valuable diamond rings, two morning swords, one with a silver handle, and a fourth cut steel inlaid with gold; a diamond stock buckle and a set of stone buckles for the knees and shoes; a pair of silver mounted pistols with rich housings; a gold headed cane, and a snuff box of tortoiseshell, mounted with gold, having the picture of a lady on the top."

In *The New Guide* already quoted, the following account is put into the mouth of a young gentleman of fashion:—

> "I ride in a chair with my hands in a muff,
> And have bought a silk coat and embroidered the cuff.
> But the weather was cold, and the coat it was thin,
> So the tailor advised me to line it with skin.

INIGO JONES, HON. H. FANE, AND C. BLAIR

> But what with my Nivernois hat can compare,
> Bag-wig, and laced ruffles, and black solitaire?
> And what can a man of true fashion denote,
> Like an ell of good ribbon tied under the throat?
> My buckles and box are in exquisite taste,
> The one is of paper, the other of paste."

Fox, when a very young man, was a prodigious dandy, wearing a little odd French hat, shoes with red heels, etc. He and Lord Carlisle once travelled from Paris to Lyons for the express purpose of buying waistcoats; and during the whole journey they talked about nothing else. (S. Rogers, *Table Talk*.)

Jane Austen's brother Edward would dress, as befitted his position, with greater variety of colour and style than his clergyman father and brother. It was the usual thing for a clergyman to dress in black, with knee-breeches and white stock, but it was not essential. In *Northanger Abbey* when Henry Tilney is first introduced to Catherine in the Lower Rooms at Bath, there is nothing in his attire to indicate that he is a clergyman, a fact which she only learns subsequently.

In ordinary civilian dress, men wore long green, blue, or brown cloth coats with stocks and frilled ruffles. In the *Man of Feeling* a man casually met with is wearing "a brownish coat with a narrow gold edging, and his companion an old green frock with a buff coloured waistcoat," while an ex-footman trying to play the gentleman has on "a white frock and a red laced waistcoat."

At that time footgear for men consisted of slippers in the house, and riding-boots for out of doors. When Beau Nash was forming the assemblies at Bath, as has been said he made a dead set against the habit some men had of wearing boots in the dancing-room. "The gentlemen's boots also made a very desperate stand against him, the country squires were by no means submissive to his usurpations, and probably his authority alone would never have carried him through, had he not reinforced it with ridicule." His ridicule took the form of a squib, one verse of which was as follows:—

> "Come Trollops and Slatterns,
> Cockt hats and white aprons,
> This best our modesty suits;
> For why should not we
> In dress be as free
> As Hogs-Norton squires in boots."

"The keenness, severity, and particularly the good rhymes of this little *morceau* which was at that time highly relished by many of the nobility at Bath, gained him a temporary triumph. But to push his victories he got up a puppet show, in which Punch came in, booted and spurred in the character of a country squire. When told to pull off his boots he replies:—'Why, madam, you may as well bid me pull off my legs. I never go without boots, I never ride, I never dance without them; and this piece of politeness is quite the thing in Bath. We always dance at our town in boots, and the ladies often move minuets in riding boots.' From this time few ventured to appear at the assemblies in Bath in riding dress." (*Life of Nash*, 1772.)

CHAPTER XIV

AT SOUTHAMPTON

FOR two and a half years, that is to say from May 1801 to September 1804, we do not hear any more of Jane Austen from her own correspondence. Then, while she was staying at Lyme, she sent a letter to her sister which is given in Mr. Austen-Leigh's *Memoir*. It will be remembered that part of the scene in *Persuasion* takes place at Lyme, where the principal characters are transported, and where Louisa Musgrove meets with her accident. Captain Wentworth's friend, Captain Harville, had settled there for the winter, and wrote such a glowing account of the fine country around that "the young people were all wild to see Lyme." The party that finally went were the heroine, Anne Elliot herself, her brother and sister-in-law, her two friends, Henrietta and Louisa Musgrove, and her quondam lover, Captain Wentworth, who was at this time paying rather more attention to Louisa Musgrove than could be borne with easiness by poor Anne, who had realised the dreadful mistake she had made in giving him up seven years before. "They were come too late in the year for any amusement or variety which Lyme, as a public place might offer; the rooms were shut up, the lodgers almost gone, scarcely any family but the residents left—and as there is nothing to admire in the buildings themselves, the remarkable situation of the town, the principal street almost hurrying into the water, the walk to the Cobb, skirting round the pleasant little bay, which in the season is animated with bathing machines and company; the Cobb itself, its old wonders and new improvements, with the very beautiful line of cliffs stretching out to the east of the town, are what the stranger's eye will seek; and a very strange stranger it must be who does not see charms in the immediate environs of Lyme to make him wish to know it better. The scenes in its neighbourhood, Charmouth, with its high grounds and extensive sweeps of country, and still more its sweet retired bay, backed by dark cliffs, where fragments of low rock among the sands make it the happiest spot for watching the flow of the tide, for sitting in unwearied contemplation; the woody varieties of the cheerful vista of Up Lyme; and, above all, Pinny, with its green chasms between romantic rocks, where the scattered forest trees and orchards of luxuriant growth declare that many a generation must have passed away since the first partial falling of the cliff prepared the ground for such a state, where a scene so wonderful and so lovely is exhibited, as may more than equal any of the resembling scenes of the far-famed Isle of Wight; these places must be visited, and visited again, to make the worth of Lyme understood."

It is wonderful that Jane should have remembered in such detail a place which she had apparently only seen on one visit, and that many years before she wrote the book in which the description is embodied, but it is not unlikely that, as the instinct of word-painting was strong within her, she wrote down some such account on the spot, and had it for reference afterwards.

Louisa's wilfulness in leaping down the steps of the Cobb, and her subsequent accident, at which Captain Wentworth deceives Anne further as to the real state of his feelings by displaying much poignant and unnecessary grief, form the chief episode in the book.

While at Lyme herself, Jane took part in the usual amusements; she went to a dance and was escorted back by "James and a lanthorn, though I believe the lanthorn was not lit as the moon was up." She walked on the Cobb, and bathed in the morning, also she looked after the housekeeping for her father and mother, who were with her in lodgings.

This was in September. In the beginning of the following year her father died, but there is no letter yet published from which we can judge any of the details or the state of her feelings at this great loss.

In the April after this event there are two letters, given by Mr. Austen-Leigh, written from Gay Street, Bath, in which no allusion is made to her father's death. She and her mother were then in lodgings. It was at the end of this year that they moved to Southampton.

Jane's pen had not been altogether idle while at Bath, for it is supposed that she there wrote the fragment *The Watsons* which is embodied in Mr. Austen-Leigh's *Memoir*.

It must also have been at this time that the MS. of *Northanger Abbey* was offered to the Bath bookseller, a transaction which is described elsewhere.

Before leaving Bath Jane went to stay with her brother, Edward Knight, at Godmersham; this was in August of the same year, 1805.

Godmersham, to which the Austen girls so often went on visits, is thus described by Lord Brabourne, who certainly had every right to know—

"Godmersham Park is situated in one of the most beautiful parts of Kent, namely, in the valley of the Stour, which lies between Ashford and Canterbury. Soon after you pass the Wye station of the railway from the former to the latter place, you see Godmersham church on your left hand, and just beyond it, comes into view the wall which shuts off the shrubberies and pleasure grounds of the great house from the road; close to the church nestles the home farm, and beyond it the rectory, with lawn sloping down to the river Stour, which for a distance of nearly a mile runs through the east end of the park. A little beyond the church you see the mansion, between which and the railroad lies the village, divided by the old high road from Ashford to Canterbury, nearly opposite Godmersham. The valley of the Stour makes a break in that ridge of chalk hills, the proper name of which is the Backbone of Kent.

"So that Godmersham Park, beyond the house, is upon the chalk downs, and on its further side is bounded by King's Wood, a large tract of woodland containing many hundred acres and possessed by several different owners."

The children of Edward and Elizabeth were now growing up. The eldest boy, Edward, was delicate, and there was some talk of taking him to Worthing instead of sending him back to school; however, he apparently grew stronger, for he returned to school again with his brother George. The next two boys were Henry and William; Jane says, she has been playing battledore and shuttlecock with the younger of the two, "he and I have practised together two mornings, and improve a little; we have frequently kept it up three times, and once or twice six."

The eldest girl, Fanny, had become almost as dear as a sister to her aunt, and the next, Elizabeth, are also mentioned in the letters; there were besides these younger children, two more boys and three girls, a fine family!

Before coming to Godmersham Jane had stayed

at Eastwell, where George Hatton and his wife Lady Elizabeth lived; their eldest son succeeded later to the title of ninth Earl of Winchilsea; Jane mentions this lad as a "fine boy," but was chiefly delighted with his younger brother Daniel, who afterwards married a daughter of the Earl of Warwick. At the time she wrote this letter, Cassandra was at Goodnestone with the Bridges. The two sisters soon after changed places, crossing on the journey, as Jane went to Goodnestone and Cassandra to Godmersham; owing to the difficulty of carriage transit, journeys must frequently have been arranged thus to save the horses double work.

Jane in writing from Goodnestone alludes much to the two Bridges girls, Harriet and her delicate sister Marianne.

There was to be a great ball at Deal for which Harriet Bridges received a ticket, and an invitation to stay at Dover, but this was suddenly put off on account of the death of the Duke of Gloucester, brother of George III. Jane opined that everybody would go into mourning on his account. Mourning was of course much more generally used then than now, and everyone seems to have rushed into it whether they belonged to the Court or not on the death of any member of the Royal Family.

During the four years that had passed since the beginning of the century, Europe had been in a continual turmoil, a turmoil that could never cease while Napoleon was at liberty. The Battle of Alexandria in the first year of the new century had taught him that the English were as formidable on land as on sea, and the Battle of the Baltic in the following month, further convinced him that there was one unconquered nation that dared oppose him. He recognised, however, that while he could not but acknowledge the superiority of Britain on the sea, and in places accessible by sea, he could do much as he pleased on the Continent, therefore a compromise was arrived at, and on March 27, 1802, the Treaty of Amiens was signed, and for the first time for many years the strain of war was relaxed in Great Britain.

The arrogance of Napoleon, however, made a continuous peace impossible, and by the spring of the next year (1803) the two nations were again ready to spring at each other's throats. Napoleon seized and detained 10,000 British travellers who were in France, and this provoked fury in Great Britain. Great preparations were now once more made in France for the long-cherished project of the invasion of England, where in a few weeks 300,000 volunteers were enrolled. The national excitement was tremendous, and Jane must have heard at least as much about the preparations for war, and the dangers of invasion, even in the frivolous society of Bath, as about dress and trivial society details.

In May 1804, Napoleon threw aside all disguise, and had himself proclaimed Emperor of the French, and by the end of the same year Spain, having thrown in her lot with France, declared war also against England. The whole of 1805 must have been one of tense excitement to everyone with a brain to understand. The future of England trembled in the balance, yet Jane's pleasant letters from Godmersham deal in nothing but domestic detail and small talk, not one allusion is there to the throes which threatened to rend the national existence.

In the autumn of 1805 both the sisters had returned to their mother, who in their absence had had the companionship of Martha Lloyd. Then came the removal to Southampton, where they went to " a commodious old-fashioned house in a corner of Castle Square."

Mr. Austen-Leigh, writing from recollection, says: "My grandmother's house had a pleasant garden bounded on one side by the old city walls; the top of this wall was sufficiently wide to afford a pleasant walk, with an extensive view, easily accessible to ladies by steps. . . . At that time Castle Square was occupied by a fantastic edifice, too large for the space in which it stood, though too small to accord well with its castellated style, erected by the second Marquess of Lansdowne, half-brother to the well-known statesman who succeeded him in the title. The marchioness had a light phaeton drawn by six, and sometimes by eight little ponies, each pair decreasing in size and becoming lighter in colour. . . . It was a delight to me to look down from the window and see this fairy equipage put together, for the premises of the castle were so contracted that the whole process went on in the little space that remained of the open square. . . . On the death of the Marquess in 1809 the castle was pulled down. Few probably remember its existence; and anyone who might visit the place now would wonder how it ever could have stood there."

Mrs. Austen was not well off, for her husband had had no private means and she herself but little, yet her son Edward was well able to help her, for Chawton alone is said to have been worth £5000 a year. There was also money in the family, for Jane some years later speaks of her eldest brother's income being £1100 a year. She and her sister must have had some little allowance also, as it was with her own money that she paid for the publication of the first of her books. Simply as she had always lived, she does not seem to have had small ideas on the subject, the couples in her books require about two thousand a year before they can be considered prosperous, and incomes of from five thousand to ten thousand pounds are not rare. She makes one of the characters in *Mansfield Park* remark, on hearing that Mr. Crawford has four thousand pounds a year, "' Those who have not more must be satisfied with what they have. Four thousand a year is a pretty estate.'"

There was apparently some question raised by her relations about the income bestowed by Jane upon the mother and daughters in *Mansfield Park*, namely, five hundred pounds a year. But having regard to all the circumstances, the style to which they were accustomed, and Mrs. Dashwood's inability to economise, this could perhaps hardly have been made less.

We hear at the close of one year at Southampton that Mrs. Austen is pleased "at the comfortable state of her own finances, which she finds on closing her year's accounts, beyond her expectation, as she begins the new year with a balance of thirty pounds in her favour."

And afterwards, " My mother is afraid I have not been explicit enough on the subject of her wealth; she began 1806 with sixty-eight pounds; she begins 1807 with ninety-nine pounds, and this after thirty-two pounds purchase of stock."

In this year, 1805, the income tax was increased from $6\frac{1}{2}$ per cent. to 10 per cent. on account of the tremendous war expenditure.

At this time an amicable arrangement had been arrived at, by which Frank Austen and his wife shared the house of the mother and sisters at Southampton, Frank himself being of course frequently away. His first wife, Mary Gibson, whom he had only recently married, lived until 1823; and is referred to by her sister-in-law as "Mrs. F. A.," doubtless to distinguish her from the other Mary, James's wife. Martha Lloyd, whom Frank married as his second wife, long, long after, seems to have been such a favourite with the family that she practically lived with the Austens at Southampton, as her own mother had died some years before.

The country round Southampton is pretty, and the town itself pleasant; we have a contemporary description of it in 1792. "Southampton is one of the most neat and pleasant towns I ever saw . . . was once walled round, many large stones of which are now remaining. There were four gates, only three now. It consists chiefly of one long fine street of three quarters of a mile in length, called the High Street. . . . The Polygon (not far distant) could the original plan have been completed, 'tis said, would have been one of the first places in the kingdom. . . . At the extremity a capital building was erected with two detached wings, and colonnades. The centre was an elegant tavern, with assembly, card rooms, etc., and at each wing, hotels to accommodate the nobility and gentry. The tavern is taken down, but the wings converted into genteel houses." (Mrs. Lybbe Powys.)

There does not seem to be any record of the first year spent here, there are no letters preserved, and we know that Jane wrote no more novels. Household affairs and altering clothes according to the mode must have filled up days too pleasantly monotonous to have anything worth recording. Southampton evidently did not inspire her, for it figures in none of her books, though its neighbour, Portsmouth, is described as the home of Fanny Price in *Mansfield Park*.

Yet in October 1805, just at the time Jane was settling into her new home, was fought the Battle of Trafalgar, which smashed the allied fleets of Spain and France, and freed Britain from any fear of invasion. As it was a naval battle, we can imagine for the sake of her brothers she must have thrilled at the tremendous news, which would arrive as fast as a sailing ship could bring it —probably a day or two after the action.

In January 1807, Cassandra was again at Godmersham, and Jane writes her several letters full of family detail as usual.

James Austen had then been staying at Southampton with his wife; perhaps they had brought with them the little son who looked out of the window at the fairy carriage and the ponies; as he was born in November 1798 he would be between eight and nine years old. His little sister Caroline certainly was there, for she is mentioned by name.

In speaking of a book Jane draws a distinction between her two sisters-in-law, "Mrs. F. A., to whom it is new, enjoys it as one could wish, the other Mary, I believe, has little pleasure from that or any other book."

The garden at Southampton was evidently the cause of much enjoyment. "We hear that we are envied our house by many people, and that our garden is the best in the town."

" Our garden is putting in good order by a man who bears a remarkably good character, has a very fine complexion, and asks something less than the first. The shrubs which border the gravel walk he says are only sweet briar and roses, and the latter of an indifferent sort; we mean to get a few of a better kind therefore, and at my own particular desire he procures us some syringas. I could not do without a syringa, for the sake of Cowper's line. We talk also of a laburnum. The border under the terrace wall is clearing away to receive currants and gooseberry bushes, and a spot is found very proper for raspberries."

In this extract the odd use of the active for the passive tense, in fashion in the eighteenth century, jars on modern ears, these and similar constructions, used throughout the novels, have had something to do with the opinions of those people who have dismissed these brilliant works as " vulgar."

Terrific fighting continued on the Continent, and in December the prestige of Napoleon was enhanced on the stubborn field of Austerlitz. In the beginning of 1806, England had the misfortune to lose by death the great minister Pitt, who had steered her through such perilous times. It is said that the news of Austerlitz was the final blow to a nature worn out by stress and anxiety. In September of the same year his talented but inferior rival, Fox, died also.

In this year was issued the famous Berlin Decree, by which Napoleon prohibited all commerce with Great Britain, and declared confiscated any British merchandise or shipping. But Britain had spirit enough to retort in the following year with a decree declaring a blockade of France, and that any of her merchant vessels were fair prizes unless they had previously touched at a British port.

The war continued without intermission throughout 1807. Austria, exhausted, had sullenly withdrawn, Prussia had plucked up spirit to join with Russia in opposing the conqueror of Europe, but in June, after the hard fought battle of Frieland, France concluded with Russia the secret Peace of Tilsit, based upon mutual hatred of England. England, however, soon found out the menace directed against her, and as the French troops marched to Denmark, evidently with the intention of summoning that country to use her fleet in accordance with their orders, England by a prompt and brilliant countermove appeared before Copenhagen first, and by bombarding the town compelled submission, and carried away the whole fleet for safety's sake. Those were glorious days for the navy, when measures were prompt and decisive, when no hesitation and shilly-shallying and fear of "hurting the feelings" of an unscrupulous enemy prevented Britain from taking care of herself.

Britain was now at war with Russia and Denmark as well as France, but the unprecedented duplicity of Napoleon in Spain in 1807 gave Britain an unexpected field on which to do battle, and allies by no means to be despised. Spain was France's ally, yet France after marching through the country to crush Portugal, quietly annexed the country of their ally in returning, and by a ruse made the whole Royal Family prisoners in France, while Napoleon's brother Joseph, King of Naples, was subsequently proclaimed King. The Spaniards were aroused, and though the best of their troops had been previously drawn off into Germany by the tyrant, they managed to give a good account of themselves, even against the invincible French. Joseph Buonaparte had been proclaimed King of Spain in June 1808. In that month Jane was at Godmersham again, and though she did not know it, this was the last visit she would pay before the death of Mrs. Edward Knight, which occurred in the following October, at the birth of her eleventh child; Jane seems to have noticed her sister-in-law was not in good health, she says, " I cannot praise Elizabeth's looks, but they are probably affected by a cold."

Mr. and Mrs. James Austen accompanied her on this visit, and her account of the arrival gives such a homely picture that, trivial as it is, it is worth quoting. " Our two brothers were walking before the house as we approached as natural as life. Fanny and Lizzy met us in the hall with a great deal of pleasant joy. . . . Fanny came to me as soon as she had seen her aunt James to her room, and stayed while I dressed . . . she is grown both in height and size since last year, but not immoderately, looks very well, and seems as to conduct

FASHIONS FOR LADIES IN 1795

and manner just what she was and what one could wish her to continue."

"Yesterday passed quite à la Godmersham; the gentlemen rode about Edward's farm, and returned in time to saunter along Bentigh with us; and after dinner we visited the Temple Plantations. . . . James and Mary are much struck with the beauty of the place."

Lord Brabourne gives a note on the Temple Plantation, it was "once a ploughed field, but when my grandfather first came to Godmersham, he planted it with underwood, and made gravel walks through it, planted an avenue of trees on each side of the principal walk, and added it to the shrubberies. The family always walked through it on their way to church, leaving the shrubberies by a little door in the wall at the end of the private grounds."

The casual sentence "Mary finds the children less troublesome than she expected," adds one more stroke to the character of that sister-in-law which Jane makes us know so well.

Mrs. Knight senior was still living, and was generous toward the other members of her adopted son's family besides himself.

"This morning brought me a letter from Mrs. Knight, containing the usual fee, and all the usual kindness. . . . She asks me to spend a day or two with her this week . . . her very agreeable present will make my circumstances quite easy; I shall reserve half for my pelisse."

It will be remembered that Mrs. Edward Knight had been a Miss Bridges, and the good-natured Harriet, her sister, was now staying at Godmersham with her own husband, Mr. Moore, whom Jane did not think good enough for her, though she admits later, "he is a sensible man, and tells a story well." She refers to her sister-in-law's opinion of her, "Mary was very disappointed in her beauty, and thought him very disagreeable; James admires her and finds him pleasant and conversable."

It was at the conclusion of this visit that Jane wrote to her sister of the pressing necessity of coming home again to meet the visitor with whom her "honour as well as affection" were engaged.

She was now thirty-two, no longer a young girl, and not at all likely to mistake the nature of attentions of which she had had her full share. However it was, whether the visitor did not come, or coming proved himself unequal to her ideal, we do not know, and in any case the romance so mysteriously suggested by these few words, must ever remain in the shadow.

Jane speaks with pleasure of her sister-in-law, Elizabeth, " having a very sweet scheme of accompanying Edward into Kent next Christmas." Alas, before that Christmas came, the loving mother, who seems to have been in every way a perfect wife and sister, was no more.

When this sad event occurred in October the sisters had again changed places, Cassandra being at Godmersham and Jane at Southampton. The first of Jane's letters of this period is congratulatory on the birth of Edward's eleventh child, and sixth son, but very shortly afterwards she writes in real sorrow at the dreadful news which has reached her of the death of her dear sister-in-law. The news came by way of Mrs. James Austen and her sister Martha, who was at Southampton.

"We have felt—we do feel—for you all as you do not need to be told; for you, for Fanny, for Henry, for Lady Bridges, and for dearest Edward, whose loss and whose sufferings seem to make those of every other person nothing. God be praised that you can say what you do of him, that he has a religious mind to bear him up and a disposition that will gradually lead him to comfort. My dear, dear Fanny, I am so thankful that she has you with her! You will be everything to her; you will give her all the consolation that human aid can give. May the Almighty sustain you all, and keep you, my dearest Cassandra, well."

"With what true sympathy our feelings are shared by Martha you need not be told; she is the friend and sister under every circumstance."

Poor Fanny was then in her sixteenth year, the time when a girl perhaps feels the loss of a sensible, affectionate mother more than any other. She acquitted herself splendidly in the difficult task that fell on her as the eldest of so many brothers and sisters. Her next sister Lizzy was at this time only eight years old, and though she seems to have felt the loss keenly, it could not be the same to her as it was to Fanny.

Mourning at that time entailed heavy crape, and Jane at once fitted herself out with all that was proper. The two eldest boys, Edward and George, were by this time at Winchester College, but when their mother died they went first to their aunt and uncle at Steventon, and on October 24 came on to Southampton. Jane's next letter is full of them. "They behave extremely well in every respect, showing quite as much feeling as one wishes to see, and on every occasion speaking of their father with the liveliest affection. His letter was read over by each of them yesterday and with many tears; George sobbed aloud, Edward's tears do not flow so easily, but as far as I can judge, they are both very properly impressed by what has happened. . . . George is almost a new acquaintance to me, and I find him, in a different way, as engaging as Edward. We do not want amusement; bilbocatch, at which George is indefatigable, spillikens, paper ships, riddles, conundrums, and cards, with watching the ebb and flow of the river, and now and then a stroll out keep us well employed."

Rhymed charades were a very common form of amusement at that date, and all the Austen family excelled in them.

It will be remembered that Mr. Elton's charade, of which the meaning was "Courtship," further misled the match-making Emma into thinking he was in love with Harriet the dowerless, while she herself, the heiress, was the real object of his attentions.

Several charades of this type made up by the Austens are still extant; the two following are Jane's own.

> "Divided I'm a gentleman
> In public deeds and powers;
> United, I'm a monster, who
> That gentleman devours."

To which the answer is *A-gent*.

> "You may lie on my first by the side of a stream,
> And my second compose to the nymph you adore;
> But if, when you've none of my whole, her esteem
> And affection diminish—think of her no more."

Which is easily read as *Bank-note*.

Both of these specimens show the gaiety of spirit so noticeable in the smallest extracts from her letters.

Her observations on her nephews put the two boys before us to the life. "While I write now George is most industriously making and manning paper ships, at which he afterwards shoots horse chestnuts, brought from Steventon on purpose; and Edward equally intent over the Lake of Killarney and twisting himself about in one of our great chairs."

Her wonderful powers as an entertainer are clearly shown in this sad time, when she strove to keep her nephews occupied to the exclusion of sad thoughts; she took them for excursions on the Itchen, when they rowed her in a boat, and she was never weary of entering into their sports and feelings; her real unselfishness came out very strongly on this occasion.

Sir Arthur Wellesley had sailed for Spain in the July of this year, and now England was in the throes of the Peninsular War; some of the very few allusions that Jane ever makes to contemporary events are to be found in reference to the Peninsular War, and these are more personal than general. On hearing of Sir John Moore's death in January 1809, she writes: "I am sorry to find that Sir J. Moore has a mother living, but though a very heroic son, he might not be a very necessary one to her happiness. . . . I wish Sir John had united something of the Christian with the hero in his death. Thank heaven we have had no one to care for particularly among the troops, no one in fact nearer to us than Sir John himself."

CHAPTER XV

CHAWTON

IN 1809 another move was contemplated. Edward Knight had found it in his power to offer his mother and sisters a home rent free; and he gave them the choice of a house in Kent, probably not far from Godmersham, or a cottage at Chawton close to his Manor House there.

The latter offer was accepted, and preparations were made to alter the cottage, which had been a steward's residence, into a comfortable dwelling. The cottage is still standing, close by the main road, and may be seen by anyone in passing; it is of considerable size, and there are six bedrooms besides garrets. It stands close to the junction of two roads, one of which passes through Winchester to Southampton, and the other through Fareham to Gosport. Chawton lies about as far north-west of Winchester as Steventon does north.

The considerable country town of Alton, which would be convenient for shopping, is only about a mile from the village. The cottage, dreary and weather-beaten in appearance, is of a solid square shape, and abuts on the high-road with only a paling in front. It is not an attractive looking dwelling, but probably at the time was fresher and brighter in appearance than it is now. It had also the advantage of a good garden.

It is now partially used for a club or reading-room and partially by cottagers. At the junction of the two roads aforesaid is a muddy pond, that which was playfully referred to by Jane in writing to her nephew, who had not been well, when she says "you may be ordered to a house by the sea or by a very considerable pond."

A short distance along the Gosport Road is the entrance gate to the Manor House, and about fifty yards up the drive is the pretty little church, considerably altered since Jane's time, with pinnacled and ivy-mantled tower. Just above it is the fine old Elizabethan house.

In 1525 one William Knight had a lease of the place; the house itself was probably built by his son John, who bought the estate, and it has remained ever since in the hands of the Knight family, if we may count adoption as ranking in family inheritance.

The move to Chawton was evidently some time in contemplation before actually taking place, for writing in December 1808, Jane says that they want to be settled at Chawton "in time for Henry to come to us for some shooting in October at least, or a little earlier, and Edward may visit us after taking his boys back to Winchester. Suppose we name the fourth of September."

Of the actual settling in at Chawton we have no details, for the next batch of letters begins in April 1811, and Jane, with her mother and sister, had been there about a year and a half.

Chawton was her home for the rest of her short life, though she actually died at Winchester. At Chawton her three last novels were written, as will be recounted in detail. It is curious that the periods of her literary activity seem to have been synchronous with her residence in the country; at Steventon and at Chawton respectively she produced three novels; at Bath only a fragment, and at Southampton nothing at all.

The life at Chawton during this and the next few years must have been part of the happiest time she ever experienced. Her first book, *Sense and Sensibility*, was published in 1811; she had tasted the joys of earning money, and, what was much greater, the joy of seeing her own ideas and characters in tangible shape; she lived in a comfortable, pretty home, with the comings and goings of her relatives at the Manor House to add variety, and she had probably lost the restlessness of girlhood. If the conjecture of which we have spoken in a previous chapter was true, she had now had time to get over a sorrow which must have taken its place with those sweet unrealised dreams in which the pain is much softened by retrospect. That she fully appreciated her country surroundings is shown by frequent notes on the garden at Chawton. "Our young piony at the foot of the firtree has just blown and looks very handsome, and the whole of the shrubbery border will soon be very gay with pinks and sweet williams, in addition to the columbines already in bloom. The Syringas too are coming out. We are likely to have a great crop of Orleans plums, but not many greengages." "You cannot imagine what a nice walk we have round the orchard. The row of beech look very pretty and so does the young quickset hedge in the garden. I hear to-day that an apricot has been detected on one of the trees." "Yesterday I had the agreeable surprise of finding several scarlet strawberries quite ripe. There are more strawberries and fewer currants than I thought at first. We must buy currants for our wine."

Thus the seasons are marked. The Austens ate

their own tender young peas from the garden, and "my mother's" chickens supplied the table.

Mrs. Austen at this time seems to have taken a new lease of life, she busied herself with garden and poultry, and did not shirk even the harder details necessitated by these occupations.

Her granddaughter Anna, James's eldest daughter, now grown up, was a constant visitor at the cottage, and speaks of Mrs. Austen's wearing a "round green frock like a day labourer" and "digging her own potatoes." Anna enjoyed the little gaieties that fell to her lot as freshly as her aunt had done at her age, indeed with even more simplicity, for Jane remarks of one ball to which she went "it would not have satisfied me at her age." And again, "Anna had a delightful evening at the Miss Middletons, syllabub, tea, coffee, singing, dancing, a hot supper, eleven o'clock, everything that can be imagined agreeable," as if the freshness of Anna's youth were very fresh indeed.

The beautiful park stretching around Chawton House, with its fine beech trees, was of course quite open to the inhabitants of the cottage, who must have derived many advantages from their near relationship to the owner.

Altogether, with the freedom from care for the future, the companionship of her sister, the increased health and energy of her mother, the solace of her writing, the comings and goings of the Chawton party, and the occasional visits to London and elsewhere, to give her fresh ideas, Jane's life must have been as pleasant as external circumstances could make it. We can picture her sauntering out in the early summer sunshine, her head demurely encased in the inevitable cap, while the long stray curl tickles her cheek as she stoops to see the buds bursting into bloom or triumphantly gathers the earliest rose. We can picture her standing about watching Mrs. Austen feeding the chickens, and giving her opinion as to their management. Then going in to the little parlour, or living-room, and sitting down to the piano while Cassandra manipulated an old-fashioned tambour frame. In this little parlour, in spite of frequent interruptions, Jane did all her writing sitting at the big heavy mahogany desk of the old style, like a wooden box, which opened at a slant so as to form a support for the paper; at this time she was revising *Sense and Sensibility* for the press, or adding something to the growing pile of MS. called *Mansfield Park*. We cannot imagine that she wrote much at a time, for her work is minute, small, and well digested; probably after a scene or conversation between two of the characters, she would be interrupted by another member of the household, and stroll up to the Manor House to give orders for the reception of some of the Knight family, or go into Alton to buy some necessary household article. Occasionally a post-chaise would rattle past, or the daily coach and waggons would form a diversion.

For six months, during the year 1813, the whole of the Godmersham party lived at Chawton, while their other house was being repaired and painted, and this intercourse added greatly to Jane's happiness. She cemented that affectionate friendship with her eldest niece Fanny, and Lord Brabourne gives little extracts from his mother's diary to show how close the companionship was between the two, " Aunt Jane and I had a very interesting conversation," " Aunt Jane and I had a very delicious morning together," " Aunt Jane and I walked into Alton together," and so on.

But during these years there was no abatement of the fierce turmoil in Europe, the Peninsular War, demanding ever fresh levies of men and fresh subsidies of money, was a continual drain on England's resources, and the beginning of 1812 found the French practically masters of Spain; but in that year the tide turned, and after continual and bloody battles and sieges in which the loss of life was enormous, Wellington drove the French back across the Pyrenees, and in the following year planted his victorious standard actually on French soil.

But the effects of the continuous wars were being felt in England, in 1811 broke out the Luddite riots, nominally against the introduction of machinery, but in reality because of the high price of bread and the scarcity of employment and money. Austria had signed the disastrous Peace of Vienna with France in 1809, and during this and the following years the Continent with small exception was ground beneath the heel of Napoleon, who in 1812 commenced the invasion of Russia which was to cost him so dearly. In 1811 there is rather a characteristic exclamation in one of Jane's letters apropos of the war: " How horrible it is to have so many people killed! And what a blessing that one cares for none of them!"

Napoleon's tyranny and utter regardlessness of the feelings of national pride in the countries he had conquered now began to bring forth for him a bitter harvest. The Sixth Coalition of nations was formed against him, including Russia, Prussia, Austria, Great Britain and Sweden. After terrific fighting his armies were forced back over the Rhine, and the mighty Empire he had formed of powerless and degraded "Republics" melted away like snow in an August sun. In March 1814, Paris, itself was forced to surrender to the triumphant armies of the Allies. In April, Napoleon signed his abdication and retired to Elba. Ever since he first appeared as an active agent on the battlefields of Europe he had kept the Continent in a perpetual ferment; cruelty, bloodshed and horror had followed in his train. His mighty personality had seemed scarcely human, and his very name struck terror into all hearts, and became a bugbear with which to frighten children.

We have two letters of Jane's in the early part of March, written from London where she was staying with her brother Henry. There is not another until June, and that is dated from Chawton. Of course it is difficult to imagine that any intermediate letters she wrote can have been entirely free from allusion to the great news at which the whole Continent burst into pæans of thankfulness, and which must have made England feel as if she had awakened from a nightmare, but as we have no proof either way it must be left open to doubt.

In the June letter she says to Cassandra, who was in London, " Take care of yourself and do not be trampled to death in running after the Emperor. The report in Alton yesterday was that they would certainly travel this road either to or from Portsmouth." This referred to the visit of the Allied monarchs to England after their triumph in Paris, and the " Emperor " was the Emperor Alexander of Russia, who but a few years ago had formed a secret treaty with Napoleon to the detriment of England!

Here we must leave political matters, to take a short review of the work which Jane had produced in the years since she had come to Chawton.

In 1811 the first of her books, *Sense and Sensibility*, was published at her own expense, and produced in three neat little volumes in clear type by T. Egerton, Whitehall. Her identity was not disclosed by the title-page, which simply bore the words " By a Lady." She paid a visit to her brother Henry in London in order to arrange the details, with which Henry helped her very much. When in London with this object she writes,

"No, indeed, I am never too busy to think of *Sense and Sensibility*. I can no more forget it than a mother can forget her sucking child, and I am much obliged to you for your enquiries. I have had two sheets to correct but the last only brings us to Willoughby's first appearance. Mrs. K. regrets in the most flattering manner that she must wait *till* May, but I have scarcely a hope of its being out in June. Henry does not neglect it; he *has* hurried the printer, and says he will see him again to-day."

Sense and Sensibility did not come out until she had returned to the country, and when she received £150 for it later on, she thought it "a prodigious recompense for that which had cost her nothing." And certainly, considering her anonymity and the small chances the book had, she had good reason to be satisfied. The gratifying reception of *Sense and Sensibility* seems to have awakened the powers of writing which had so long lain dormant from want of encouragement. In 1812 she began *Mansfield Park*, perhaps in some ways the least interesting, though by no means the least well constructed, of her novels. Edmund and Fanny are both a little too mild for the taste of most people, and are far from taking their real place as hero and heroine. However, Edmund's blind partiality for Miss Crawford is very natural, and, as Henry Austen himself said, it is certainly impossible to tell until quite the end how the story is going to be finished. The minor characters are throughout excellent; it is one of Jane's shining qualities that no character, however small the part it has to play, remains unknown, she seems able to describe in a touch or two some human quality or defect which at once brings us into intimate relations with either man or woman. Mr. Rushworth's self-importance, "I am to be Count Cassel and to come in first in a blue dress, and a pink satin cloak, and afterwards have another fine fancy suit by way of a shooting dress. I do not know how I shall like it . . . I shall hardly know myself in a blue dress and pink satin cloak," is excellent.

Lady Bertram's character might be gathered from one sentence in the letter which she sends to Fanny, telling of her elder son's dangerous illness : " Edmund kindly proposes attending his brother immediately, but I am happy to add Sir Thomas will not leave me on this distressing occasion as it would be too trying for me."

Mrs. Norris, with her sycophantic speeches towards her well-to-do nieces, her own opinion of her virtues, her admonitions to Fanny, her habit of taking credit for the generous acts performed by other people, her spunging, and trick of getting everything at the expense of others, is the most striking figure in the book. When poor Fanny, having been neglected and left alone all day, the odd one of the party, is returning with the rest rather drearily from Rushworth Park, Mrs. Norris remarks—

" Well, Fanny, this has been a fine day for you, upon my word! Nothing but pleasure from beginning to end! I am sure you ought to be very much obliged to your Aunt Bertram and me for contriving to let you go. A pretty good day's amusement you have had." This, when she has done her best to stop Fanny's going at all, depicts her character in unmistakable colours. On another occasion she tells the meek Fanny, " The nonsense and folly of people's stepping out of their rank and trying to appear above themselves makes me think it right to give you a hint, Fanny, now that you are going into company without any of us, and I do beseech and entreat you not to be putting yourself forward, and talking and giving your opinion as if you were one of your cousins, as if you were dear Mrs. Rushworth or Julia. That will never do, believe me. Remember wherever you are you must be the lowest and last." In the same book Sir Thomas Bertram's conference with his niece on the proposals he has received for her from Mr. Crawford is a wonderful commentary on the opinions of the time, but is too long to quote in entirety. That Fanny should refuse a handsome eligible young man, merely because she could neither respect nor love him, was quite incredible, and not only foolish but wicked. Sir Thomas speaks sternly of his disappointment in her character, " I had thought you peculiarly free from wilfulness of temper, self-conceit and every tendency to that independence of spirit which prevails so much in modern days, even in young women, and which, in young women, is offensive and disgusting beyond all common offence."

We know what Jane herself thought of coercion of this kind, and how fully her sentiments were on the side of liberty of choice.

Among the other excellencies of *Mansfield Park* we may note the sketch of Fanny's home at Portsmouth, with her loud-voiced father and noisy brothers so distressing to her excessive sensitiveness. With all these merits, and to add to them that of excellent construction, *Mansfield Park* may rank high in spite of its somewhat colourless hero and heroine. We cannot, however, leave Edmund and Fanny in the same certainty of a happy future as we may leave others of the heroes and heroines in the novels; they may rub along well enough, but we feel they cannot but be intolerably dull, though perhaps so long as people are not aware of their own dulness they may enjoy happiness of a negative sort!

Henry Austen read *Mansfield Park* in MS. while

travelling with his sister, and she notes with pleasure, " Henry's approbation is hitherto even equal to my wishes. He says it is different from the other two, but he does not think it at all inferior. He has only married Mrs. Rushworth. I am afraid he has gone through the most entertaining part. He took to Lady Bertram and Mrs. Norris most kindly, and gives great praise to the drawing of all the characters. He understands them all, likes Fanny, and, I think, foresees how it will all be." And she adds later, " Henry is going on with *Mansfield Park*. He admires H. Crawford ; I mean properly, as a clever pleasant man, I tell you all the good I can, and I know how much you will enjoy it." " Henry has this moment said he likes my M. P. better and better; he is in the third volume ; I believe now he has changed his mind as to foreseeing the end ; he said yesterday at least he defied anybody to say whether H. C. would be reformed or forget Fanny in a fortnight."

The first two extracts are from a letter given in Mr. Austen-Leigh's *Memoir*.

In 1813 came the publication of *Pride and Prejudice*, apparently at Mr. Egerton's risk. This was evidently Jane's own favourite among the novels, and her references to it are made with genuine delight.

" Lady Robert is delighted with P. and P., and really was so, I understand, before she knew who wrote it, for, of course she knows now." " I long to have you hear Mr. H's opinion of P. and P. His admiring my Elizabeth so much is particularly welcome to me." " Poor Dr. Isham is obliged to admire P. and P. and to send me word that he is sure he shall not like Madam D'Arblay's new novel half so well. Mrs. C. invented it all of course." The book had come out quite in the beginning of the year, for in a letter dated Jan. 29, 1813, given by Mr. Austen-Leigh, she writes—

"I hope you received my little parcel by J. Bond on Wednesday evening, my dear Cassandra, and that you will be ready to hear from me again on Sunday, for I feel that I must write to you to-day. I want to tell you that I have got my own darling child from London. On Wednesday I received one copy sent down by Falkner with three lines from Henry to say that he had given another to Charles and sent a third by the coach to Godmersham. . . . The advertisement is in our paper to-day for the first time: 18s. He shall ask £1, 1s. for my two next and £1, 8s. for my stupidest of all."

Mansfield Park was finished in the same year, and came out under the auspices of Mr. Egerton in 1814, though the second edition was transferred to Mr. Murray. Before the publication of *Emma,* Jane had begun to be known in spite of the anonymity of her title-pages. The only bit of public recognition she ever personally received was accorded to her while she was in London, and must be told in the account of her London experiences.

CHAPTER XVI

IN LONDON

DURING the years when she lived at Chawton, Jane stayed pretty frequently in London, generally with her brother Henry. She was with him in 1811, when he was in Sloane Street, going daily to the bank in Henrietta Street, Covent Garden, in which he was a partner.

Mr. Austen-Leigh says of Henry Austen, "He was a very entertaining companion, but had perhaps less steadiness of purpose, certainly less success in life, than his brothers."

Jane was evidently very fond of Henry, and fully appreciated his ready sympathy and interest in her affairs. In speaking of her young nephew George Knight, she says: "George's enquiries were endless, and his eagerness in everything reminds me often of his uncle Henry."

Henry was at this time married to his cousin Eliza, widow of the Count de Feuillade, who has already been mentioned, and Eliza was evidently vivacious and fond of society, so her sister-in-law had by no means a dull time when staying with her. But how different were Jane's visits to London, unknown, and certainly without any idea of the fame that was to attend her later, to those of her forerunners and contemporaries who had been "discovered," and who on the very slightest grounds were fêted and adored. The company of Mrs. Austen's friends, a little shopping, an occasional visit to the play, these were the details which filled up the daily routine of Jane's visit. She made the acquaintance of many of her sister-in-law's French friends, and enjoyed a large musical party given by her, where, "including everybody we were sixty-six," and where "the music was extremely good harp, pianoforte, and singing," and the "house was not clear till twelve."

It is not difficult to reconstruct the London that she knew. Rocque's splendid map of the middle of the eighteenth century gives us a basis to go upon, though houses had been rapidly built since it was made. Even at Rocque's date, London reached to Hyde Park Corner, and the district we call Mayfair was one of the smartest parts of the town. St. George's Hospital stood at the corner as at present, and a line of houses bordered the road running past it, but beyond this, over Belgravia, were open fields called the Five Fields crossed by the rambling Westbourne stream, and traversed by paths.

Sloane Street itself had been planned in 1780, and was called after the famous Sir Hans Sloane, whose collection formed the nucleus of the British Museum. It was therefore comparatively new in Jane's time. To the south, near the river, there were a good many houses at Chelsea, that is to say south of King's Road, and Chelsea Hospital of course stood as at present. Next to it, where is now the strip of garden open to the public, and lined by Bridge Road, stood the waste site and ruins of the famous Ranelagh Rotunda, which had been in its time the scene of so much gaiety; only a few years previous to Jane's visit to Sloane Street it had been demolished and the fittings sold.

Vauxhall, however, the great rival of Ranelagh, was still popular, and continued, with gradually waning patronage, until after the middle of the nineteenth century. It does not appear that Jane ever went there, however.

As for Knightsbridge, if we imagine all the great modern buildings such as Sloane Court and the Barracks done away with, and picture a long unpaved road stretching away into fields and open country westward, with a few small houses of the brick box type on both sides, we get some idea of the district. Sloane Street was then in fact quite the end of London; not long before it had been dangerous to travel to the outlying village of Chelsea without protection at night, and it was not until another fourteen years had passed that the Five Fields were laid out for building.

In the London of that date, many things we now take as commonplace necessaries were altogether wanting, and if we could be carried back in time it would be the negative side that would strike us most; for instance, there was very little pavement, and what there was was composed of great rounded stones like the worst sort of cobble paving in a provincial town. Most of the roads were made of gravel and dirt; Jane mentions a fresh load of gravel having been thrown down near Hyde Park Corner, which made the work so stiff that "the horses refused the collar and jibbed." Grosley tells us many little details which are just what we want to know, of the kind which in all ages are taken for granted by those who live amid them, so that they need a stranger to record them.

He gives us first an account of his arrival in London by coach over Westminster Bridge.

"I arrived in London towards the close of the day. Though the sun was still above the horizon, the lamps were already lighted upon Westminster Bridge, and upon the roads and streets that lead to it. These streets are broad, regular, and lined with high houses forming the most beautiful quarter of London. The river covered with boats of different sizes, the bridge and the streets [were] filled with coaches, their broad footpaths crowded with people."

The group of buildings on the west of the bridge belonged of course to the old Palace, where, in the chapel of St. Stephen, sat the House of Commons. The Abbey would be much as it is now, also St. Margaret's Church. The splendid Holbein gate standing across Whitehall had been removed about fifteen years before Grosley's visit. He tells us that: " Means, however, have been found to pave with free-stone the great street called Parliament Street. The fine street called Pall Mall is already paved in part with this stone; and they have also begun to new pave the Strand. The two first of these streets were dry in May, all the rest of the town being still covered with heaps of dirt."

The dirt is what strikes him most everywhere: " In the most beautiful part of the Strand and near St. Clement's Church, I have seen the middle of the street constantly foul with a dirty puddle to a height of three or four inches; a puddle where splashings cover those that walk on foot, fill coaches when their windows happen not to be up, and bedaub all the lower parts of such houses as are exposed to it. The English are not afraid of this dirt, being defended from it by their wigs of a brownish curling hair, their black stockings, and their blue surtouts, which are made in the form of a nightgown."

On each side of the road ran a kind of deep and dirty ditch called the kennel, into which refuse and rubbish was thrown, and from which evil and unwholesome odours came. When vehicles in passing splashed into this, a shower of filth would bespatter the passersby behind the posts, therefore it was of no small consequence to keep to the wall, and the giving up of this was by no means a mere matter of form, and frequently produced quarrels between hot-tempered men. Toward the end of the century, however, swords were not usually worn, except by physicians, therefore these quarrels were not always productive of so much harm as they might have been.

The streets were full of enormous coaches, sometimes gilt, hung on high springs, drawn by four, and even six horses; footmen, to the number of four or six, ran beside them, and the wheels splashed heavily in the dirt described, sending up the mud in black spurts. It was early in the nineteenth century that a new kind of paving was tried, blocks of cast-iron covered with gravel, but this was not a success. Besides the large coaches there were hackney coaches, which would seem to us almost equally clumsy and unwieldy. Omnibuses were not seen in the metropolis until 1823, but there was something of the kind running from outlying places to London, for Samuel Rogers tells a story as follows:—

"Visiting Lady —— one day, I made inquiries about her sister. 'She is now staying with me,' answered Lady ——, 'but she is unwell in consequence of a fright which she got on her way from Richmond to London.' On enquiry it turned out that while Miss —— was coming to town, the footman observing an omnibus approach, and thinking she might like to see it, suddenly called in at the carriage window, 'Ma'am, the omnibus!' She, being unacquainted with the term, and not sure but an omnibus might be a wild beast escaped from the Zoological Gardens, was thrown into a dreadful state of agitation by the announcement, and this caused her indisposition."

Hackney coaches were in severe competition with sedan chairs, for to call a chair was as frequent a custom as to send for a hackney coach. The chairmen were notorious for their incivility, just as the watermen had previously been, and as their successors, the cabmen, became later, though now the reproach is removed from them.

The rudeness of chairmen is exemplified in *Tom Jones*, for when Tom found himself after the masqued ball unable to produce a shilling for a chair, he " walked boldly on after the chair in which his lady rode, pursued by a grand huzza from all the chairmen present, who wisely take the best care they can to discountenance all walking afoot by their betters. Luckily, however, the gentry who attend at the Opera House were too busy to quit their stations, and as the lateness of the hour prevented him from meeting many of their brethren in the street, he proceeded without molestation in a dress, which at another season would have certainly raised a mob at his heels."

These chairs were kept privately by great people, and often were very richly decorated with brocade and plush ; it was not an unusual thing for the footmen or chairmen of the owner to be decoyed into a tavern while the chair was stolen for the sake of its valuable furniture. The chairs opened with a lid at the top to enable the occupant to stand up on entrance, and then were shut down ; in the caricatures of the day, these lids are represented as open to admit of the lady's enormous feather being left on her head.

It was of course quite impossible for a lady to go about alone in the streets of London at this date, and even dangerous sometimes for men. The porters, carriers, chairmen, drunken sailors, etc., ready to make a row, are frequently mentioned by Grosley, and scuffles were of constant occurrence. George Selwyn in 1782 was so " mobbed, daubed, and beset by a crew of wretched little chimney-sweeps " that he had to give them money to go away.

These pests were under no sort of control, as there were no regular police in the streets.

"London has neither troops, patrol, or any sort of regular watch; and it is guarded during the night only by old men chosen from the dregs of the people; who have no other arms but a lanthorn and a pole; who patrole the streets, crying the hour every time the clock strikes; who proclaim good and bad weather in the morning; who come to awake those who have any journey to perform; and whom it is customary with young rakes to beat and use ill, when they come reeling from the taverns where they have spent the night." (Grosley).

It is bewildering to find that this sort of thing continued until George the Fourth's reign, when Sir Robert Peel's Metropolitan Police Act was passed. And in that lawless rowdy age, one wonders how the town ever got on without police; probably there were numerous deaths from violence. It carries us back almost to the Middle Ages to realise that so late as 1783 the last execution took place at Tyburn; Samuel Rogers recollected as a boy seeing a whole cartful of young girls in dresses of various colours on their way to execution for having been concerned in the burning of a house in the Gordon Riots. Though some of these details belong to an age prior to that when Jane stayed in London, yet they lingered on until the nineteenth century with little change.

In 1811 gas was just beginning to be used in lighting the streets! The town was in a strange transitional state. Pall Mall was first lighted with a row of gas-lamps in 1807, and on the King's birthday, June 4, the wall between Pall Mall and St. James's Park was

CHARING CROSS, 1795

brilliantly illuminated in the same way, but gas generally was not placed in the thoroughfares until 1812 or 1813, and meantime oil-lamps requiring much care and attention were the only resource.

It was a noisy, rattling, busy, dirty London then, as much distinguished for its fogs as it is at present.

M. Grosley was much struck with the fogs: "We may add to the inconvenience of the dirt the fog-smoke which, being mixed with a constant fog, covers London and wraps it up entirely. . . . On the 26th of April, St. James's Park was incessantly covered with fogs, smoke, and rain, that scarce left a possibility of distinguishing objects at the distance of four steps."

He speaks at another place of—

"This smoke being loaded with terrestrial particles and rolling in a thick, heavy atmosphere, forms a cloud, which envelopes London like a mantle, a cloud which the sun pervades but rarely, a cloud which, recoiling back upon itself, suffers the sun to break out only now and then, which casual appearance procures the Londoners a few of what they call glorious days."

In regard to the main streets and squares in the West End, the greatest difference noticeable between the London of 1811 and of the present time would be the network of dirty and mean buildings over-spreading the part where is now Trafalgar Square. In the middle of these stood the King's Mews, which had been rebuilt in 1732, and was not done away with until 1829. At the corner where Northumberland Avenue joins Charing Cross, was the splendid mansion of the Duke of Northumberland, which remained until 1874.

Another great difference lay in the fact of there being no Regent Street, for this street was not begun until two years after Jane's 1811 visit. Bond Street was there and Piccadilly, and across the entrance to the

Park, where is now the Duke of York's column, was Carlton House, the home of the obstreperous Prince of Wales.

In M. Grosley's time, Leicester House, in Leicester Fields, was still standing, but in 1811 it had been pulled down. Grosley lodged near here, and his details as to rent, etc., are interesting.

He says that the house of his landlord was small, only three storeys high, standing on an irregular patch of ground, and rented at thirty-eight guineas a year, with an additional guinea for the water supply, which was distributed three times weekly. In this house two or three little rooms on the first storey, very slightly furnished, were let to him at a guinea a week.

The touch about the water supply points to another deficiency; all the present admirable system of private taps and other distributing agencies, also the network of drains, sewers, etc., had yet to be evolved, for sanitation was in a very elementary condition.

Many of the shops were still distinguished by signs, for though the custom of numbering, in place of signs, had been introduced, it had made way but slowly, thus we find Jane referring to "The tallow chandler is Penlington, at the Crown and Beehive, Charles Street, Covent Garden."

It would be particularly pleasant to know where she did her own shopping in which she was femininely interested, but it is difficult to infer. But beyond the fact that "Layton and Shears" was evidently the draper whom she patronised, and that "Layton and Shears is Bedford House," and that "Fanny bought her Irish at Newton's in Leicester Square," we do not get much detail. But we glean a few particulars from this visit, and one of a later date.

Grafton House was evidently a famous place for

shopping, for she and Fanny frequently paid visits there before breakfast, which was, however, generally much later than we have it, perhaps about ten; Jane says, "We must have been three quarters of an hour at Grafton House, Edward sitting by all the time with wonderful patience. There Fanny bought the net for Anna's gown, and a beautiful square veil for herself. The edging there is very cheap. I was tempted by some, and I bought some very nice plaiting lace at three and fourpence." Again she says, "We set off immediately after breakfast, and must have reached Grafton House by half past eleven; but when we entered the shop the whole counter was thronged and we waited full half an hour before we could be attended to."

"Fanny was much pleased with the stockings she bought of Remmington, silk at twelve shillings, cotton at four shillings and threepence; she thinks them great bargains, but I have not seen them yet, as my hair was dressing when the man and the stockings came."

It was quite the fashion at that time to patronise Wedgwood, whose beautiful china was much in vogue. The original founder of the firm had died in 1795, and had been succeeded by his son.

"We then went to Wedgwood's where my brother and Fanny chose a dinner set. I believe the pattern is a small lozenge in purple, between lines of narrow gold, and it is to have the crest."

This identical dinner set is still in the possession of the family.

Mrs. Lybbe Powys also mentions Wedgwood. "In the morning we went to London a-shopping, and at Wedgwood's as usual were highly entertained, as I think no shop affords so great a variety."

In the spring of 1813 Jane was again in London, and visited many picture galleries. The fact of having

Fanny with her was enough to enhance greatly her pleasure in these sights.

Mrs. Henry Austen had died in the early part of this year, leaving no children. Henry, of course, eventually married again, as did all the brothers with the exception of Edward Knight, but it was not for seven years; his second wife was Eleanor, daughter of Henry Jackson. The house in Sloane Street was given up after his wife's death, and he went to Henrietta Street to be near the bank. It was here Jane came to him.

A collection of Sir Joshua Reynolds' paintings was being exhibited in Pall Mall, though the great painter himself was dead. With her head full of *Pride and Prejudice*, which had recently been published, Jane looks in vain to discover any portrait that will do for Elizabeth Bennet, and failing to find one, she writes playfully, " I can only imagine that Darcy prizes any picture of her too much to like it should be exposed to the public eye. I can imagine he would have that sort of feeling—that mixture of love, pride, and delicacy."

She, however, is more successful in finding one of Jane Bingley, Elizabeth's sister, " Mrs. Bingley's is exactly herself—size, shaped face, features and sweetness; there never was a greater likeness. She is dressed in a white gown with green ornaments, which convinces me of what I had always supposed, that green was a favourite colour with her."

Kensington Gardens were at that time the resort of many of the fashionable; Jane mentions frequently walking there, though we doubt if she were attracted by the scenes of struggle and confusion that sometimes took place.

From *The Times* of March 28, 1794, we learn, " the access to Kensington Gardens is so inconvenient to the visitors, it is to be hoped the politeness of those who have the direction of it will induce them to give orders for another door to be made for the convenience of the public; one door for admission, and another for departure would prove a great convenience to the visitors. For want of this regulation the ladies frequently have their clothes torn to pieces, and are much hurt by the crowd passing different ways."

"Two ladies were lucky enough to escape through the gate of Kensington Gardens, on Sunday last, with only a broken arm each. When a few lives have been lost perchance then a door or two may be made for the convenience of the families of the survivors."

This shows that there was a wall or high paling running completely round the Gardens.

We find mentioned also the seats or boxes scattered up and down the grass-plots, and moving on a pivot to catch the sun, a convenience it would be well to restore.

When one realises the crowds that habitually frequented the place it seems as if there must be some mistake in the record that a man was accidentally shot in 1798 when the keepers "were hunting foxes in Kensington Gardens!"

The Serpentine was made out of the Westbourne in 1730, and the gardens reclaimed, having been up to then a mere wilderness. During the reign of George II., the Gardens were only open to the public on Saturdays, but when the Court ceased to reside at Kensington Palace, they were open during the spring and summer. The Broad Walk seems to have been the most fashionable promenade, and doubtless there was frequently to be seen here some such crowd as that described by Tickell, when

> "Each walk with robes of various dyes bespread
> Seems from afar a moving tulip bed,
> Where rich brocades and glossy damasks glow,
> And chintz, the rival of the showery bow."

During most of her visits to London, Jane went several times to the theatre, chiefly to Covent Garden and Drury Lane, which were then considered far the best, though there were many others existing, among which were the Adelphi, which had been opened in 1806; Astley's Amphitheatre for the exhibition of trained horses, which was very popular; the Haymarket, or Little Theatre, taken down in 1820; the Lyceum, which was then the opera house, having been enlarged in 1809; the Olympic, which belonged to Astley, and where there was the same style of show as at his other theatre; the Pantheon, Oxford Street, chiefly for masquerades and concerts, reopened as an opera house in 1812 and sold up in 1814; the Queen's, near Tottenham Court Road, not much known or frequented; a description which also applies to the old Royalty in Well Street and others. Among places of amusement must also be enumerated the Italian Opera House, which stood where His Majesty's Theatre is at present. It was opened in 1705, burnt down in 1789, and rebuilt the following year.

Of the two principal theatres, Covent Garden had been opened by Rich in 1737, it was afterwards greatly enlarged and improved, and in 1803 John Kemble became proprietor. Only five years later it was burnt to the ground. The new theatre, built on the same site, was reopened in 1809, when the prices were raised: they had been, boxes 4s.; pit 2s 6d.; first gallery 1s. 6d.; upper gallery 1s. There were then no stalls, and persons of "quality" had to go to boxes. The prices demanded by Kemble were: boxes 7s.; pit 3s.; gallery 2s.; while the upper gallery remained the same. A fearful riot broke out on the first night of the new prices, and the mob would hear no explanations, listen to no reason. The members who banded themselves

THE LITTLE THEATRE, HAYMARKET

together adopted the name of O.P., for Old Prices, and would not allow the play to proceed, making an indescribable din with whistles, cat-calls, and shrieks. After weeks of dispute, a compromise was arrived at, the higher price being retained in the case of the boxes.

At an earlier date some of the audience had actually been seated on the stage among the performers; and there were still in Jane's time boxes on the stage, but outside the curtain. We can see this in the illustration of the Little Theatre, Haymarket, where the pit comes right up to the footlights, there being no stalls, and the patrons of the pit are seated on backless benches not divided into compartments.

We gather from contemporary literature that it was a common thing to go to rehearsals of the performances at the opera, and that there was a coffee-room attached, which formed at least as great an attraction to the idle rich, who loved to chatter sweet nothings, as the piece itself.

Kemble was the brother of Mrs. Siddons, and did as much as any man for the improvement of the stage; when he first began his career, he was struck by the ludicrous conventionality of the dresses, which were as much a matter of form as the custom of representing statues of living men "in Roman habit." He and the great Garrick killed this foolish custom.

The conventionalism in matters of dress upon the stage is noticed by the ubiquitous M. Grosley thus—

"On the stage the principal actresses drag long trains after them, and are followed by a little boy in quality of a train-bearer, who is as inseparable from them as the shadow from the body. This page keeps his eye constantly upon the train of the princess, sets it to rights when it is ever so little ruffled or disordered, and is seen to run after it with all his might, when a violent emotion makes the princess hurry from one side of the stage to another."

Drury Lane Theatre has an older record than Covent Garden. It dates from 1663, and in 1682 was the only theatre in London, being considered sufficient for the joint representations of the two old established companies of players, The King's and The Duke's. It was many times rebuilt, being more than once destroyed by fire; in fact nothing is more striking in the annals of theatres than the astonishing number of times nearly every theatre has been burnt down. The third house was burnt in February 1809, and its successor opened in 1812, with a prologue by Lord Byron. During Jane Austen's first recorded visit to London, therefore, it would be in course of rebuilding, though on subsequent visits it would be very fashionable, being new.

Just as in novels during the lifetime of Jane Austen, there was an enormous change from the grandiloquent and conventional, to the natural and simple, and the same in poetry, so it was on the stage. The absurd conventionalism, the unsuitable dresses, no matter what, so long as they were grand, were exchanged for easy declamation and natural attitude.

Garrick, as we have said, was one of the first actors to begin this movement, and it is no wonder that he won the applause of London, and that crowds came to hear him, so that in 1744, when he was to act Hamlet, servants were sent at three o'clock in the afternoon to keep places for their employers, for there were then no such things as reserved seats. Fine actors and actresses abounded in the eighteenth century; Mrs. Siddons, who was born in 1755, did not give her farewell performance in Lady Macbeth until 1812, and lived

THE REV. GEORGE CRABBE

long after. Both Mrs. Oldfield and Peg Woffington, however, had passed away before Jane's time.

It was an age when people were wild about acting, and private theatres were a common hobby, many a young spark ruined himself in this extravagance, and *The Times* of 1798 mentions that there were no fewer than six private theatres in London and Westminster.

The plays commented upon in Jane's letters seem to us very dull, " Fanny and the two little girls are gone to take places for to-night at Covent Garden; *Clandestine Marriage* and *Midas*. The latter will be a fine show for L[izzie] and M[arianne]. They revelled last night in *Don Juan* whom we left in hell at half past eleven. We had Scaramouch and a ghost, and were delighted. I speak of them; my delight was very tranquil, and the rest of us were sober minded. *Don Juan* was the last of three musical things. *Five Hours at Brighton*, in three acts, and the *Beehive* rather less flat and trumpery."

"We had good places in the box next the stage box. . . . I was particularly disappointed at seeing nothing of Mr. Crabbe. I felt sure of him when I saw the boxes were fitted up with crimson velvet. The new Mr. Terry was Lord Ogleby, and Henry thinks he may do, but there was no acting more than moderate."

In the following year, 1814, her comments are, "We went to the play again last night. The *Farmer's Wife* is a musical thing in three acts, and, as Edward was steady in not staying for anything more, we were home before ten. Fanny and Mr. J. P. are delighted with Miss S—— all that I am sensible of . . . is a pleasing person and no skill in acting. We had Mathews, Liston, and Enery; of course some amusement." "Prepare for a play the very first evening,

I rather think Covent Garden, to see Young in *Richard*."

Miss S—— was probably Miss Stephens, a singer who made her debut in 1812 in concerts, and appeared on the stage at Covent Garden in 1813; she afterwards became Countess of Essex. She was considered "unsurpassed for her rendering of ballads." Jane mentions her again—

"We are to see the *Devil to Pay* to-night. I expect to be very much amused. Excepting Miss Stephens, I daresay *Artaxerxes* will be very tiresome."

The Mathews she mentions was Charles Mathews senior.

Liston was at first master of St. Martin's Grammar School, Leicester Square, but became a popular actor, and at the time of her writing was appearing at Covent Garden. But by far the best actor she records having seen is Kean. "We were quite satisfied with Kean, I cannot imagine better acting, but the part was too short and excepting him and Miss Smith,—and she did not quite answer my expectation,—the parts were ill-filled and the play heavy. We were too much tired for the whole of *Illusion* (*Nourjahad*), which has three acts; there is a great deal of finery and dancing in it, but I think little merit. Elliston was Nourjahad, but I think it is a solemn sort of part, not at all calculated for his powers. There was nothing of the best Elliston about him, I might not have known him but for his voice," and later, "I shall like to see Kean again excessively, and to see him with you too. It appeared to me as if there were no fault in him anywhere; and in his scene with Tubal there was exquisite acting."

In another place she says that so great was the rage for seeing Kean that only a third or fourth row could be got, and that "he is more admired than ever."

This is very different from Miss Mitford's account of her first impressions of the great actor: "Well, I went to see Mr. Kean and was thoroughly disgusted. This monarch of the stage is a little insignificant man, slightly deformed, strongly ungraceful, seldom pleasing the eye, still seldomer satisfying the ear—with a voice between grunting and croaking, a perpetual hoarseness which suffocates his words, and a vulgarity of manner which his admirers are pleased to call nature . . . his acting will always be, if not actually insupportable, yet unequal, disappointing and destructive of all illusion."

But, as in her account of Darcy and Elizabeth, we have seen that Miss Mitford preferred the stereotyped and conventional to the natural, of which Jane Austen was so ardent an admirer, therefore we cannot feel much surprise at the difference between the two opinions.

Jane evidently enjoyed good acting, but was critical and not a great lover of the drama unless it was very well done; this we might expect, for naturalness was her admiration, and naturalness she would only find in first-rate performers such as Kean.

CHAPTER XVII

FANNY AND ANNA

THE nephews and nieces at Godmersham were rapidly growing into men and women. Edward and George on leaving Winchester went to Oxford; the luxurious way in which they were brought up evidently sometimes annoyed their aunt, who was accustomed to see the younger generation more repressed; she says of them—

"As I wrote of my nephews with a little bitterness in my last, I think it particularly incumbent on me to do them justice now, and I have great pleasure in saying they were both at the Sacrament yesterday; now these two boys, who are out with the foxhounds, will come home and disgust me again by some habit of luxury or some proof of sporting mania."

While Jane was at Godmersham in 1813, her brother Charles, his wife, and little daughters were there too. It was the custom then—though not an invariable one but a matter of inclination—for a captain in the Navy to take his wife and children voyaging with him. It will be remembered that in *Persuasion* Captain Wentworth says he hates "to hear of women on board," and Mrs. Croft, whose husband is an Admiral, declares "women may be as comfortable on board as in the best house in England. I believe I have lived as much on board as most women and I know nothing superior to the accommodation of a man-of-war."

Charles Austen's wife and children seem to have spent a good deal of time on board with him; and Cassy, the eldest girl, a delicate quiet child, suffered from seasickness during rough weather. Jane says affectionately of her, " Poor little love! I wish she were not so very Palmery, but it seems stronger than ever. I never knew a wife's family features have such undue influence." Cassy was not quite happy among her cousins, " they are too many and too boisterous for her." Jane speaks of her and her mother as being " their own nice selves, Fanny looking as neat and white this morning as possible, and Charles all affectionate, placid, quiet, cheerful good humour."

Alas, in September of the following year Mrs. Charles Austen died in childbirth. Her husband, who was a very domestic man, felt the loss severely; subsequently he married her sister Harriet, and became the father of two boys in addition to his little daughters.

In 1814, Edward Knight was annoyed by a claimant to the Chawton estate, and it appears from what Miss Mitford says on the subject in her letters, that this was in consequence of old Mr. Knight's not having fulfilled some technical point in connection with the property. As Chawton was worth about £5000 a year, the matter was serious, and that it was not altogether a fancy originating in the mind of the claimant, is shown by the fact that after protracted discussions, Edward Knight did, in 1817, pay him a sum of money to settle the matter.

We have no letters of Jane's before November 1815; but she was probably at home at Chawton with her sister and mother, when the news that Napoleon had escaped from Elba burst upon the world like a thunderclap! The call to arms rang throughout Europe, and then followed the terrible Hundred Days which ended on June the eighteenth with the Battle of Waterloo.

Alison in his *Epitome of the History of Europe* says, "No one who was of an age to understand what was going on can ever forget the entrancing joy which thrilled through the British heart at the news of Waterloo. The thanks of Parliament were voted to Wellington and his army; a medal struck by government was given to every officer and soldier who had borne arms on that eventful day; and not less than £500,000 was raised by voluntary subscriptions for those wounded in the fight, and the widows and orphans of the fallen."

We wonder if the household at Chawton contributed its mite among the rest? Jane's heart surely must have thrilled in unison with those of her countrymen!

Louis XVIII. was once more placed on the throne of his fathers, and Napoleon was sent to St. Helena. He arrived there on November the sixteenth, and by that date Jane was again in London nursing her brother Henry.

Between 1814 and 1816 many charming letters passed between Jane and her young niece Fanny, and as these contain more of the personal element than any of the others that have been preserved, they are among the most interesting of all. At the beginning of these letters Fanny was twenty-one, which in those days was considered quite a staid age for an unmarried girl. In one of her letters she tells her aunt that her feelings had cooled towards someone, who at one time she had thought of marrying.

Jane's answer is full of sense and sympathy, and gives us much insight into her own views on the relations of the sexes. "What strange creatures we are," she writes, "it seems as if your being secure of him had made you indifferent. . . . There was a little disgust I suspect at the races, and I do not wonder at it. His expressions then would not do for one who had rather more acuteness, penetration, and taste, than love, which was your case, and yet after all I *am* surprised that the change in the feelings should be so great. He is just what he ever was, only more evidently and uniformly devoted to *you* . . .

"Oh dear Fanny! Your mistake has been one that thousands of women fall into. He was the *first* young man who attached himself to you. That was the charm, and most powerful it is. . . . Upon the whole what is to be done? You have no inclination for any other person. His situation in life, family, friends and above all his character, his uncommonly amiable mind, strict principles, just notions, good habits, *all* that *you* know so well how to value, *all* that is really of the first importance, pleads his cause most strongly. You have no doubt of his having superior abilities, he has proved it at the University, he is, I dare say, such a scholar as your agreeable idle brothers would ill bear a comparison with. The more I write about him the more strongly I feel the desirableness of your growing in love with him again. . . . There *are* such beings in the world, perhaps one in a thousand, as the creature you and I should think perfection, where grace and spirit are united to worth, where the manners are equal to the heart and understanding, but such a person may not come in your way, or, if he does, he may not be the eldest son of a man of fortune, the near relation of your own particular friend and belonging to your own country. . . . And now my dear Fanny, having written so much on one side of the question I shall turn round and entreat you not to commit yourself farther, and not to think of accepting him unless you really do like him. Anything is to be preferred or endured rather than marrying without affection; and if his deficiencies of manner strike you more than all his good qualities, if you continue to think strongly of them, give him up at once . . .

"When I consider how few young men you have yet seen much of; how capable you are of being really in love; and how full of temptation the next six or seven years of your life will probably be, I cannot wish you, with your present very cool feelings, to devote yourself in honour to him. It is very true that you never may attach another man his equal altogether; but if that other man has the power of attaching you *more*, he will be in your eyes the most perfect.

"You are inimitable, irresistible. You are the delight of my life. Such letters, such entertaining letters as you have lately sent! such a description of your queer little heart! such a lovely display of what imagination does! . . . You are so odd, and all the time so perfectly natural, so peculiar in yourself, and yet so like everybody else. It is very, very gratifying to me to know you so intimately. . . . Oh what a loss it will be when you are married! You are too agreeable in your single state. I shall hate you when your delicious play of mind is all settled down into conjugal and maternal affections . . .

"And yet I do wish you to marry very much because I know you will never be happy till you are," and later on, apropos of someone else, she adds: "Single women have a dreadful propensity for being poor, which is one very strong argument in favour of matrimony, but I need not dwell on such arguments with you, pretty dear. To you I shall say, as I have often said before, Do not be in a hurry, the right man will come at last; you will in the course of the next two or three years meet with somebody more generally unexceptionable than anyone you have yet known, who will love you as warmly as possible, and who will so completely attract you that you will feel you never really loved before."

But it was not until 1820 that Fanny married, as his second wife, the Rt. Hon. Sir Edward Knatchbull, 9th Bt., who had already five sons and one daughter, the eldest boy being twelve years old. Six years after the marriage, the daughter married Fanny's brother Edward. She herself lived to nearly ninety, and was the mother of five sons and four daughters, and in 1880 her eldest son was created Baron Brabourne; and he, as has been already stated, was the editor of the volumes of *Letters*.

But Jane's sympathetic advice was called for by more than one niece passing through the difficult time between girlhood and womanhood; Anna, her eldest brother James's daughter, was a frequent visitor at Chawton, and though she does not seem ever to have taken quite the same position in her aunt's affections as Fanny did, she was yet a lively, amusing, pleasant girl.

She had evidently determined to follow in her aunt's footsteps, as was most natural, and had attempted to write a novel herself; Jane's treatment of her tentative efforts was very kind, some of the letters to the would-be authoress are preserved, and nothing could be gentler. "I am very much obliged to you for sending me your MS. It has entertained me extremely; indeed all of us. I read it aloud to your grandmamma and aunt Cass, and we were all very pleased. The spirit does not drop at all. Now we have finished the second book or rather the fifth: Susan is a nice animated little creature, but St. Julian is the delight of our lives. He is quite interesting. The whole of his break off with Lady Helena is very well done." She then goes in great detail into all the characters, making various suggestions: "You are but now coming to the heart and beauty of your story. Until the heroine grows up the fun must be imperfect, but I expect a great deal of entertainment from the next three or four books, and I hope you will not resent these remarks by sending me no more."

Then she gives one or two characteristic touches.

"Devereux Forester's being ruined by his vanity is extremely good, but I wish you would not let him plunge into a 'vortex of dissipation.' I do not object to the thing but cannot bear the expression; it is such thorough novel slang, and so old that I daresay Adam met with it in the first novel he opened."

In 1814, Anna was engaged to Benjamin Lefroy, whom she married in November. After her marriage she first lived at Hendon, but in the following year she and her husband took a small house near Alton, so that she was within a walk of Chawton. She still went on with her novel-writing. And Jane continued to criticise her progress—

"We have no great right to wonder at his [Benjamin Lefroy's] not valuing the name of Progillian. That is a source of delight which even *he* can hardly be quite competent to."

"St. Julian's history was quite a surprise to me. You had not very long known it yourself I suspect. His having been in love with the aunt gives Cecilia an additional interest with him. I like the idea, a very proper compliment to an aunt! I rather imagine indeed that nieces are seldom chosen but out of compliment to some aunt or other. I daresay Ben was in love with me once, and would never have thought of you if he had not supposed me dead of scarlet fever."

Anna became the mother of six daughters and one son, and lived until 1872.

CHAPTER XVIII

THE PRINCE REGENT AND *EMMA*

IN October 1815, Henry Austen was dangerously ill. He had by this time moved into another house, which was in Hans Place, quite near his former residence in Sloane Street, though the connection with the bank in Henrietta Street was still kept up. Both his sisters were with him at first, and an express was sent for his brother Edward, so critical was his state considered to be, but he rallied, and afterwards, when he was out of danger, Edward and Cassandra went on to Chawton, and Jane was left to nurse him back to complete health. The ideas of medicine at that time were primitive, and consisted chiefly of unmitigated blood-letting, an extraordinary custom, which must have been responsible for many a weak body's giving up the ghost.

This incredible system is exemplified in the following anecdote. When Mrs. Lybbe Powys' son Philip had a coach accident she comments on his treatment thus: " He has not, since the accident, tasted a bit of meat, or drunk a drop of wine, had a perpetual blister ever since, and blooded every three or four days for many weeks." Well may the editor of the book remark, " Truly Mr. Powys' enduring this treatment was a survival of the fittest ! "

There was then a wide distinction between the Physician and the Apothecary, which may be noticed in

Jane's playful repudiation: "You seem to be under a mistake as to Mr. H. you call him an apothecary. He is no apothecary, he has never been an apothecary; there is not an apothecary in the neighbourhood—the only inconvenience of the situation perhaps—but so it is, we have not a medical man within reach. He is a Haden, nothing but a Haden, a sort of wonderful nondescript creature on two legs, something between a man and an angel, but without the least spice of an apothecary. He is perhaps the only person not an apothecary hereabouts."

As it happened, this nursing of her brother brought her into public notice, for the physician who attended Henry Austen was also a physician of the Prince Regent's. At that time, though Jane's name had not appeared on the title-page of her books, there was no longer any secret as to the writer's identity, and the doctor told her one day that the Prince of Wales, who had been made Regent in 1811, was a great admirer of her novels; this is the only good thing one ever heard of George IV., and one cannot help doubting the fact; it is hard to imagine his reading any book, however delightful. The physician, however, added that the Prince read the novels often, and kept a set in every one of his residences, further, he himself had told the Prince that the author was in London, and he had desired his librarian to wait upon her. The librarian, Mr. Clarke, duly came, and Jane was invited to go to Carlton House, but it does not seem that the Prince himself deigned to bestow any personal notice upon her, or that he even saw her; she saw Mr. Clarke and Mr. Clarke alone, and therefore one begins to feel tolerably sure that it was from Mr. Clarke the whole thing originated. This worthy man deserves some credit, but that he was lacking in any sense of humour or knowledge of life was evidenced

THE GARDEN OF CARLTON HOUSE

by his ponderous suggestions as to future books, one of which was that Jane should "delineate in some future work the habits of life, character, and enthusiasm of a clergyman, who should pass his time between the metropolis and the country, who should be something like Beattie's minstrel"; and when this was rejected, "an historical romance illustrative of the august house of Cobourg, would just now be very interesting." Jane's reply is full of good sense and excellently expressed. "You are very kind in your hints as to the sort of composition which might recommend me at present, and I am fully sensible that an historical romance, founded on the House of Cobourg, might be much more to the purpose of profit or popularity than such pictures of domestic life in country villages as I deal in. But I could no more write a romance than an epic poem. I could not sit seriously down to write a serious romance under any other motive than to save my life; and if it were indispensable for me to keep it up, and never relax into laughing at myself or at other people, I am sure I should be hung before I had finished the first chapter. I must keep to my own style and go on in my own way; and though I may never succeed again in that, I am convinced that I should totally fail in any other." (Mr. Austen-Leigh's *Memoir*.) She, however, gladly agreed to dedicate her next work to His Royal Highness. The next work was *Emma*, then nearly ready for publication. Mr. Murray was the publisher, and the dedication, which had been graciously accepted, appeared on the title-page.

The state of the Court at that time is abundantly pictured in numerous memoirs, diaries, journals, etc., not the least among which is that of Miss Burney, Jane's contemporary and sister authoress. George III. had one very striking virtue—striking in his time and position and especially in his family—he seems to have lived a good domestic life. He had been married young, to a princess who had no beauty to recommend her, and his first feelings on seeing her had been those of disappointment, but being a sensible, kindly man, he had soon learnt to value the good heart and nature of the girl who had come so far to marry a man she had never seen. Their numerous family linked them together, and though the sons were a constant source of trouble and notorious in their wild lives, the tribe of princesses seem to have endeared themselves to everyone by their gracious manners. Poor old George himself, with his well-meant, "What? What? What?" and his homely ways, could never offend intentionally, and the "sweet queen," as Miss Burney so fulsomely calls her, though fully conscious of her own dignity, and not disposed to make a fuss about the hardships inseparable from the position of her waiting-women, was yet at the bottom kind-hearted too.

As for most of the princes, however, their ways were a byword and scandal. In every contemporary book we read of their being drunk, and otherwise disgracing themselves.

The Prince of Wales and the Duke of York were the worst, and the Dukes of Clarence and Kent seem to have been the best. At Brighton, where the Prince of Wales had established his pavilion, orgies of drink and coarseness went on that disgusted even those accustomed to very free manners; the princes appeared in public with their mistresses, and reeled into public ball-rooms. The Prince's treatment of his own ill-used wife is well known. Purely from caprice, and without a shadow of justification, she, the mother of his only child Princess Charlotte, was dismissed from her home, and forbidden any of the privileges or respect due to her rank, a course of treatment which made England despised among the nations. Of the other two we read:—

"The duke of Kent is certainly one of the most steady looking of the princes, perhaps he may be heavy, but he has unquestionably the most of a Man of Business in his Appearance."

And Horace Walpole says—

"My neighbour, the Duke of Clarence, is so popular, that if Richmond were a borough, and he had not attained his title, but still retained his idea of standing candidate, he would certainly be elected there. He pays his bills regularly himself, locks up his doors at night, that his servants may not stay out late, and never drinks but a few glasses of wine. Though the value of crowns is mightily fallen of late at market, it looks as if His Royal Highness thought they were still worth waiting for; nay, it is said that he tells his brothers, that he shall be king before either; this is fair at least." He was afterwards William IV.

The Prince of Wales mixed freely in political intrigues of the worst kind, and took part in faction politics. As a man he was a contemptible creature without character or intellect, but, in spite of all his faults, he had a certain number of admirers, because as a young man he was graceful and obliging in manners, and personal graciousness in a sovereign covers a multitude of sins.

It is incongruous that a pure sweet story such as *Emma* should have been dedicated to a man whose faults and vices were such as the clean-minded author could never have conceived, but the dedication probably served the purpose of advertising this, the last novel that Jane herself was to see issued to the public.

Emma ranks very high indeed among the novels, but it relies for its position on a different sort of excellence from that which distinguishes *Pride and Prejudice;* there is in it, as we might have expected, more finished workmanship and less of the brilliancy of youth. The book is not so lively as *Pride and Prejudice*, and its somewhat slow opening, unlike Jane's usual style, is enough to discourage some readers who expect to be plunged into a scene such as that which begins her first novel, or which comes very soon in *Sense and Sensibility*. *Emma* has, however, more plot than is usual with Jane Austen's writings, it is more deliberately constructed, and yet the whole scene takes place in a quiet country village without once changing.

The heroine Emma, whose domestic importance as the only unmarried daughter of a wealthy widower has given her a full idea of her own value, has developed her individuality very strongly. She is not spoilt, but all her words and actions betoken one accustomed to impress her will on her surroundings, in a way not often allowed to unmarried girls at home. The motif is her matchmaking propensity, which again and again brings her to grief; this affords opening for many of the humorous touches in which the author delights.

The book is very rich in secondary characters. The garrulous, kind-hearted Miss Bates, with her rattling tongue, is one of the strongly individualised comic characters which Jane generally manages to insert. She ranks with Mr. Collins, with Mrs. Norris, and the lesser specimens of the same gallery, Mrs. Allen and Mrs. Jennings. She is admirably true to life, just such a garrulous, empty-headed, good-hearted, tiresome creature as many a governess of the old school has degenerated into in the evening of her life.

Emma's father, the valetudinarian Mr. Woodhouse, has been said to be overdrawn, but the great merit of Jane's work is that she does not exaggerate; traits to be found in people that any of us might number among our acquaintance are so skilfully depicted as to appear prominent; she selects true if extreme types, and does not draw monstrosities such as those in which Dickens's books abound, and of which one can only say they *may* have existed, once, at one time, but are as rare as the exhibits in a dime museum.

Mr. Woodhouse's married daughter, Mrs. Knightley, is excellently done; her sympathy with her father's tastes is only kept in check by her affection for husband and children, which forces her to attend to them and forget herself; yet the enjoyment with which she sips her gruel, when allowed to have it, is real enjoyment, and she would have certainly lived on gruel too had she been an old maid.

The hero, Mr. Knightley, is one of the few sensible men among Jane's heroes, and he with his experience and strength of character, is, as has been said elsewhere, the only true mate for Emma. Knightley has been criticised as a prig, but he is far from that. He was a stern elderly man apparently at least forty-five in age, though we are told he was only thirty. Emma herself has more ability than her rival, Elizabeth Bennet, in *Pride and Prejudice;* her mind has more depth and application: we could imagine Emma reading and studying, whereas, pleasant as Elizabeth might have been as a companion, her forte was general intelligent interest not depth, and we could not picture her deeply absorbed in any book but a novel. Emma was one of Jane's own favourite heroines, and she said of her, " I am going to draw a heroine whom no one but myself will much like." It is true that for the generality of men Emma would, in real life, have been just a little too strong, but she is none the less interesting to read about.

Mr. Elton has already been commented on in the chapter on clergymen; a more perfect match than he and his vulgar flashy wife would be difficult to find. As for Jane's traits of character in regard to the hero and his brother, her genius cannot be better expressed than in the words of Mr. Herries Pollock, who calls it "the finely touched likeness and unlikeness between the brothers Knightley. At every turn of phrase, at every step so to speak, one knows which is the better man, and yet the point is never pressed by the author." Though on the whole the book has less *verve* than *Pride and Prejudice*, it is rich in observation and quiet humour.

It was published by Mr. Murray in December 1815. Jane says of it—

"My greatest anxiety at present is that this fourth work should not disgrace what was good in the others. But on this point I will do myself the justice to declare that, whatever may be my wishes for its success, I am strongly haunted with the idea that to those readers who have preferred *Pride and Prejudice* it will appear inferior in wit, and to those who have preferred *Mansfield Park* inferior in good sense." (Mr. Austen-Leigh's *Memoir*.)

A reviewer in *The Quarterly* of the autumn 1815 includes *Emma* with other works of the same writer. It has been supposed, therefore, that the proof sheets must have been in the hands of the *Quarterly* reviewer before the work was actually issued. Mr. Austin-Dobson, by application to Mr. Murray, cleared up the difficulty, for he ascertained that, owing to exceptional delays, the number of the Review bearing date October 1815 did not in reality come out until March 1816, and that therefore *Emma* had actually appeared before its production.

The reviewer was Sir Walter Scott, as is stated by Lockhart in a note to the *Life*, who adds that *Emma* and *Northanger Abbey* were in particular great favourites of Scott's. In his summary at the end of the article, Sir Walter Scott says—

"The author's knowledge of the world and the peculiar tact with which she presents characters that the reader cannot fail to recognise, reminds us something of the merits of the Flemish school of painting. The subjects are not often elegant and certainly never grand; but they are finished up to nature, and with a precision which delights the reader." "The faults on the contrary arise from the minute detail which the author's plan comprehends. Characters of folly or simplicity such as those of old Woodhouse and Miss Bates, are ridiculous when first presented, but if too often brought forward, or too long dwelt upon, their prosing is apt to become as tiresome in fiction as in real society."

In this we cannot agree, to accuse Jane of it is to accuse her of lacking the very gift in which she was pre-eminent—selection. The merit of her bores is that they never bore, but are only amusing. She never proses, and her few paragraphs of quotation from the sayings of Miss Bates set that lady before us as clearly or more clearly than if fifty pages from the actual life had been given by the phonograph.

From what Jane says she apparently saw this article in March 1816 when she was back at Chawton; for she writes: "The authoress of *Emma* has no reason, I think, to complain of her treatment in it, except in the total omission of *Mansfield Park;* I cannot but be sorry that so clever a man as the reviewer of *Emma* should consider it as unworthy of being noticed."

That Jane was satisfied with her treatment by Mr. Murray may be seen by her handing over to him the conduct of the second edition of *Mansfield Park*. She writes in one place, "I had a most civil note in reply from

Mr. Murray. He is so very polite indeed that it is quite over-coming."

At this time she must have begun the last and shortest of her books, *Persuasion*, which she finished in August of the same year. And with this we enter on the last phase, the gradual decline and sinking of the bright spirit, which had added so greatly to the happiness of thousands it had never known.

CHAPTER XIX

LAST DAYS

THE evening of Jane's life had set in, but yet it had not occurred even to those who loved her best that they must inevitably lose her. She was in her forty-first year; recognition from the public had just begun to be accorded to her; in the novels she had lately written no sign of decay could be detected. It is true that in both *Emma* and *Persuasion* there is a particular maturity of rendering, and a kindlier tone that marks perhaps a difference, but not degeneracy. If the word seriousness can ever be used of such clear-cut, brilliant work as hers, we might say that a certain sweet seriousness pervaded these two, which are more alike in tone than any of the other novels. *Persuasion* has been called the "most beautiful of all the novels"; it has many excellencies, not the least among which is the character of the heroine, whose girlish weakness develops into a loyal steadfastness. She has also that endearingness that perhaps certain others of the heroines lack. In fact, of all the principal female characters that of Anne Elliot has most of that nameless and indefinable charm, which comes from a combination of qualities such as firmness, gentleness, unselfishness, sympathy and sweetness, a charm which is more lovable than any number of stereotyped graces. Though Anne was at one time weak, we feel that she outgrows it, that it was the weakness of immaturity, not of character, and that her loyalty fully redeems it.

Jane herself says of Anne Elliot, "You may perhaps like the heroine as she is almost too good for me," yet the too-good note seems less obtrusive with Anne than with Fanny Price, whose exceeding surface meekness does sometimes produce a little exasperation. Anne and Fanny have the most in common among the heroines of the novels, yet what a difference is there! Fanny has many virtues, but her intense nervous sensitiveness makes one feel her self-consciousness, and underlying all her shrinking there was a quality of obstinacy that is felt without being insisted upon. It is just the subtle difference that Jane knew so well how to make, the feeling perhaps is that Fanny is not quite a gentlewoman, that she would be difficult to get on with, however meek and self-effacing on the surface, while Anne could never be anything but a delightful companion.

Incidentally some parts of *Persuasion* have already been referred to, Louisa Musgrove's fall on the Cobb, the scenes that take place in Bath, the touching words of Anne when she feels that she has hopelessly lost her lover, which strike a deeper note of feeling than any other in the whole range of the novels. It remains therefore but to say that there is no secondary character to equal those of Miss Bates or Mr. Collins, that the secondary characters are in all cases less sharply defined than those usually depicted by Jane, but that Captain Wentworth is equal to his good fortune, and that as a pair of lovers he and Anne stand unrivalled.

Persuasion was finished in July 1816, but Jane was not satisfied with it, perhaps her own failing health and the sense of tiredness that went with it, had made her lose that grip of the action that she had hitherto held so well; she felt the story did not end satisfactorily, that it wanted bringing together and clinching so to speak; Mr. Austen-Leigh says: "This weighed upon her mind, the more so probably on account of her weak state of health, so that one night she retired to rest in very low spirits. But such depression was little in accordance with her nature, and was soon shaken off. The next morning she woke to more cheerful views and brighter inspirations; the sense of power revived and imagination resumed its course. She cancelled the condemned chapter and wrote two others, entirely different, in its stead."

These were the tenth and eleventh chapters, and contained the scene in which Anne so touchingly expresses her ideas on the theme of woman's love. There is no question that the story as it now stands is improved by the change, and that her instinct was true. Mr. Austen-Leigh gives the cancelled chapter in his *Memoir*, and it certainly is "tame and flat" compared with the others, and had she not made the substitution it might justly have been said that *Persuasion*, however charming, did show signs of failing power.

This book was not published until after her death, when it appeared in one volume with *Northanger Abbey*, the first to which her name was prefixed, this came out in 1818 with a Memoir by her brother Henry. Up to the time of her death she had received nearly seven hundred pounds for the published books, which, considering her anonymity, and entire lack of publicity and influence, must have appeared to her, and indeed was, wonderful, though in comparison with the true value of the work very little indeed.

In December 1816 her brothers, Henry and Charles, were both at Chawton, and she speaks of their being in good health and spirits. She got through the winter well, and wrote to a friend in January, "Such mild weather is, you know, delightful to us, and though we have a great many ponds and a fine running stream through the meadows on the other side of the road, it is nothing but what beautifies us and does to talk of. I have certainly gained strength through the winter, and am not far from being well. And I think I understand my own case now so much better than I did, as to be able by care to keep off any serious return of illness."

She had taken to using a donkey-carriage in good weather, and doubtless this was a great boon, though she was able to walk one way either to or from Alton without over-fatigue, and hoped to be able to manage both ways when the summer came. In January also she mentions that her brother Henry, who was now ordained, was coming down to preach. "It will be a nervous hour for our pew, though we hear that he acquits himself with as much ease and collectedness as if he had been used to it all his life."

Her last completed book *Persuasion* was not her last work, even in declining strength the motive power was unabated.

"Upon a fitful revival of her strength, at the beginning of 1817, she fell eagerly to work at a story, of which she wrote twelve chapters. It has no name, and the plot and purpose are undeveloped. But some of the personages sketched have more than promise. There is a Mr. Parker with fixed theories as to the fashionable watering place he hopes to evolve out of a Sussex fishing village; there is a rich and vulgar Lady Denham, who will certainly disappoint her relatives by the testamentary disposition of her property, and there are two maiden ladies who thoroughly 'enjoy' bad health, and quack themselves to their heart's content. Whatever the plot to be unravelled, there is no sign that the writer's hand had lost its cunning." (Mr. Austin Dobson's preface to Macmillan's edition of *Northanger Abbey*.)

We are told by Mr. Austen-Leigh that the date on the last chapter of this MS. was March 17, which, "as the watch of a drowned man denotes the time of his death, so does this final date seem to fix the period when her mind could no longer pursue its accustomed course."

It was in March that her own family began to think seriously of the malady that was so insidiously making inroads on her vitality. Her niece Caroline, Anna's half-sister, and sister of the Mr. Austen-Leigh to whose *Memoir* the world is so much indebted, was then a child of twelve; she came about the end of March to stay at Chawton, but found her aunt so ill that she could not be taken in, so she was sent on to her half-sister Anna Lefroy; in her private records she gives the following account from recollection: "The next day we walked over to Chawton to make enquiries after our aunt, she was then keeping her room, but said she would see us and we went up to her. She was in her dressing-gown, and was sitting quite like an invalid in an arm-chair, but she got up and kindly greeted us, and then pointing to seats which had been arranged for us by the fire, 'There is a chair for the married lady, and a little stool for you, Caroline.' . . . I was struck by the alteration in herself. She was very pale, her voice was weak and low, and there was about her a general appearance of debility and suffering, but I have been told that she never had much acute pain. She was not equal to the exertion of talking to us, and our visit to the sick room was a very short one, aunt Cassandra soon taking us away. I do not suppose we stayed a quarter of an hour, and I never saw aunt Jane again."

It was in May that Jane was persuaded to go with her sister to lodgings in Winchester for the sake of further medical advice, and she never returned to Chawton, though probably that was the last thought that would have occurred to her on leaving it, for she was never inclined to be analytical or valetudinarian, and certainly she was one of the last to affect illness, or become an invalid for fancy. Cassandra cannot have known how soon she was to be bereaved of that dear sister whose life had run in such harmony with her own, and though anxiety must have darkened her heart, Jane's own sanguineness would buoy her with fresh hope, and the weeks the sisters passed together in Winchester must have been singularly peaceful.

The house in which Jane stayed still stands, it is in College Street, close to the great archway that marks the entrance to the College precincts. She says of it herself, "Our lodgings are very comfortable, we have a neat little drawing-room with a bow window overlooking Dr. Gabell's garden."

Here her life and strength slowly ebbed away; day by day she was longer chained to her sofa from increasing weakness. The elementary medical knowledge of her day was powerless to help her, though her life, humanly speaking, could probably have been prolonged if medical science had then known what it knows now.

Day by day through the bow window overlooking the street, would come the sound of boyish voices, the clatter of boyish feet, and she could see the greenery of the trees in the garden beyond the wall. She had plenty of companionship, Cassandra was ever with her, and Mrs. James Austen helped in the nursing.

The slight sharpness arising from unusual penetration, which had sometimes marked Jane's comments in earlier days, had all died down, she said gratefully to her sister-in-law, "You have always been a kind sister to me, Mary," and of her own dear Cassandra she said, " I will only say further that my dearest sister, my tender, watchful, indefatigable nurse, has not been made ill by her exertions. As to what I owe her, and the anxious affection of all my beloved family on this occasion, I can only cry over it, and pray God to bless them more and more."

And on July 18, when all the trees were at their greenest, and the bright sunshine lighted up the walls of the hoary abbey, she passed away. We can add nothing to her sister's account, written in the agony of the first bereavement, to her who was now closest to her heart, her niece, Fanny Knight.

" My dearest Fanny,—Doubly dear to me now for her dear sake whom we have lost. She did love you most sincerely. . . . Since Tuesday evening when her complaint returned, there was a visible change, she slept more, and much more comfortably ; indeed during the last eight and forty hours she was more asleep than awake. Her looks altered and she fell away, but I perceived no material diminution of strength, and, though I was then hopeless of her recovery, I had no suspicion how rapidly my loss was approaching.

" I have lost a treasure, such a sister, such a friend as never can have been surpassed. She was the sun of my life, the gilder of every pleasure, the soother of every sorrow, I had not a thought concealed from her, and it is as if I had lost a part of myself.

" . . . She felt herself to be dying about half an hour before she became tranquil and apparently unconscious. During that half hour was her struggle, poor soul ! She said she could not tell us what she suffered, though she complained of little fixed pain. When I asked her if there was anything she wanted, her answer was she wanted nothing but death, and some of her words were, 'God grant me patience; pray for me, oh, pray for me!' Her voice was affected, but as long as she spoke she was intelligible.

"I hope I do not break your heart, my dearest Fanny, by these particulars, I mean to afford you gratification while I am relieving my own feelings. I could not write so to anybody else. . . . On Thursday, when the clock struck six, she was talking quietly to me. I cannot say how soon afterwards she was seized again with faintness, which was followed by the sufferings which she could not describe, but Mr. Lyford who had been sent for, had applied something to give her ease, and she was in a state of quiet insensibility by seven o'clock at the latest. From that time till half past four when she ceased to breathe, she scarcely moved a limb, so that we have every reason to think with gratitude to the Almighty, that her sufferings were over. A slight motion of the head with every breath remained till almost the last. I sat close to her with a pillow in my lap to assist in supporting her head which was almost off the bed, for six hours; fatigue made me then resign my place to Mrs. J. A. for two hours and a half, when I took it again, and in about an hour more she breathed her last.

". . . There was nothing convulsed which gave the idea of pain in her look; on the contrary, but for the continual motion of the head, she gave one the idea of a beautiful statue, and even now in her coffin, there is such a sweet serene air over her countenance as is quite pleasant to comtemplate."

And later on after the funeral she wrote again, "Thursday was not so dreadful a day to me as you imagined. . . . Everything was conducted with the greatest tranquillity, and but that I was determined that I would see the last, and therefore was upon the listen, I should not have known when they left the house. I watched the little mournful procession the length of the street, and when it turned from my sight, and I had lost her for ever, even then I was not over-powered, nor so much agitated as I am now in writing of it. Never was a human being more sincerely mourned by those who attended her remains than was this dear creature. May the sorrow with which she is parted with on earth be a prognostic of the joy with which she is hailed in heaven! ... Oh, if I may one day be reunited to her there!"

Cassandra herself survived for twenty-eight years, and spent her last days in the cottage at Chawton endeared to her by recollections of her mother and beloved sister.

Jane's resting-place in the Cathedral is almost opposite the tomb of the founder, William of Wykeham. A large black slab of marble let into the pavement marks the spot, it bears an inscription including the following words: "The benevolence of her heart, the sweetness of her temper, and the extraordinary endowments of her mind obtained the regard of all who knew her, and the warmest love of her immediate connexions."

Subsequently her nephew Mr. Austen-Leigh inserted a brass on the wall near with an inscription which runs as follows: " Jane Austen, known to many by her writing, endeared to her family by the varied charms of her character, and ennobled by Christian faith and piety, was born at Steventon in the county of Hampshire Dec. 16, 1775, and buried in this cathedral July 24, 1817. 'She openeth her mouth with wisdom and in her tongue is the law of kindness.'"

In 1900 a memorial window was inserted as the result of a public subscription; it was designed and executed by C. E. Kemp. In the head of the window is a figure of St. Augustine whose name in its abbreviated form is St. Austin. In the centre of the upper row of lights is David with his harp. Below his figure, in Latin, are the words, "Remember in the Lord Jane Austen who died July 18, A.D. 1817." In the centre of the bottom row is the figure of St. John, and the remaining figures are those of the sons of Korah carrying scrolls, with sentences in Latin, indicative of the religious side of Jane Austen's character, namely, "Come ye children, hearken unto me; I will teach you the fear of the Lord." "Them that are meek shall He guide in judgement, and such as are gentle them shall He teach His way." "My mouth shall speak of wisdom and my heart shall muse on understanding." "My mouth shall daily speak of Thy righteousness and Thy salvation."

That Jane was so deeply and dearly loved by her own people speaks much for her worth. She and Cassandra, especially Cassandra, were very reticent in their expression of feeling, but seldom has heart been knit to heart as were theirs. The love of sisters has not often formed the theme of song or romance; we hear of a mother's love for her son, of a brother for a brother, but the love of sisters is, when it exists in perfection, as strong as these, as pure in its spring, and more full of feeling. Sisters whose hearts are open to one another, who have shared the same experiences, look on the world from a similar standpoint, and the breaking of such ties is severe agony. At only forty-one Jane had passed away still in the highest maturity of her powers, leaving behind her but six completed books, all short, but each one perfect in itself. This is what will be said of her— She did what she attempted to do perfectly. The books are all instinct with the same qualities, the precision of word and phrase, the genius for knowing what to select and what to leave unsaid, but not one is a repetition of another, in the whole gallery of characters each one is distinct.

She was a real artist. Her work lay apart from and outside of herself. We do not find a picture of herself under different names playing heroine in different sets of circumstances; each heroine stands by herself, and in her women's portraits she reaches her high-water mark—Elizabeth Bennet, Emma Woodhouse, Fanny Price, Anne Elliot, Catherine Morland, Elinor Dashwood, we know each one as a friend, and each one is completely differentiated.

So brilliant, so perfect, so stamped with its own individuality is each of the books, that one wonders what she could possibly have produced next to take rank with its forerunners. Within so small a compass, with such a narrow stage on which to set the *dramatis personæ*, how did she manage to make so great a variety?

It is in keeping with her character and work that there should be no decline, no falling off, that all should be good; it is true that some of the novels are preferred by one, some by another; some are stronger in one point, some in another, but neither decay nor improvement can justly be found between first and last. This is genius. Genius cannot grow nor can it be cultivated, it is there, and its work is done without effort and without labour. If Jane had not died at so early an age, her life would not have seemed so complete, so rounded as it did. Her dying in the full plenitude and maturity of power is in keeping with the level excellence of her work.

Her life had been a happy one, free from mind worries, free from great sorrows, her affections had wide play, her tastes full development; she was happy in the love of one very near and dear, and if she missed great ecstasies, she at least had no hideous sorrows to endure in the sin or vice of those near to her. Her one great sorrow was perhaps the death of her father, but he was not young, and in the natural course of events his death cannot be called unexpected. Sunny, well-occupied, surrounded with the refinements that a sensitive mind appreciates, she lived out a life on a high uniform level. Her books supplied a motive and mainspring that otherwise might have been felt to be lacking by one so energetic. If, as has been said, happiness on earth demands "someone to love, something to do, and something to hope for," she had all these, and much more.

TABULAR STATEMENT OF DATES OF NOVELS

Name.	Begun.	Finished.	Published.
Pride and Prejudice (First Impressions)	Oct. 1796	Aug. 1797	Early in 1813
Sense and Sensibility (Elinor and Marianne)	Nov. 1797	1798	June 1811
Northanger Abbey	1798	1803	1818
Mansfield Park	1812	Mar. 1814	July 1814
Emma	1814 or 1815	1815	Dec. 1815
Persuasion	1815 or 1816	Aug. 1816	1818

RECORD OF JANE AUSTEN'S RESIDENCES

	From	To
Steventon, Hants	*b.* Dec. 16, 1775	Spring 1801
Bath— 4 Sydney Terrace Green Park Buildings 25 Gay Street	Spring 1801 Autumn 1804 March 1805	Autumn 1804 1805
Southampton	End of 1805	1809
Chawton, Hants	Autumn 1809	*d.* July 18, 1817

TABLE OF NEAR RELATIONS MENTIONED IN THE BOOK

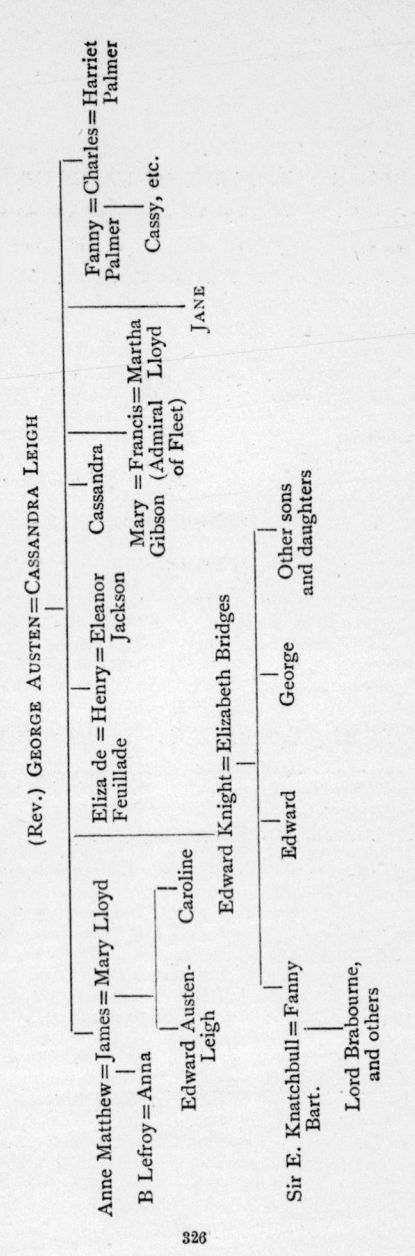

(Rev.) GEORGE AUSTEN = CASSANDRA LEIGH

| Anne Matthew = James = Mary Lloyd | Eliza de = Henry = Eleanor Feuillade Jackson | Cassandra | Mary = Francis = Martha Gibson (Admiral Lloyd of Fleet) | Fanny = Charles = Harriet Palmer Palmer |

B Lefroy = Anna Caroline

Edward Austen-Leigh

Edward Knight = Elizabeth Bridges

Sir E. Knatchbull = Fanny   Edward   George   Other sons and daughters
Bart.

Lord Brabourne, and others

JANE

Cassy, etc.

326

INDEX

Acting, 291–295.
Alexander, Emperor, 272.
Alexandria, Battle of, 253.
Alger, J. G., on travel, 10–11.
Allen, Ralph, 111.
Amiens, Treaty of, 254.
Art of the period, 8–9.
Ashton, John, on the press-gang, 206–207; on feminine costume, 240.
Austen family—
  Connections, 16.
  Genealogical table of, 326.
Austen, Anna (niece), *see* Lefroy.
Austen, Caroline (niece), on Jane's illness, 317.
Austen, Cassandra (sister), Jane's attachment to, 18, 19, 31, 116, 322; engagement of, 19; Jane's letters destroyed by, 20; visits to Goodnestone and Godmersham, 253, 258, 262–263; at Winchester, 317–319; letters after Jane's death, 319–321; last days of, 321; *cited*—on the sea-side romance, 131–132; otherwise mentioned, 166–167, 303.
Austen, Cassy (niece), 297.
Austen, Adm. Charles John (brother), marriages of, 19, 297; naval career of, 19, 197, 199, 208; at Godmersham, 296; at Chawton (1816), 315; mentioned, 107.
Austen, Mrs. Charles (Fanny Palmer), 19, 297.
Austen, Edward (brother), *see* Knight.
Austen, Adm. of the Fleet Francis (brother), marriages of, 19, 256; naval career of, 151, 196–199; shares the home at Southampton, 256; otherwise mentioned, 148, 149.

Austen, Mrs. Francis (Mary Gibson), 256, 258.
Austen, Mrs. Francis (Martha Lloyd), popularity of, with the Austens, 17, 256–257, 263; marriage of, 19, 256; at Bath, 254; at Southampton, 256–257.
Austen, Rev. George (father), career of, 15–16; retirement to Bath, 212–213; hobbies, 213; income, 215; death, 133, 213, 223; characteristics, 41, 62; otherwise mentioned, 59, 177.
Austen, Mrs. (mother), health of, 59–60; income of, 255, 256; at Chawton, 269; mentioned, 184.
Austen, Rev. Henry (brother), marriages of, 18, 288; Jane's literary affairs managed by, 18, 193, 272; Memoir by, prefixed to *Northanger Abbey*, 57–58, 194, 315; sponsor to Edward Cooper (junior), 118; Jane's visits to, 278, 288, 298, 303; illness of, 303–304; at Chawton (1816), 315; in Orders, 316; career of, 149; estimate of, 278; *cited*—on *Mansfield Park*, 273, 276; otherwise mentioned, 148, 293.
Austen, Mrs. Henry (Eliza de Feuillade), 18, 112, 278, 288.
Austen, Mrs. Henry (Eleanor Jackson), 18, 288.
Austen, Rev. James (brother), marriages of, 17; at Steventon, 212–213; visit to Southampton, 258; visit to Godmersham (1808), 260–262; otherwise mentioned, 194, 214.
Austen, Mrs. James (Mary Lloyd), Jane's attitude towards, 214, 258, 261, 318–319; on Harriet Moore, 262.

INDEX

Austen, Jane—
  Career — parentage and family, 15–19; childhood, 23, 26, 31; school days, 31, 32; home life, 71; early writings, 77–78; visits to relatives, 19, 66, 105, 119, 133, 148–151; offers of marriage, 129, 131; romance, 131, 262, 268; *Pride and Prejudice*, 176, 184–185; *Sense and Sensibility*, 185, 188–189; *Northanger Abbey*, 189, 193–194; removal to Bath, 212–213, 215–218; Green Park Buildings and Gay Street, 223; at Lyme, 249–251; visit to Godmersham (1805), 251; move to Southampton, 251, 254; visits to Eastwell and Goodnestone, 253; at Southampton, 257–258; at Chawton, 267–270; visits to London, 278–279, 286–288; theatre-going, 290, 293–295; at Godmersham (1813), 296; nursing Henry (1815), 298, 303–304; interview with Prince Regent's librarian, 304–305; failing health, 314–319; last work, 316–317; at Winchester, 318; death, 319–320; tomb and memorials, 321–322.
  Characteristics—
    Appearance, 58.
    Asperity, 129.
    Cheerfulness, 58, 129, 324.
    Critical faculty, 185.
    Fastidiousness, 129, 132.
    Health, 58–59.
    Humour, 1, 181.
    Narrowness of vision, 50, 254.
    Penetration and grasp of detail, 1, 9, 49, 81, 95, 129, 132, 318.
    Practicality, 58.
    Selective faculty, 311.
    Superficiality, 58.
    Vivacity and wit, 123, 129.
  Comparison of, with Fanny Burney, 87, 97; with George Eliot, 100–101; with Charlotte Brontë, 103–104; with Maria Edgeworth, 181–182.
  Estimates of, unfavourable, 128.
  Portrait of, at 15, 32; later, 57.
Austen-Leigh, James Edward (nephew), birth of, 194; name of Leigh assumed by, 17, 216; *Memoir* of Jane Austen by, 17; memorial brass inserted by, 321; *quoted*—on Steventon, 13, 14; on Jane's popularity with children, 23; on Jane's accomplishments, 32–33; on furniture, 63; on Jane's early writings, 78; on the Coopers, 118; on minuets, 126; on the sea-side romance, 131–132; on the home at Southampton, 255; on Henry Austen, 278; on *Persuasion*, 314–315, 317; *cited*—on minuet-dancing, 223; letters in the *Memoir*, 249, 276; *The Watsons* in the *Memoir*, 251; cancelled chapter of *Persuasion* in the *Memoir*, 315.

Baillie, Joanna, 172.
Balls—
  Bath, at, 222–225.
  Country, 119–120.
  Dances at, 121 (*see also* Dancing).
  Dress at, 124–127; masculine, 126.
  Etiquette of, 121–123.
  Evelina, account in, 121–123.
  Formality of, 121.
  Partners at, 121–123.
Bateson, Mary, *cited*, 238.
Bath—
  Abbey, 219.
  Assembly Rooms, 220–221.
  Austens' removal to, 212–213, 215–218; house in Sydney Place, 219; table of residences, 325.
  Balls at, 222–225.
  Characteristics of the town, 219.
  House-hunting in, 215–218.
  Nash's renovation of, 220–221, 247–248.
  New Guide on, 224.
  Pump Room, 219–220.
  Society of, reproduced in *Northanger Abbey*, 189–190.
Besant, Sir Walter, *quoted*—on eighteenth-century morals, 95; on franking of letters, 113–114; on wigs, 235–236.
"Blue-stocking," origin of epithet, 7.
Boothby, Capt. Charles, *quoted*, 156–157.
Brabourne, Lord, family of, 18, 301; *cited*—on the Coopers, 117–118; on Fanny Knight, 270; *quoted*—on Godmersham, 251–252, 261.

INDEX

Brasbridge, Joseph, *cited*, 114.
Bridges, Harriet, *see* Moore.
Bridges, Louisa, 148, 149.
Bridges, Marianne, 253.
Brontë, Charlotte, compared with George Eliot, 100–102; with Jane Austen, 103–104.
Brydges, Sir Egerton, on Jane's appearance, 57.
Burnet, Bishop, *quoted*, 47.
Burney, Fanny, works of, 86–87, 97; Macaulay's criticism of, 164–165; Walpole's criticism of, 165; lively environment of, 164; *cited*—on the Court, 305–306.
Byron, 173.

Cage, Lewis, 148, 149.
Camilla, 165.
Campbell, Thomas, 173.
Caps, 230–232.
Card games, 5, 127.
Cecilia, 86, 87, 97, 165, 176.
Charades, 264.
Chawton Cottage, Austens' home at, 266–270.
Chawton House—
  Acquisition of, by Edward Knight, 17.
  Lawsuit concerning, 128, 297.
  Value of, 255, 297.
Cheverels of Cheverel Manor, The, 8, 65, 67, 77; travelling described in, 154–155.
Children—
  Books for, 28.
  Jane's attitude towards, 23–24; her popularity with, 23; her delineation of, 24–27.
  Treatment of, 22, 27.
Churches, 38–39.
Clarence, Duke of (William IV.), 307.
Clarentine, 168.
Clarke, Mr., 304–305.
Clergy—
  Examination of, for Orders, 46–47.
  Jane's references to, 43.
  Livings of, 42.
  Position of, 34–37, 44–45.
  Types of, 40–43.
Coaches, 156–158, 282.
Coals and coal mines, 64–65.
Cœlebs in Search of a Wife, estimate of, 167; *quoted*, 27, 30; *cited*, 96.

Coleridge, 173.
Comedy of Jane Austen, character of, 1, 88.
Cooper, Dr., 117, 119.
Cooper, Edward, 117–118.
Cooper, Jane (Lady Williams), 118.
Country Clergyman—cited, 40.
Country gentlemen, 91.
Cowper, William, Jane's partiality for, 14, 58, 169, 170, 258; *quoted*—on the clergy, 37, 40; on condition of labourers, 74.
Crabbe, 170–171, 293.

Dancing, 121, 123–124, 126–128; the waltz, 121; the minuet, 126, 223; the quadrille, 127–128, 149; the Boulangeries, 149.
Deportment, 121.
Dobson, Austin, *cited*, 186, 189; *quoted*, 316.
Dockwra, William, 109–111.
Dress—
  Academic, 239.
  Ball, 125–127.
  Caps, 230–232.
  Cloaks, 240.
  Excesses in, 229–230.
  Fabrics, 241–242; cost of, 242–243.
  Feminine costumes, 73, 239–241.
  Fruit-wearing, 229.
  Headgear, 230–234; feathers, 125, 232, 234, 283; wigs, 235–236, 239.
  Hoops, 244.
  Jane Austen's lack of reference to, in the novels, 4; particular description of, in a letter, 243.
  Masculine, 126, 245–247.
  Mamaloucs, 231.
  Night-caps, 232–233.
  Nomenclature of, 243.
  Pelisses, 241.
  Pockets, absence of, 244.
  Scantiness of, 240.

Edgeworth, Maria, works of, 87; *Emma* presented to, 172; Jane Austen compared with, 181–182.
Education of girls, 29–31.
Eighteenth-century period, scope of, 3.
Eliot, George, Charlotte Brontë and Jane Austen compared with, 100, 101.

INDEX

Emma—
  Characters of, 308–310; children, 24, 26; clerical character, 43, 48; Mrs. Bennet, 61; Harriet, 139–142.
  Date of, 98.
  Dedication of, 163, 305, 307.
  Length of, 80.
  Love depicted in, 136.
  Personal appearance of heroine in, 57.
  Persuasion compared with, 313.
  Pride and Prejudice compared with, 99, 308–310.
  Scott's review of, 134–135, 310–311.
  Otherwise mentioned, 69–70, 83–84, 91, 97, 115, 135.
Entertainments, 120.
Evelina, 87, 164, 186; *cited*, 121–122.

Fairchild Family, The—*cited*, 28–29.
Fashion (*see also* Dress)—
  Bare necks, 220, 240.
  Excesses of, 229–230, 240, 244.
  Hair-dressing, 233–236, 239.
Ferrier, Miss, 82, 98, 174.
First Impressions, see *Pride and Prejudice*.
Flirtation, 119, 129–130.
Food, prices of, 70–71, 77.
Foreign affairs, outline of, 49–56, 253–254, 259–260, 270–272, 297–298.
Fox, George, 247, 259.
French Revolution and Reign of Terror, 50–53.
Furniture, 63.

Gardening, 71–72.
Garrick, David, 161, 291, 292.
Gas, 284–285.
Geography of the period, 6–7.
George III., King, 94, 235, 305–306.
Gibson, Mary (Mrs. F. Austen), 256, 258.
Gloucester, Duke of, 253.
Godmersham—
  Acquisition of, by Edward Knight, 17, 148.
  Description of, 251–252.
  Temple Plantation, 261.
Goodnestone, visits to, 253.

Gordon, Duchess of (1791), 56.
Gosse, Edmund, on eighteenth-century literature, 169.
Grosley, M., *quoted*—on English breakfasts, 66; on wages, 72; on coaching, 157–158; on King George III., 235; on London, 280–281, 283–286; on the stage, 291–292.

Hair-dressing, 231, 233–234; feathers, 125, 232, 234, 283; wigs, 235–236, 239; powder, 237–239.
Hastings, Warren, 56.
Hats and bonnets, 234.
Hatton, George, 253.
Highwaymen, 158–160.
Hill, Constance, *cited*, 46.
Hill, Rowland, 109, 111.
Housekeeping, 65.

Inchbald, Mrs., 172.
India, affairs of, 55–56.
Ireland, union of, with England, 55.

Jackson, Eleanor (Mrs. H. Austen), 18, 288.
Jane Austen and Her Contemporaries—*quoted*, 92.
Johnson, Dr. Samuel, Jane's partiality for, 58, 169; Fanny Burney influenced by, 164–165; wigs of, 236; otherwise mentioned, 164, 171.

Kean, Charles, 294–295.
Kemble, 291.
Kensington Gardens, 288–289.
Kent, Duke of, 307; letter of, to Mr. Creevy, 94.
Kentish Country House, A—*cited*, 182–183.
Knatchbull, Lady (Fanny Catherine Knight) (niece), Jane's attachment to, 18, 252, 270, 288; shopping with, 287; letter to, on marriage, etc., 298–301; Cassandra's letters to, after Jane's death, 319–321; estimate of, 260–261, 263; marriage and family of, 18, 301; mentioned, 19.
Knight, Mr., presents Steventon to George Austen, 16; adopts Edward Austen, 17, 148; mentioned, 59.
Knight, Mrs., 17, 148, 261.

INDEX

Knight, Edward (brother), adopted by his cousin, 17, 148; marriage of, 18; Jane's visits to (1796), 148–151; (1805), 251–252; (1808), 260–261; lawsuit concerning Chawton, 128, 297; family of, 252; offers Chawton Cottage to his mother, 266; otherwise mentioned, 133, 255, 287, 293, 303.
Knight, Mrs. E. (Elizabeth Bridges), 133, 148; death of, 260, 262–263.
Knight, Edward (nephew), 150, 263–264, 296.
Knight, Fanny (niece), see Knatchbull.
Knight, George (nephew), 263–264, 296.

Labourers—
  Condition of, 73–75.
  Wages of, 76.
Lackington (bookseller), 114.
Lady Susan, 99.
Landor, W. S., 239.
Langdale, Lord, *quoted*—on travel, 10; on night-caps, 233.
Latournelle, Mrs., 31.
Lefroy, Mrs. Benjamin (Anna Austen) (niece), at Chawton, 269; novel-writing by, 301–302; marriage of, 302; *cited*, 131–133; mentioned, 17.
Lefroy, Tom, 107, 119, 129–130.
Leigh, Rev. Thomas (grandfather), 16, 118.
Leigh-Perrot, Mrs., 119, 216.
Letters of Jane Austen—
  Contemporary events, lack of reference to, 5, 9.
  Date of earliest published, 106, 117.
  Pettiness in, 214–215.
  Style of, 107.
Letters of the period—
  Carriage of, 109–111.
  Cost of transmission of, 109, 111, 114, 116.
  Fetching of, 115–116.
  Form of, 108.
  Franking of, 112–115.
  Importance of, as news-carriers, 6.
  Style of, 106–107.
Liston, 293, 294.
Literature of the period—
  Leading works of, classified, 171–174.
  Novels, *see that title*.

Lloyd, Martha, see Austen, Mrs. F.
London of the period—
  Coaches in, 282.
  Dangers of, 283–284.
  Dirt of, 281–282.
  Extent of, 279–280.
  Fogs of, 285.
  Kensington Gardens, 288–289.
  Lighting of, 284–285.
  Paving in, 280–282.
  Postage arrangements in, 109–110.
  Press-gang in, 207.
  Rent, etc., in, 286.
  Shops in, 286.
  Streets in, 285.
  Theatres in, 290–292; private, 193.
  Watchmen in, 284.
Love, 135–139, 146–147.
Lyme, 249–251.

Macaulay, Lord, *quoted*—on Jane Austen's art, 84; on novels previous to Miss Burney's, 86; on Miss Burney's environment, 164; on her work, 164–165.
Mail-coaches, 111–112.
Mansfield Park—
  Characters of, 210–211, 273–275; children, 26–27; clerical characters, 43–46; Fanny Price, 314.
  Date of, 98.
  Education described in, 29–30.
  Minuet described in, 126.
  Publication of, 277.
  Scene of, 257, 275.
  Second edition of, 311.
  Writing of, 270, 273.
  Otherwise mentioned, 4, 62, 82–83, 104, 145, 256, 310.
Marriage—
  Jane Austen's view of, 137, 144–146.
  Modern attitude towards, 139.
Marriage, 82, 98, 174.
Matches, sulphur, 64.
Mathews, Charles, 293, 294.
Meal times, 65–67, 162.
Meals, 68.
Mitford, Miss, description of Jane Austen given to, 128; list of books read by, 168–169; publication of *Our Village* by, 174; *quoted*—on M. St. Quintin's, 31–32; on the waltz, 121; on morning calls, 162;

INDEX

on *Waverley*, 173 ; on *Pride and Prejudice*, 181-182 ; on Kean, 295 ; *cited*—on *Self Control*, 167 ; on the Chawton lawsuit, 297.
Mitford, Mrs., recollections of Jane Austen by, 128.
Montagu, Mrs., 7.
Moore, Mrs. (Harriet Bridges), at Godmersham, 261-262 ; mentioned, 148, 149, 253.
Moore, Sir J., 265.
Moore, Thomas, 173.
Morals, 94-95.
More, Hannah, fêting of, 161 ; popular estimate of, 172 ; plays by, 162-163 ; *quoted* — on Mrs. Montagu, 7 ; on children, 27 ; on mail-coaches, 112 ; on abolition of letter-franking, 114-115 ; on dress, 243 ; *cited*—on fruit-wearing, 229-230 ; *Cœlebs in Search of a Wife*, see that title.
Morning calls, 162.
Mothers as depicted by Jane Austen, 60-62, 89-90, 188.
Mourning, 253.
Murray, Mr., 310-312.

Names, female, 90.
Napoleon Bonaparte, 53-54, 253-254, 259-260, 271, 297, 298.
Nash, Beau, 220-223, 247-248.
Navy—
  Bounties, system of, 206.
  Captains accompanied by their families, custom of, 296.
  Corruption in, 204.
  Hardships of, 201-205.
  Interest, abuse of, 208-209.
  Mutiny in, 209-210.
  Officers' careers in, 201.
  Press for, 206-207.
  Prize-money in, 207-208.
  Victories of, 199-200.
New Guide, The — *quoted*, 224, 246-247.
Night-caps, 232-233.
Northanger Abbey—
  Ball described in, 225-226.
  Biographical Memoir prefixed to, 58, 90, 194.
  Date of, 98.
  Estimates of, 189, 193.
  Local colour in, 227.

Northanger Abbey—continued.
  Preface to, by Jane Austen, 194.
  Publication of, 315.
  Publisher's neglect of, 193, 251.
  Scene and characters of, 189-193.
  Otherwise mentioned, 4, 13, 43, 47, 82, 88, 119, 124, 145, 224-225, 247.
Novelists prior to Jane Austen, 85.
Novels of Jane Austen (*see also separate titles*)—
  Character the main feature of, 4, 102.
  Characters of, 91-92 ; children, 24-27 ; mothers, 60-62, 89-90, 188 ; male characters, 186, 210-211 ; secondary characters, 308.
  Comedy of, 1, 88.
  Humanity of, 81, 84.
  Humour of, 81.
  Individuality of, 323.
  Modernity of, 5.
  Refinement of, 94-95.
  Religion, lack of mention of, 90.
  Scenery ignored in, 14.
  Selective art exhibited in, 82, 95, 311.
  Style of, 97.
  Tabular list of, 325.
Novels of the period—
  Character of, 85-86, 168.
  Gosse's classification of, 169.
  Jane Austen's reading of, 166.

Omnibuses, 282.
Our Village, 174.

Palmer, Fanny, see Austen, Mrs. C.
Papendick, Mrs., *quoted* — on plate and services, 69 ; on hair-powder, 238 ; on dress, 231, 241.
Parish visiting, 73.
Perrot, see Leigh-Perrot.
Persuasion—
  Characters in, 210-211 ; Anne Elliot, 314.
  Date of, 98.
  Estimate of, 313.
  Local colour in, 227-228.
  Love depicted in, 137-138.
  Publication of, 315.
  Scene of, 249-250, 314.
  Writing of, 312, 314-315.
  Otherwise mentioned, 24, 62, 90, 208, 224-225, 296.

Petrel (ship sloop), 198–199.
Plate and services, 68–69.
Pollock, Mr., *cited*, 92, 310.
Porter Jane, 166.
Post office, development of, 109–111, 115.
Post-boys, 111.
Powys, Mrs. Philip Lybbe (Caroline Girle), 117, 119; *quoted* — on Steventon inn, 12; on Holkham, 67; on an evening party, 127; on highway robbery, 160; on boy officers, 209; on Bath balls, 223–224; on Southampton, 257; on Wedgwood's, 287; on medical treatment, 303.
Pride and Prejudice—
  Characters of — Mr. Collins, 35–36, 183–184; Elizabeth, 58, 81, 95–96, 123, 178–180, 182; Darcy, 179–181; Jane Bingley, 288.
  Date of, 98.
  Emma compared with, 308–310.
  First Impressions the original title of, 99, 176.
  Improbability in, 187.
  Opinions on — by Sir W. Scott, 182; by Miss Mitford, 181–182; by Jane Austen, 184–185.
  Publication of, 276–277.
  Publisher's refusal of, 177.
  Social caste in, 92–93.
  Otherwise mentioned, 58, 81–82, 124, 128, 145.
Prince Regent, *Emma* dedicated to, 163, 305, 307; librarian of, 304–305; character of, 306–307; home of, 286.

Radcliffe, Mrs., 88, 172, 189.
Residences of Jane Austen, table of, 325.
Roads, state of, 75, 116, 151–154.
Rogers, Samuel, *Pleasures of Memory* published by, 173; omnibus story of, 282; *quoted*—on novels, 168; on hair-powdering, 239; *cited*—on head-dresses, 234; on Fox, 247; on executions, 284.
Romance, Scott's plea for, 134–135.
Rowling, life at, 148–150.

St. Vincent, Battle of, 200.

Scott, Sir W., review of *Emma* by, 134–135, 310–311; authorship of *Waverley* imputed to, 173; *cited*— on *Pride and Prejudice*, 182.
Secker, Archbishop, *cited*, 35, 38.
Sedan chairs, 282–283.
Self Control, opinions on, 167–168.
Selwyn, George, *cited*, 283–284.
Sense and Sensibility—
  Anonymous issue of, 163.
  Characters of—children, 24–26; Elinor, 136; male characters, 186–187; minor characters, 188.
  Date of, 98.
  Estimate of, 189.
  Improbability in, 187.
  Letter form of, 185.
  Marriage, views on, depicted in, 142–144.
  Origin of, 78.
  Publication of, 268, 272–273.
  Revision of, 270.
  Title of, 177.
  Otherwise mentioned, 26, 43, 47, 61–62, 83, 89, 91, 135, 136, 308.
Servants, wages of, 72–73.
Seward, Anna, 172.
Sheridan, R. B., old age of, 164; plays of, 172.
Sherwood, Mrs., 28, 31.
Shopping, 286–287.
Siddons, Mrs., 292.
Sloane, Sir Hans, 279.
Social England—*cited*, 238.
Society of the period, entrée of, 161.
Southampton, 251, 254.
Southey, Robert, 173.
Stephens, Miss, 293, 294.
Steventon Rectory—
  Description of, 12.
  Sale of furniture of, 218.
  Situation of, 12–14.
Style of the eighteenth century, 97, 258.
Swords, wearing of, 124–125, 282.

Tea, price of, 77.
Téméraire, mutineers on, 209.
Theatres, 290–292; private, 293.
Thompson, Capt. Edward, on the navy, 202–203.
Thomson, Richard, *quoted*, 156.
Tilsit, Peace of, 259.

INDEX

Times of the period—
    "Baby officers" satirised in, 209.
    Dress fashions satirised in, 125, 244.
    Form of, 107–108.
    Kensington Gardens exit advocated by, 288–289.
    Press-gang's activities described in, 206–207.
    Private theatres mentioned in, 293.
Tips, 150–151.
Trafalgar, Battle of, 257.
Travel—
    Conditions of, 9–11.
    Ladies, by, 159.
    Methods of—post, 151, 158–159; by waggon, 153–154; by private chaise, 154–155; by coach, 155–158.

United States of America, secession of, 56.

Vicar of Wakefield, The—*cited*, 34.

Walpole, Horace, letters of, 108, 113; death of, 171; *quoted*—on church-going, 39; on the French Revolution, 51; on village merry-makings, 75–76; on highway robbery, 160; on Fanny Burney, 165; on the Duke of Clarence, 307; *cited*—on Twickenham, 115; on dress, 245.
Watsons, The, 66, 99, 251; child character in, 26.
Wedgwood, 287.
Whateley, Archbishop, *quoted*, 84, 87, 189.
Wigs, 235–236, 239.
Winchester, 78, 317–319, 321.
Women, advancement in position of, 7.
Wordsworth, William, 173.

York, Duke of, post office the monopoly of, 109–110; robbed by highwaymen, 160; character of, 306.
Young, Arthur, *quoted*—on French clergy, 37; on roads, 152; *cited*—on food prices, 70; on wages, 73, 76.

Printed by MORRISON & GIBB LIMITED, *Edinburgh*